Jon Driscoll

Get it Kicked!

The Battle for the Soul of English Football

First published by Pitch Publishing, 2022

Pitch Publishing
9 Donnington Park,
85 Birdham Road,
Chichester,
West Sussex,
PO20 7AJ
www.pitchpublishing.co.uk
info@pitchpublishing.co.uk

A CIP catalogue record is available for this book
from the British Library.

ISBN 978 1 80150 193 4

Typesetting and origination by Pitch Publishing
Printed and bound in Great Britain by TJ Books, Padstow

Contents

'It's difficult to change what's in your blood, in your body, and all the history of playing that way, and you change it for what? Because of one guy from another country who's had success in the past? It's stupid. It's an analysis English people have to do.'

Pep Guardiola, 2018

Introduction

THE BALL rockets over the crossbar and smacks into the metal fence that shrieks and reverberates. The goalkeeper, and I hope this choice of verb isn't too harsh, toddles off to collect the ball that very nearly gave him a haircut. His centre-backs split to their designated stations either side of the posts, inside the penalty area, of course. The full-backs are wider still; a defensive midfielder hovers in the D on the edge of the box. They're going to 'play out from the back' even though the previous five attempts didn't end well. The keeper plonks the ball down in the six-yard box and side-foots it behind for a corner.

The coach was being 'assessed for his badges', the reason for this unfortunately ill-matched friendly, which was fascinating and embarrassing in equal measure. It was roughly 10-0 before the end of the first quarter when the coaches could step in. The intervention that mattered was that the stronger team eased off. We will never know what the score would have been if the kids had followed their ruthless instincts.

Maybe they should have been left to get on with it. Kids get over losing football matches quickly enough if adults don't make a fuss. If the weaker team had lost 30-0, so what? The 'growth mindset' individual would suck it up, accept their opponents were bigger and better players and get to work improving their skills and tactics. In the real world, it seemed fair to intervene; it was the adults who had sent them into a mismatch, so it was their fault – along with the new coaching philosophy of English football, or more accurately, its dogmatic implementation.

7

Was the coach failing the kids? Playing that way is easy if you've got Kevin De Bruyne, Phil Foden and João Cancelo. Principles are fine if you're not the one getting a pasting. Surely, the kids needed alternatives. What's the shame in kicking the ball away from danger when you're facing a coordinated press of bigger, stronger players who have been taught the same as you?

Or is that wrong? If we coach 11-year-old kids to revert to 'Plan Hoof' whenever they face a better team, how will they ever learn? Is that attitude why the nation that invented football has failed so often for so long? Are we too afraid, so fragile in defeat that we're incapable of learning from it? That team could have had a centre-back lump the ball up the pitch and scrapped for the seconds but what would that have taught them?

Football coaching in England is light years ahead of where it was when I was young. On the most basic level there is far more of it. My son is a far better player than I was, but he does currently have five FA-qualified coaches: three in his Junior Premier League team and two in his grassroots team. There were some brilliant coaches in the past but if you spend time around kids' football now, you'll meet a tracksuited army, equipped with tiers of coaching certificates. The electronic information age has seen a surge in shared practice which is wonderful, although it tends to come with the new parroted language of coaching. If you can't explain it in your own words, you don't fully understand. As former England women's international and now TV pundit Sue Smith put it, 'A lot of it is old stuff repackaged, a new name for something we all know. The low block is a team sitting back in their own half, mid-block means they're a bit further forward.'

There has been a concerted effort to shift English football from its crash-bang-wallop tradition. The authorities advocate possession football. The people are less sure. The title of this book was inspired by my memory of an old guy in the crowd when I was watching Darlington play Cambridge United at Feethams some decades ago. Bursting with rage and frustration, and desperate for the ball to be further up the pitch, he screamed, 'Get it kicked, man, Darlo!' If English football has a soul, then it is straddling those extremes.

When football was better

I am 50 years old. That should help you assess the lens through which I view football. We are all susceptible to nostalgia, remembering long childhood summers when everything was fascinating and new. I used to pay £1 to get into Ayresome Park. I loved the sense of community, and the excitement of going without my dad. When I take the filter off, I know lots of games were bad, with keepers picking up back-passes and strikers being flagged offside dozens of times. Before I ever went to a football match, I had learned at school that Charlie Amer, owner of Middlesbrough FC, was a bad man.

Daniel Wood runs a Twitter account called 'When Football Was Better' in which he shares old match footage and funny articles from the glory days of football magazines. He's got 81,000 followers and rising. I wondered whether I would encounter a dinosaur, railing against the modern world but I didn't.

'When I set it up, I thought I was disillusioned with modern football and that things were better in the past,' he told me. 'But were they really? Quality of football better? No. Pitches better? No. Safer? No.

'I think it boils down to nostalgia. Everything seems better with the rose-tinted spectacles of the past. Telly seemed better when you were a kid, food was better, the weather was better. As a child growing up in the '80s, I was captivated by football, and it was a massive part of my life. So many of my childhood memories centre on football, reading magazines, watching, playing the game or football computer games. I had a brilliant time growing up, so I'm bound to view that period as special.

'I'm not sure I, nor my followers, who I assume are a similar age to me, really believe that football was better but it's the memories we love. It's true the focus on the FA Cup and the Football League outside of the top flight has diminished as football has become a multibillion-pound industry. The naivety and working-class nature of the football I grew up with has been lost forever. In lieu of ever getting that back I like to reminisce, and it seems to be popular as my number of followers would attest to. It's an honour to have the amount I have, including many of my heroes and important footballing figures. But not Gary Lineker, I'm desperate for him to follow me!'

To convince myself I'm not just a middle-aged man shouting at clouds, I have conducted a series of interviews with people in and around English football. They were all great, giving up their time to teach me something about the game. I have watched matches from England at the Euros to the snappily titled Southern League Division One Central League, from kids in the park to academy games, and via the magic of YouTube revisited what English football really looked like in the past. It wasn't all hoofball.

I am optimistic. England's youth teams look as good as anyone's, and Gareth Southgate's senior side has reached the World Cup semi-final and the Euros final. We are genuine contenders to win the World Cup. The Premier League is top of the UEFA rankings and our clubs are regularly in European finals although declining competitiveness could threaten its long-term strength. But change comes at a cost; what have we lost, and was it worth it?

'The English footballer is very brave and strong and committed and there are always enough high-class players in his team to cause concern in any opponent. It is a national characteristic.'

Johan Cruyff

No one objects to improving players' technique, but the truth is revealed in the emphasis. When you are up against it, if your team is weaker and resources are limited, where do you turn? When time is short, how do you spend it? If we aim for a sophistication that doesn't come naturally, will we end up as a poundshop Spain? After all, people around the world love to watch English football, a trend that predated the updated coaching models. Are we losing the elements of English football that Cruyff admired?

Les Ferdinand was the first person to mention the bulldog spirit:

'We've lost that traditional English never-say-die mentality. Going back through the years, you'd say we weren't the most gifted nation in terms of technical ability but anyone who played against an English side in Europe knew they'd played against an English side because we would go for 95, 96, 97 minutes at full throttle. I think we've lost that mentality but that's how I would describe our sort of football: the mentality was like a British bulldog spirit. We never say die, we never know when to give up and we give our all for 90-odd minutes.'

Ferdinand was a traditional English centre-forward, voted PFA Players' Player of the Year in 1995/96 for his part in Newcastle's infamous Premier League near miss, but he is not an old pro clinging to his glory days. He is Queens Park Rangers' director of football, overseeing the development of young players, trying to build up the club he served with such distinction as a player.

Interestingly, he chose to define English football by what it has lost:

'We've looked at the brand we had and said what we need to compete in Europe is to improve technically. Now, I would never have disagreed with that. I would have said, "Yes 100 per cent, if we can add the technique to what we have, that would take us where we want to go," but where we've looked for improvement in the technique of players, we've lost that bit of what we had.'

There is a tendency in both the media and coaching community to conflate two different concepts: possession-based football and attractive football. It is boring to watch ineffective long-ball football, but I've seen plenty of awful matches between possession-based teams. A fully firing Pep Guardiola outfit moves the ball quickly and scores freely but watching an ill-equipped team doggedly shifting the ball around their own half can be achingly dull.

We'll start with a quick history lesson, a tale of how England invented football then got beaten at it frustrating frequently.

Notes on devolution! I refer to English and
Welsh football as the same thing when talking
about leagues and academies. We have shared
a club structure for all our lifetimes, and I don't
say anything specifically about Welsh league
football. Internationally, of course, we are rivals
and I know lots of Welsh people love to see the
England national team suffer and I am all for
that; there is no point to football without rivalry.
I checked with Cardiff-born Matt Crocker, one
of the architects of the England DNA, whether
Welsh football should be considered separately.
He smiled but looked slightly baffled. Scotland,
however, has always had a separate structure.
In the history section I have tried to use 'British'
when I deliberately want to include Scottish
football and switch to England/English for a
clearer distinction. When I was young there were
brilliant Scottish players throughout the English
Football League but that is not so noticeable
now, with some noble exceptions. I checked with
football data analyst Dave Carbery, a proud Scot
and Stirling Albion fan and as he put it, 'The
money is so different so it's hard to replicate
what's happening down south.' I don't analyse
recent developments in Scottish football but if
you want to, I'll read your book.

1

A potted history of English football

'I hate sophisticated football.'

Graham Taylor, 1982

ENGLISH FOOTBALL was a hard man's sport from the off. It evolved from the incredibly dangerous folk game where teams, or mobs if you prefer, moved a ball towards a distant target by any means necessary. It just about survived various attempts to outlaw it by authorities who had a problem with the frequency of injury and death.

Towns, villages, and public schools all had their own rules so when people started travelling to play, there were arguments. Some wanted to catch the ball and run with it, or to hack their opponents' shins, literally. It came to a head in 1863 when the newly formed Football Association tried to write unified laws. At the fifth meeting Blackheath's Francis Maude Campbell declared that to abolish running with the ball and hacking would 'do away with all the courage and pluck from the game'. He added, 'I will be bound to bring over a lot of Frenchmen who would beat you with a week's practice.' At the sixth meeting he lost the argument and withdrew his club. The split wasn't clean, and it wasn't until 1871 that the Rugby Football Union was formed with its own distinct laws.

The 1863 football code didn't look like the modern game; it was more of a football/rugby hybrid. Australian rules football travelled an alternative path and gives us an idea of how things could have turned out. It took more law changes for the sport we know and love to emerge – the one still referred to as soccer, by rugby fans, Australians, Americans, and old posh people. Campbell was certain the public would reject the softer game: he was hopelessly wrong. Football boomed and the resourceful Victorian Brits took it to the world.

In Europe, the 'Scottish' game with more passing and movement was influential and in South America the game developed its own style with ball skills highly prized. The Brits were the best for a while, judging by results of touring teams, although the difference in the perception of fair play often flared into mini diplomatic incidents.

There has always been a duality in British attitudes to internationalism. Some early footballers took our great game to the world – note the anglicised team names of Athletic Club and AC Milan. Check the early history of European clubs for English coaches.

The rival instinct was to pull down the shutters on the outside world and its different interpretations of football. Nowhere was this starker than in the decision by the home nations not to play at the World Cups in 1930, 1934 and 1938. There is a profound fragility about proclaiming yourself the best while refusing to prove it.

Hugo Meisl, Austrian player, referee, writer, administrator, and manager of his national team from 1919 to 1937, wrote of English football, 'To us Middle Europeans, the attacking play of the British professional, seen from the aesthetic point of view, seems rather poor.

'Although their passing, swift and high, is rather lacking in precision, the English players compensate for this by the rare potency and great rapidity of their attacks.'[1]

Lancastrian Jimmy Hogan became known as the spiritual father of central European football. He believed the English long-ball game developed from a change to the laws. Under the 1863 code any attacker ahead of the ball was offside, except at

---

1 Quoted in *Inverting the Pyramid*

goal kicks; picture rugby union. A change in 1866 meant that attackers needed three opponents to play them onside but by the 1920s there was a problem: the offside trap. Teams were playing with two defenders, one of whom could sweep while the other stepped up to catch opponents offside. A decline in goals led to action. From 1925, just two players from the defending team could play an attacker onside (one of those is almost always the goalkeeper). At first there was a goal glut; these were the days of George Camsell scoring 59 in a season for Middlesbrough and Everton's Dixie Dean breaking his record with 60 a year later. Coaches soon adapted. Arsenal's Herbert Chapman was the most effective. In short, the old 2-3-5 formation was replaced by the WM with the centre-half withdrawn into defence. The Gunners won the title in 1931 and 1933, before Chapman's untimely death. Hogan, looking at his homeland from afar, thought the success of Chapman's system did great harm to the English game,[2] 'Other clubs tried to copy Chapman but they had not the men and the result was, in my opinion, the ruination of British football with the accent on defence bringing about the big kicking game which put to an end the playing of constructive football. Through this type of game, our players lost the touch and feeling for the ball.'

Chapman also experienced a sense of loss, but he blamed the changed nature of society after World War One:

'Football today lacks the personalities of 20 or 30 years ago. This, I think, is true of all games, and the reason for it is a fine psychological study. The life which we live is so different: the pace, the excitement, and the sensationalism which we crave are new factors which have had a disturbing influence. They have upset the old balance mentally as well as physically, and they have made football different to play as well as to watch. And they have set up new values. The change has, in fact, been so violent that I do not think the past, the players and the game, can fairly be compared with the present.'

That is not the last time you will read such sentiments.

---

2   More history of tactics at *Inverting the Pyramid*, by Jonathan Wilson

Walter Winterbottom

England played in the first football international in 1872 but no one in power saw the need for a national team manager until 1946. This was years after Chapman had revolutionised tactics and won titles with Huddersfield and Arsenal. It was after Vittorio Pozzo had guided Italy to two World Cup wins. The FA, with its blend of amateurish toffs and middle-class administrators, was sceptical of grubby professionalism. Throughout English football there was a reluctance to be seen to try too hard although once the whistle was blown, endeavour and spirit were prized.

A committee picked the England team while managers and 'trainers' from clubs were hired to oversee games on an ad hoc basis. The figure of the trainer was still around in the 1970s – a hybrid of first-team coach and physio – the man with the bucket and sponge.

The job went to Walter Winterbottom, a teacher who had played part-time for Manchester United and met FA secretary Sir Stanley Rous in the RAF during the war. His appointment was as 'Director of Coaching' with the England job tacked on.

Winterbottom wrote, 'The Football Association first became "coaching-minded" when in 1934, it sent a few well-known players on coaching visits to selected schools and minor clubs.' His 1952 book *Soccer Coaching* is remarkably basic to the modern eye, 'Power in his boot is essential to the full-back, but the defender who boots the ball haphazardly upfield is no friend of his forwards.'

Winterbottom didn't pick the England team despite being its manager for 139 games. They won 78 of those but his era was defined by high-profile defeats. When England finally entered the World Cup in 1950 it ended in humiliation. The players were unprepared for Brazil: exhausted from travel and spooked by unfamiliar food. They beat Chile but lost to a ragtag USA team of semi-professionals, and then to Spain. Stanley Matthews and Tom Finney both asked to stay to watch games and learn from other countries. The FA told them it wasn't worthwhile.

Nothing was learned. The World Cup was thousands of miles away in trying conditions and despite the popularity of football among the working classes, it didn't dominate newspaper sports coverage. So, when Hungary visited Wembley in 1953, most observers expected a comfortable home victory despite the visitors being the Olympic champions on a 24-match unbeaten run. As future England manager Bobby Robson put it, 'England had never been beaten at Wembley – this would be a 3-0, 4-0 maybe even a 5-0 demolition of a small country.'

Hungary's 6-3 victory destroyed the notion of English invincibility. A lot of the analysis has focused on the respective tactics and formations: Robson said, 'Our WM formation was kyboshed in 90 minutes of football.' I think that misses the point. The Hungarians were better at everything. They resembled a modern football team while England looked like a re-enactment society. The WM formation wasn't the problem – it was that England's players were stuck rigidly in slots. The Hungarians had played together far more, they were technically superior and mostly fitter. Even their lightweight footwear brought a sceptical response from England captain Billy Wright – before the game, not after he had been dumped on his backside by Ferenc Puskás's drag-back. A rematch in Budapest the following year finished 7-1 to Hungary.

Poor old Walter. He has gone down in history as a dinosaur, defined by his failings. Yet he had the whiff of a plan. Brian Glanville wrote in his obituary for *The Guardian* in 2002 that when Winterbottom took on his dual role in 1946, 'He found himself confronted by a welter of prejudice and ignorance. If the FA coaching scheme may in later years have ossified into a new orthodoxy, initially it had much to offer; and much to contend with. At many clubs, training still consisted of endless running round the track, with nothing seen of the ball, the theory being that the less the players saw of it during the week, the more they would want it on a Saturday.'

Winterbottom's descriptions of players' roles were not those of a kick-and-rush merchant, 'The centre-half who does no more than shadow the opposing centre-forward around the field is not doing anything like his full job. He is the pivot, for ever on the alert, his judgement always being tested.'

On the inside-forward, 'Often he is the most hard-worked member of the team, but he needs superb ball play as well as mere running fitness. He must be adept at working his way out of "smothered" conditions, often starting with his back towards goal. Above all, he must be a thinker, for he is the major tactician in attack.'

Winterbottom even advocated for deep-lying forwards – in a book published a year before, Hungary's Nandor Hidegkuti played a famously pivotal role in dismantling England. But Winterbottom had an air of defeatism, 'Remoulding the tactics of a team is not always a simple matter. After discussing an idea – and even rehearsing it – the players may still be unable to incorporate it successfully into their game. Once the whistle blows for the kick-off, previous habits start to assert themselves and the new tactic is forgotten.'

The longest-serving England manager was an earnest man stuck between FA toffs and working-class players, unable to communicate freely with either, but affable enough to survive until 1962. He nudged English football in the right direction and although he was no inspirational leader or deep philosopher, he was a better influence than some who followed.

Hungary never did win the World Cup: they lost the 1954 final, unable to replace the injured Puskás and facing a West Germany team possibly fuelled up on amphetamines. Just 13 years after their mauling by the Magical Magyars, England were crowned world champions.

'England can play football. England have got it in the bag.'

If we don't understand how and why something worked, there is a good chance it's doomed to become dogma. We do something because we're told it worked in the past. If Jimmy Hogan was right, we can draw a line from Chapman's innovative WM formation through a generation of copycat managers and arrive at the static setup of Winterbottom's England of the 1950s. There was an anti-intellectual streak in English football: a preference for the working-class 'do-er' over the middle-class thinker. While it is important to value experience, an unwillingness to continually reassess your actions can make success a curse.

He was an odd man, Alf Ramsey. He spoke in a weirdly affected posh voice which was occasionally exposed by his poor grammar.[3] His upbringing was so humble it is hard to envisage now we have social security. He grew up in Dagenham when it was an Essex village, in a cottage with no electricity, inside toilet or hot water. He left school at 14 and, despite being a talented footballer, had two years out of the game because his job delivering groceries by bicycle involved working on Saturdays. Joining the army in World War Two rescued his career. He played in organised matches and his ability was spotted, which led to him joining Southampton when professional football returned. He was in his mid-20s but lied about his age and was meticulous about his fitness.

In 1949 he moved to Tottenham under Arthur Rowe, the inventor of 'push and run', which made systematic use of one-twos; passing and moving into space was still a relatively novel idea. Spurs were promoted from the Second Division in 1950 and won the Football League 12 months later. Success didn't last and Ramsey's low point with Spurs came in the 1953 FA Cup semi-final when he tried to dribble the ball out of his penalty area in the last minute, only to lose it and hand Blackpool the winning goal.

He won 32 international caps, including the 1950 defeat against the USA in which he claimed England had suffered a year's worth of bad luck in 45 minutes. His last match was the 1953 defeat by Hungary. Ramsey pushed against the tide,

3   I recommend the documentary *Sir Alf Ramsey: England Soccer Team Manager* and Leo McKinstry's biography *Sir Alf*

maintaining England lost because they had conceded from long-range shots. That didn't explain the 7-1 defeat the following year or England's lacklustre World Cup campaign.

Ramsey became a manager in 1955 with Third Division South side Ipswich Town. Progress was unspectacular at first. They were promoted in 1957 then consolidated in the Second Division until they went up in 1961. The 1961/62 season was a sensational one for the Suffolk club as they claimed their only Football League title, largely credited to Ramsey's tactics of using a deep-lying wide midfielder to deliver accurate balls over opposition defences. Their success didn't last, and they finished 17th the following season as opponents adapted. In October 1962 Ramsey agreed to replace Winterbottom as England manager but still led Ipswich until the end of the campaign. Ramsey insisted on picking the England team himself and told the media his side would win the 1966 World Cup on home soil.

His biographer, Leo McKinstry, wrote, 'He was a tough demanding character, who could be strangely sensitive to criticism, a reserved English gentleman who was loathed by the establishment, an unashamed traditionalist who turned out to be a tactical revolutionary, a strict disciplinarian who was not above telling his players to "get rat-arsed". His ruthlessness divided the football world; his stubbornness left him the target of abuse and condemnation. But it was his zeal that put England at the top of the world.'

The road to glory began with defeat against France in a two-legged contest for a place in the last 16 of the European Championship, England's first participation in the tournament, having been typically dismissive of the first edition in 1960. Ramsey was undeterred.

His legacy is two-fold: winning the World Cup and scrapping wingers. As time goes on, the first of those takes precedence, which seems fair. Winterbottom abandoned the WM and the side Ramsey inherited had, reputedly, been playing a 4-2-4 with two central forwards and two wingers. It took a while but his experiments with 4-3-3 convinced him it was

England's best option although it wasn't popular with older observers and the journalists with whom Ramsey shared a tetchy relationship. They missed the likes of Matthews, the dribbling right-winger who largely stayed out on his flank until fed the ball, then dazzled defenders and onlookers alike. They wanted Jimmy Greaves, who had a remarkable international scoring record as a young man but whose injury allowed Ramsey to pair up the hard-working forwards Roger Hunt and Geoff Hurst. Hurst's hat-trick in the final is one of the cornerstones of the English football story but his fitness and willingness to run were critical to Ramsey's plan. The West Ham striker's touch map for the 1966 final is spread remarkably evenly throughout the West German half.

The formation for the final was shown on TV as 4-3-3, although by the time I was watching football Ramsey's team had become known as the founding fathers of the English 4-4-2. Gordon Banks was in goal. The back four was obvious: George Cohen and Ray Wilson were full-backs with Bobby Moore and Jack Charlton in central defence. The midfield was shown as Nobby Stiles, Bobby Charlton and Martin Peters. A nominal front three was Hurst, Hunt, and Alan Ball.

I can see why people came to describe it as a 4-4-2: Ball was a midfielder, 21 years old and hugely energetic. Peters was another newcomer, and it was obvious why Ramsey liked him too: when possession was lost, he would run back into midfield and be ready to defend. Bobby Charlton was also hard-working and at 28, much younger than he looked. His England career crossed over with the likes of Finney, starting as a left-winger but he adapted to the changing times. I rank him as the country's greatest ever player.

Stiles was the most controversial presence. The FA asked Ramsey to drop the Manchester United man after he injured France's Jacques Simon in the group stage. Ramsey stood by Stiles, partly out of principle, but mainly because he wanted a midfield spoiler. In 2006 Ball described Stiles as a holding midfielder but in the first half of the World Cup Final, he doesn't look like that to me: he vacated the space in front of defence to join attacks, leaving England wide-open to counter attacks. He wasn't alone in that – the game was end-to-end to an extent you never see now in high-level football. In the second half he was more cautious in something more like a 4-1-3-2. George Cohen described England's tactical progression through the tournament, 'We went into a "loose" 4-4-2 from again a "loose" 4-3-3. You were able to adapt but with the front runners who were two very strong but very brave players.'

The game was fast moving, and players would rest out of possession so there was less pressure on whoever had the ball. Both keepers kicked aimlessly from time-to-time but there was no co-ordinated long-ball game. The South American teams complained about the refereeing in that tournament but there wasn't the brutal tackling that came later.

The attitude of the crowd is fascinating. With England 2-1 up in the last ten minutes, Jack Charlton turned and passed the ball back to Banks and was booed by the home supporters. England showed almost no sign of 'parking the bus', or in other words match management. The crowd chanted 'We want three!' when it was 2-1 and 'We want four!' when it was 3-2 with time running out in extra time. I find it touchingly naive, which might be a sign of how we have been conditioned to accept defensive-minded football. Ramsey's adversaries blamed him.

If an England manager were to win the World Cup now, they would be a national hero and it is amazing how unpopular Ramsey was with sportswriters, his fellow managers, and the FA. In his notorious live TV argument with Brian Clough, Sir Alf's successor Don Revie said, almost as an aside, 'I never got close to Ramsey. He was a cold man.'

There was more to the widespread hostility than Ramsey's prickly personality. Historian Frank McLynn was scathing in *The Guardian* in 2005, six years after Ramsey's death, blaming him for football's defensive shift:

'He was a humourless boor, he was the epitome of negativity and his legend far outstrips his actual achievement. No man without a sense of humour is ever any damn good, and Ramsey raised humourlessness to a fine art.

'As a manager, Ramsey turned football into a negative contest of attrition, predicated on the massed defence. Watch any England game from his era and it always appears that there are at least 22 white shirts clustered around the penalty area. The Ramsey method was simple: defend in such depth that the opposition eventually becomes exhausted or just plain bored, and then one of the mediocre England forwards can slip out and score a single goal.

'There were in fact four better teams than England in the 1966 finals (Hungary, the Soviet Union, West Germany and Argentina), but the hosts secured a remarkably simple path to the final. England avoided their main rivals in the group stage but then faced a formidable Argentina team, who had qualified with the West Germans, in the quarter-finals. Man for man, the Argentinians were superior to Ramsey's squad and they had in their captain, Antonio Rattín, the finest midfielder in the world at that time. How to sweep away this obstacle? With ten minutes left in the first half, a German referee sent Rattín off for "violence of the tongue", even though the referee spoke no Spanish.

'The ten-man Argentina team struggled on, only to succumb – you've guessed it – 1-0. In a match being played the same day, an English referee sent off two Uruguayans in their match against West Germany, handing the Germans an easy victory.

'The 1966 World Cup was a murky business that has never been cleared up satisfactorily, but it is on this dubious foundation that Ramsey's reputation as a saviour has been built ... It is difficult to see what there is worthwhile about the absurd Ramsey cult that still exerts such a powerful sway. If we are going to accept a humourless, cynical, negative opportunist as one of our sporting heroes, of what calibre will the villains have to be?'

You get the idea. McLynn wasn't alone. Hostility grew as Ramsey failed to add to his World Cup success. England lost the semi-final of the 1968 Euros to Yugoslavia, then to West Germany in the 1970 World Cup quarter-final, and again to the same opposition in a two-legged quarter-final in the 1972 Euros. He was sacked after England's failure to qualify for the 1974 World Cup. The final qualifier against Poland in October 1973 seared a mark on the collective English football conscience for a generation: I'm too young to have watched the game live but it was referenced for years. Having lost in Poland, England had to win at Wembley qualify. Brian Clough, working as a TV pundit, described the Polish keeper Jan Tomaszewski as a 'clown' and produced a nail that he said was 'either going in Poland's coffin or Sir Alf's'.

It went in Sir Alf's. All England fans of a certain age know it finished 1-1 after a mistake by Peter Shilton gave Poland the lead and the home side could only reply with Allan Clarke's penalty.

I have now watched the game and England were excellent. Full-backs Paul Madeley and Emlyn Hughes attacked, centre-backs Roy McFarland and Norman Hunter were comfortable bringing the ball forward, Colin Bell was a top-class midfielder and there was a fluid front three of Clarke, Mick Channon, and Martin Chivers. They missed good chances, hit the post, Poland cleared the ball off the line twice and Tomaszewski was inspired. The idea that Ramsey single-handedly sucked the joy out of English football seems nonsensical on that evidence. Poland finished third at the 1974 World Cup, losing only to hosts West Germany on a boggy pitch in what was effectively a semi-final. England would have had a chance of winning that World Cup – international football tournaments are decided on fine margins.

'We'll go on getting bad results, getting bad results.'

So did England's 1966 World Cup win, courtesy of Ramsey's pragmatism, set us on a path of negativity, paradoxically leading to these years of hurt? The declining rate of goals per game at World Cups suggest there was a general move towards cagier, defensive football. If you want to blame a single factor, I'd suggest *catenaccio* – the Italian system which raised defending to a high art. It can be thought of as a particular lop-sided formation preferred by Italian clubs in this period, or more generally as a philosophy – pick more defenders than attackers, like every manager does now.

Dave Bowen, the Wales manager contemporary to Ramsey, reflected to Leo McKinstry how the old-school winger was doomed, 'We all followed Ramsey. The winger was dead once you played four defenders. Alf saw that and it just took the rest of us a little longer to understand … with four defenders the backs can play tight on the winger and he's lost his acceleration space. Without that the winger's finished.'

By the time I was watching football in the late 1970s, it seemed everyone played 4-4-2. Old programmes and cigarette cards described players as 'inside-right' or 'left-half', but I didn't know what that meant.

Ramsey was immediately followed by Joe Mercer, who had won the league with Manchester City but ruled himself out of the England job in the long term because he considered himself too old at 60 and had sciatica. After one of his seven matches in charge, he gave a passionate defence of English football, offering one of the best deconstructions I've heard.

He said, 'I believe, I really believe English football played at its best, played naturally, pushing forward, and playing and being tight in defence and compact, setting the thing up, getting on the end of movements, goals and goalmouth incidents. All right, we mightn't have the technique and skill of the Brazil and the Ajax and people like that, but the game is about other things. It's about heart and courage and organisation and belief. I believe in England.'

Not everyone did. Pomposity had given way to self-doubt. English football was unsure whether to revel in the attributes we supposed defined us or ape European or South American sophistication. Revie followed Mercer and while his tenure was a shambles, he had been one of the greats of club management and his analysis was as sharp as his tongue. Shortly before taking the job, he said, 'It changed in 1966 when Alf Ramsey felt he had no wingers and decided to play without them which tactically was very, very good in my opinion because he felt he didn't have the wingers to attack full-backs and get round the back of them, so he used full-backs. He used George Cohen and Ray Wilson and he had Bobby Moore as a sweeper and used three in the middle of the field. It was very effective. He made Alan Ball come back from a front position to make four in the middle of the field, so it made it tight at the back when they lost possession of the ball. It demanded a lot of running, that system. I think a lot of teams in England at club level, because it had been successful at World Cup level, decided to copy it but I don't think a lot of clubs had the players to exploit the going forward system. Then we had the Germans and Dutch and they play a vastly different game completely, but they've got all-purpose players and that's what I'd eventually like to see with England.'

Revie failed to realise his vision. Results were poor as he chopped and changed his team and his plans. In 1977 he quit for a better-paid job in the UAE, leaving Ron Greenwood in charge as England failed to reach the 1978 World Cup.

Greenwood had won the FA Cup and UEFA Cup Winners' Cup with West Ham in the mid-1960s but had been 'upstairs' as the club's general manager for three years when the FA chose him over Clough as Revie's replacement. England qualified for the 1980 Euros but were knocked out at the group stage and then scraped through qualification for the 1982 World Cup. On the eve of the tournament, he was interviewed for the BBC by his old Brentford club-mate Jimmy Hill. Greenwood espoused a similar philosophy to Revie, and many who have followed, 'My whole philosophy has been based on the best of British and the best from the continent. I think it's ideal if you can marry them.'

Easier said than done. Hill asked him who would win the tournament and Greenwood identified Brazil, who would gain cult status but lose to a pragmatic Italy team:

'When you look at them with their skill, finesse, everything about them, the way they play, the fluid approach about their game, it was enlightening, it was frightening almost. We envy the Brazilians that, but they envy us this quality that we've got, this resilience which is our characteristic.'

Greenwood had been a 31-year-old Chelsea player when he watched Hungary dismantling England in 1953, setting him on his pathway to managing his national team:

'I knew there was more to football than running round a track and seeing them that day epitomised to me what I felt football was all about. It was to do with thought, and it was to do with movement. Their movement and passing was so precise, and the shooting, but I don't think people saw what was happening off the ball. They're only seeing people on the ball, and they could see big triangles and English football went through a stage with triangles, but they were stationary. The art of football is to move triangles about and that's what they did that day, it was a great influence on me, and I thought that's the way the game should be played.'

Greenwood's influence can be traced to England's modern coaching philosophy. Trevor Brooking played for him at West Ham and England and was later the FA's director of football development. Greenwood's train of thought, from that 1982 interview, is almost a blueprint for what followed, eventually:

'Lower down, I would like to see people playing man-for-man football where I'm constantly trying to dribble past and you're trying to stop me and vice versa.

'There are two facets to football: you have the ball, or you haven't. In man-to-man football, from an early age, you're in constant contact and once you've beaten him then you can run because there's space. It's helping to develop the right habits. Later on, they can talk about tactics.

'What's happening at football clubs and in schools is that kids of eight or nine are being taught about tactics. There are more tactics than we have in international games. They all like to play so create situations where they're practising within that.

'Your small-sided games will come in, because there's constant contact: five vs five, seven vs seven, whatever. You'll still have goals and your goalkeeper but there's a constant repetition: I'm having to beat you and you're having to stop me. Then you're trying to beat me and I'm having to stop you. You don't need any teaching, any advice from the sidelines, just leave them alone and let them play.'

Make the language more inclusive and the FA could sign that off now. Unfortunately, youth coaching in England was very much in the wrong hands. It was a shame, too, that Greenwood's England played dull football, despite his intentions, 'Football is becoming too mundane and too predictable every match you watch is the same. Get some new ideas. Get people thinking about it and get rid of the fear in football and at the same time entertain the public.'

They were eliminated after drawing both second-phase group games 0-0, their play characterised by slinging in crosses from unproductive areas. Ray Wilkins put it down to nerves brought on by high expectations. Mick Channon, whose international career had ended in 1977, lamented on ITV, 'We didn't have people who could go past people. We didn't have people who could score goals.'

English football would have been far better served if Greenwood had become its technical director rather than its team manager.

The best of times, the worst of times

The England team and English football are not the same, and there have been two other periods in which we can legitimately claim to be on top of the world. We will get to the current Premier League later but let me dwell briefly on my childhood days when it seemed perfectly natural that an English club would win the European Cup. Starting from 1976/77 the champions of Europe were Liverpool, Liverpool, Nottingham Forest, Nottingham Forest, Liverpool, Aston Villa, Hamburg, Liverpool. Teams usually played 4-4-2, but with exceptions such as Forest's 4-5-1 in the 1980 final against Hamburg. The run ended horrifically when the 1985 Heysel Stadium disaster triggered a thoroughly deserved ban. Blame the hooliganism that had been raging for years.

Garry Birtles was part of Nottingham Forest's two European Cup-winning teams, both led by the charismatic Clough. He says the glory days of English club football were not about the long ball, 'We got it down and played. Cloughie wasn't worried about what you couldn't do; he was worried about what you could do. When you went out on to the pitch, he made you feel a million dollars. It was very rare that we played it in the air although we could because Tony Woodcock was quick, and I had a little bit of pace, but we had two widemen in Martin O'Neill and John Robertson, and we tried to play through and round teams. Liverpool were the best club team in the world, although for two years they couldn't beat us. I still think that side was possibly better than Liverpool now.

'It's often forgotten and decried that era. There were some great teams and not just Liverpool. There weren't many teams who outmuscled you or tried to go through you. We all could play. At Forest we had Archie Gemmill, Ian Bowyer, John McGovern, great passers of the ball. They talk about attacking full-backs now, but Viv Anderson was doing it then. Kenny Burns and Larry Lloyd at the back were the retainers, if you like, but Burnsy had played up front and was a great passer of the ball. Brian Clough in the second semi-final, we were playing 4-4-2, but we were getting battered in the first ten minutes, so he changed it to 4-5-1. It's a myth that's only happening that way now.'

Tony Gale made his debut for Fulham in 1977 and moved to West Ham in 1984. 'There were so many skilful players in my time,' he recalls. 'Alan Devonshire from my West Ham side, who'd run with the ball, would be worth about £200m now because players couldn't touch him. We played with intensity. In football now you get some intense games, and you get slow games where people are tactically sitting with 11 behind the ball which really didn't happen in the old days. Everybody went at everybody.'

The games do look end-to-end compared with now, but English success was built on sound defence. The seven European Cup-winning teams played 61 matches and conceded just 33 goals while six consecutive finals finished 1-0. Goals were also becoming scarcer in domestic football. In 1960/61, there were

3.73 per game in the First Division and champions Tottenham scored 115 in their 42 matches. In 1965/66 there were 3.15 per game. By the end of the decade, goals were going out of fashion and Revie's Leeds won the title in 1968/69 by scoring 66 in 42. The low point was 1970/71 (2.36) and goalscoring has never hit the pre-1966 heights again. We can't blame it all on Ramsey, but he was part of the trend of football becoming more defensive. It wasn't just an English phenomenon: at the 1954 World Cup there were 5.38 goals per game; by 1990 that figure was 2.21. FIFA was wise to change the offside and back-pass laws. English football did strike out by awarding three points for a win from 1981/82. It made no difference in the first season but there was a four-year spell with more goals in the mid-1980s.

No club retained the English title between Wolves in 1959 and Liverpool's successes of 1975/76 and 1976/77. The Merseysiders were largely dominant from the mid-1970s through the '80s but with challenges from Forest, Villa, Everton, and Arsenal. The games are worth watching. Play was noticeably faster than the mid-60s, although ragged compared to today; possession swapped over, and teams could break against each other quickly. I've just watched a game from Aston Villa's title-winning season in 1980/81 in which commentator John Motson remarks on the patience of the build-up play when to me it looked as though the ball was crossed as the first opportunity. They recycled possession once when Middlesbrough's Mark Proctor put pressure on Gordon Cowans, so he passed to Tony Morley who crossed. Contrast that with modern teams recycling possession time and again probing for opportunities. There were still players who were described as wingers, but unlike Stanley Matthews they didn't wait for their moment. They were skilful or pacy wide midfielders, who weren't expected to regularly track deep into their own half. Teams got the ball wide and looked for crossing opportunities.

The state of pitches makes the quality of play remarkable. At times there was little choice but to get the ball off the ground, as Ray Lewington remembers, 'English football was known for being more direct than European leagues and that was due to the state of the pitches and climate, as much as preference. Most teams started the season passing a lot more but when you got to winter coaches would say you can't play through the middle, get it over the top. We tried to play football at Chelsea, but when you got to October/November the pitches were getting so bad, playing primarily through the middle was impossible.'

Tackling was robust but less violent than it became although there existed then as now the common narrative that 'you can't tackle any more'. English football in the 1970s and early '80s was packed with paradoxes: the atmosphere at games was better than now if you value singing and roaring crowds, but it came with the sad stain of hooliganism and throughout the period of European domination, attendances were dwindling. The football authorities, police and governments failed ordinary football fans until after the 1989 Hillsborough disaster which heralded the Taylor Report and a vast improvement in stadiums and fan welfare. A period of glory for English football on the pitch was one of shame off it. It wasn't just football to blame – the attitude of the establishment contributed, reaching a grim climax at Hillsborough which claimed 97 lives while another 766 people were injured.

Heroic failure

Bobby Robson's enduring popularity in England's collective consciousness represents his remarkable renaissance. He was treated abominably by the tabloids while he was the national team manager – human collateral in a circulation war which saw him ridiculed and abused. But after the 1990 World Cup he left on a high and was thereafter football's favourite uncle, especially in a successful spell at Newcastle from 1999 to 2004. I interviewed him at Villa Park when I was working for BBC Radio 5 Live and afterwards, he took me to task – with great vigour – over the rise of the football phone-in, which he felt gave a voice to ignorant people.

Our desire for neat narratives serves us badly when we assess Robson's England. I remember most of the games as dull, his team fearful and overcautious but they reached quarters and semis of successive World Cups and their legend grows with time.

He started with failure: drawing 0-0 at home to Greece and losing to Denmark meant England missed out on Euro 1984 with the Wembley crowd singing 'What a load of rubbish!' In three major tournaments, Robson's men played 14 games and won only three in normal time: Poland, Paraguay, and Egypt. They beat Belgium and Cameroon in extra time. They scored only 16 goals and with three periods of extra time included that was the equivalent of 15 matches. They conceded 14 – the games were boring compared to club football with the performances at Euro 1988 especially abject.

John Barnes was an exhilarating left-winger for his clubs, but not for England. It was a similar story with Glenn Hoddle who was revered in France after he moved to Monaco but was never a settled presence for his country. He was a technical, creative midfielder – not a natural fit for 4-4-2 and was often shoehorned in for his 53 caps. Robson's caution also held back Paul Gascoigne, the most gifted English player I've seen, who didn't start in a competitive international until the 1990 World Cup when he was 23. Gascoigne was as reckless as he was brilliant, and his career was blighted by injury and wild behaviour. The conservatism of English football still discourages individualism, and it is striking how many of our more creative players have been difficult characters.

For the most part, England played 4-4-2; the main concession to the international football environment was a turgid tempo. Again, it wasn't long-ball football. Robson and his assistant Don Howe did change formations, but it was tinkering rather than strategic. For example, in 1986 winger Chris Waddle started the tournament and was allowed to switch flanks while Bryan Robson, Wilkins and Hoddle covered the midfield.

I don't want to heartlessly trash the childhood memories of middle-aged England fans so let's get to the glorious failures.

Facing elimination from the Mexico World Cup after losing to Portugal and drawing with Morocco without a goal scored, England switched to a 4-4-2 with wide midfielders rather than wingers, and Gary Lineker became a hero, hitting a hat-trick against Poland and two more against Paraguay.

The infamous quarter-final against Argentina allowed England to depart with dignity, telling tales of skulduggery and what might have been. Another slow game on a sweltering afternoon was defined by Diego Maradona. His first goal was obviously handball – although not so obvious that it was spotted by either the officials or the BBC commentators. The second showed off an unshackled genius as Maradona danced through England's midfield and defence to score the 'goal of the century'. At 2-0 down Robson threw on Barnes and Waddle to attack from wide: Barnes set up Lineker's goal and another chance that was miraculously cleared off the line. Argentina beat Belgium in the semi-final and West Germany in the final. If only!

Four years on, Robson's England failed gloriously at Italia '90. This time they came through a stupefying group stage thanks to a 1-0 win over Egypt and were rewarded with a welcoming path to the semi-finals. The players persuaded Robson to abandon the 4-4-2 and use three centre-backs and wing-backs, in what could be described as either a 3-4-3 or a 5-4-1. David Platt's volley in the 120th minute against Belgium is one of English football's iconic moments and the quarter-final against Cameroon was a rare great game – although check out England's savage tackling.

In the semi-final against West Germany, Gazza's tears as he was shown a yellow card that ruled him out of a potential final secured his legend. Pearce and Waddle missed penalties in the shoot-out and 40-year-old Shilton didn't get close to a save. England fans have fond memories of Robson's World Cups, with good cause, but as each major tournament rolls around and I have come to regard the growing nostalgia as a rewriting of history. Tournaments are short and luck matters; the obsession with finishing with a scapegoat or neat narrative puts a cap on how much we learn.

Robson is a much-loved epitome of English football's gallant failure. He believed our players had to adjust their style to win major tournaments but also said English football – with its fast-paced First Division – would be 'all at sea' if it tried to develop the more technical game played by the countries that were winning competitions. Under Robson, England went close, but even the most ardent patriot couldn't think they were the best in the world.

Stewart Robson – no relation – was an England youth international who played for Arsenal, West Ham and Coventry in the 1980s and '90s. I asked him why club success from 1976 to 1984 was never translated into international glory.

He replied, 'There was an element that people didn't enjoy playing for England. There were club cliques and the players from when I was playing often thought it was a holiday as well, "We're away, we're going on a piss-up." They'd all go to a club in Tottenham and be absolutely smashed and they were training the next day. Players found there was a lot of pressure they didn't really want. The Wembley crowd didn't always help. The newspapers didn't always help.'

I asked the same question of Terry Gibson, another player from that era. He said, 'I don't recall the national team playing that 4-4-2 as well as club teams. Clubs had perfect players for the roles. England were always trying to adapt, to get the best players in without really coming up with a successful system.

'Liverpool were excellent technically but strong and powerful. Villa, Forest had really good technical players. European teams in two-legged affairs couldn't deal with the muddy pitches, the conditions we played in. There's no doubt the Football League teams were more powerful and that led to success.'

Bobby Robson's reign spanned from the early 1980s when English clubs were riding high to 1990, five years into the European ban after Heysel. Gibson saw our teams struggle tactically after that:

'We played the 4-4-2 and it was rigid, two wingers, two midfielders, back four, only one full-back at a time pushed forward. That period of Liverpool, Forest, Villa winning European cups led to continental sides coming up with alternatives. They started playing with an extra man in midfield and kept the ball more, getting players between those rigid lines. English players were facing teams who were technically better. While we were doing 12-mile runs, they were doing loads of touches on the ball. The technical players and the different tactical systems they employed made it more difficult for the English teams.

'They put players in unusual positions. Peter Beardsley was probably the only person in my whole career who dropped off the front and he was referred to as a "cheat" – in an endearing way, but that's how the position was seen. No one else in England played between midfield and attack; it gave a midfielder a problem or a defender a problem. English 4-4-2 was about personal or partnership duels in every area of the pitch and whenever it was like that English teams won their duels.'

The best manager England never had

The story of how Brian Clough didn't become England manager shines a light on to the dysfunctional world of English football. When Don Revie quit in 1977, five men were interviewed, and Clough was the best qualified by far. He had won a First Division title with Derby County in 1972 and his Nottingham Forest side were top, but the FA chairman Sir Harold Thompson, by all accounts an unpleasant man, was determined to block him. Thompson had treated Ramsey with disdain, fallen out with Revie and disliked the bombastic Clough. Another member of the FA's International Committee, Manchester City chairman Peter Swales, said years later they knew Clough was the best qualified, 'He gave the best interview of all the candidates – confident, full of common sense and patriotic.' True to form, the FA appointed Greenwood who hadn't managed a team for three years but was cheery and diplomatic.

Had Clough taken over England in 1977, he would never have won the European Cup with Forest, so I would argue that 1982 would have been the perfect moment but that time he wasn't even a candidate. Ipswich boss Robson had managed the

England B side part-time and was regarded by the FA as the heir apparent.

Would Clough have done better than Greenwood or Robson, and changed the course of England's football history? He was a shrewder tactician and stronger personality. He was the TV co-commentator for the Euro qualifying defeat at home to Denmark in 1983 and gave some clues about what his England team would have been like. He criticised Robson's side for not looking like a product of the English First Division – 'the best league in the world' as he put it, with ample justification. 'Challenging for the ball that's on the floor ... good tackles ...white shirts moving forwards. We've got to get white shirts into the box ... They've got no idea how to defend against people who get the ball wide and are very, very brave.' And there was detail, 'We're 1-0 down and [centre-backs] Butcher and Osman haven't broken sweat. We might as well move up 15 yards and let them earn their corn.'

I asked Garry Birtles why England failed to translate club success into international football, and he didn't miss a beat before identifying the failure to appoint his old mentor to the top job:

'Brian Clough was the best manager in the country. Everybody in the country wanted him to get the job but the FA. The FA bottled it, big style. If he'd been in charge things might have been different. I worked under him, and I honestly think England would have won something. That was the biggest travesty ever from the FA.'

I told Birtles about Swales's account of Clough's interview and for him it summed up the FA's negative influence on the national team:

'What a disgrace, absolutely ridiculous! So, it has to be a dull character to be the England manager? Oh dear, that's why we haven't won anything for so long. It's all "what ifs" and it's sad because I think things would've been totally different.'

Now that people in football are so measured, even defensive, in their comments, Clough's candour seems incredible. For that reason alone, he was never seriously considered for the England job. It is an example of the chasm between the working-class 'football men' and the 'non-football people' such as Thompson, the Oxford University-educated son of a colliery manager. Clough would have caused trouble and plenty of it. Behaving himself for the duration of an interview was one thing but he was outrageously undiplomatic about players, administrators, club owners, and even his managerial contemporaries. He wasn't an FA sort of chap, just the best English manager of his generation.

Destroyer-in-chief

Hypotheticals don't tell us whether Clough or anyone else would have done better than Greenwood or Robson. There was a widely held view that the English system wasn't producing players with the necessary technique and know-how to win international tournaments. The blame was generally laid at the door of the notorious Charles Hughes, the FA's director of coaching and education, dubbed by one newspaper as the 'Doctor Death of the Beautiful Game'.

Hughes joined the FA in 1964 as assistant director of coaching and manager of the England amateur side. Despite Winterbottom's efforts there was widespread scepticism of the value of coaching. In some ways, Hughes was ahead of his time: he and his friend Wing Commander Charles Reep saw the benefit of analysing matches statistically. Hughes also spent three years going through 16mm films of FA Cup finals and international matches. Unfortunately, they reached robust conclusions from a sliver of information and their analysis of the data they had was flawed. I suspect it simply fuelled Hughes's existing beliefs. Jimmy Hogan might have believed English football was lost to the long-ball game decades earlier, but we had produced Matthews, Charlton and Greaves. Now the coaching programme was in the grip of a man officially advocating what he termed 'direct play'.

Incongruously, Hughes's 1990 book *The Winning Formula* has a picture of Maradona on the front cover – a man who had taken

11 consecutive touches to score his second goal against England four years earlier. The tone was relentless and hectoring, 'Soccer has always been long on opinions and short on facts; analysis has been rare or non-existent. Throughout the history of the game, coaches and managers have made claims and propounded theories based on opinions rather than facts.' Hughes successfully sold books and led courses for coaches around the world.

He insisted his work wasn't an endorsement of kick-and-rush but added, 'The logical result of possession play is a succession of goalless draws,' and 'few players or spectators enjoy bouts of prolonged midfield play.'

It is very proscriptive. This, essentially, is how to play:

- Look to see if there's a pass behind the defence on
- Diagonal passes over the defence are the most lethal passes of all
- 1. Over the top 2. To a forward's feet 3. Other forward passes. 4. Switch 5. Passing back – the last resort.

The 'prime target area' was a space four yards to 12 yards and the width of the six-yard box:

'If crosses are made early into the prime target area it will inevitably lead to more goals being scored … All the facts point to the conclusion that when the number of consecutive passes in a move exceeds five, the chances of creating a scoring opportunity at the end of the move decrease.'

The reductive nature of Hughes and Reep's study led them to undervalue technical ability. Data analysis is great for processing huge numbers, but Hughes and Reep weren't dealing with huge numbers. The human brain is a wonderful computer and a player who has made hundreds of appearances has amassed a wealth of knowhow. Experienced professionals must have looked at the basic nature of Hughes's analysis and decided that improvising was a better bet.

Can we not knock it?

Long-ball football can work, as Wimbledon showed when they charged headlong through the English leagues from the Fourth

Division in 1982/83 to the top flight by 1986. Having only been elected to the league in 1977, they won the FA Cup in 1988. We will look at Terry Gibson's breakdown of their tactics later.

Watford's journey was similar. With pop star Elton John as chairman, Graham Taylor joined in the Fourth Division in 1977 and they were in the top flight by 1982. They finished second in their debut season, qualifying for the UEFA Cup. In 1984 they lost the FA Cup Final. When they were on the verge of promotion to the First Division, Taylor was interviewed by John Motson on *Match of the Day* and made a passionate defence of direct football:

'We want to go forward, and we want to get the ball in the box as often as possible. As regards style I leave it to the experts. I've seen us described as a kick-and-rush side. If it's as simple as that maybe everyone should kick and rush.'

Motson asked whether Watford would need more sophistication in the top flight, which triggered Taylor:

'More sophisticated? I hate that word being used where football is concerned. Football is a simple game. It's not a sophisticated game. It's a game for the man on the terraces. It's a game to excite the people. Whatever level of football I watch, the man on the terrace when he sees something that's going to create excitement, and usually it's in and around the penalty box, he will start to take great interest. He's not interested, in my opinion, watching people play 15, 16 consecutive passes in their own half. If we try to tell him he has to become more sophisticated, then what he'll say to us is, "I'm not going to bother coming to watch you because I just want to get excited." I hate sophisticated football.'

In 1987 Taylor was lured to Second Division Aston Villa and got them up at the first attempt before they finished 17th and second. He hadn't won a trophy and his style was controversial and unpopular with outsiders, but he had won a lot of matches despite spending very little money.

Unfortunately, Taylor's limitations were brutally exposed during three years in charge of England. They qualified for Euro

'92 but were awful in the tournament, drawing the first two games 0-0 before losing to hosts Sweden, as Taylor substituted Lineker in his final international, one short of equalling Bobby Charlton's scoring record.

Worse followed as England failed even to qualify for the 1994 World Cup – finishing below both Norway and the Netherlands in their group. Taylor was unlucky to lose Stuart Pearce and Alan Shearer to injury, but he called up Carlton Palmer and rejected Peter Beardsley and Chris Waddle. Barnes's frustrating inability to replicate his club form continued and though Paul Gascoigne played when fit, a serious knee ligament injury suffered in the 1991 FA Cup Final, and his self-destructive lifestyle, made him a more limited player.

This is Stewart Robson's analysis, 'Graham Taylor picked players who were good at that style of football. They weren't good footballers. They were runners and very determined. The skill was supposed to come from the wide areas which it had at Watford. Charles Hughes was to the fore then, and he got Taylor in to be his sort of manager. That was why we started to go downhill in terms of international football for a while. We were picking the wrong tactics and the wrong players.'

At least we discovered that long-ball football didn't work at international level.

Taylor was harassed and mocked in the newspapers to an inhuman extent. His humiliation was compounded after he had left the job when the fly-on-the-wall documentary *The Impossible Job* showed him struggling to deal with the emotions of England's failure, 'Do I not like that!' he intoned as hope withered. I worked with Taylor in radio; he was a gentleman, genuinely kind and good company but the more sober criticism of his England team was well-founded. The most revealing cry in the documentary was, 'It's got to go big!' Norway thrived on long-ball football; England didn't. Our biggest teams and best players were not long-ball merchants. Though English football was more direct and, by then, less creative than its major rivals, it was a baffling decision to appoint a manager who had never hidden his allegiance to the long ball.

The revival of English football is often attributed to the 1990 World Cup, but this is simplistic to a fault. Fans turned against England again during Taylor's reign and our football was mocked as dull and unsophisticated. The start of the Premier League and the surge in televised football were bigger factors. The rise of TV is still lamented by some traditionalists, but few people seriously advocate turning back the clock. I will look at the rise of the Premier League later but for now let's focus on the England team's triumphs and tribulations in the last 30 years.

Christmas tree come early

The abject failure of the Taylor era was replaced by a return of glorious failure under his successor. Terry Venables was Dagenham-born like Ramsey but far more cosmopolitan. He won La Liga and reached the European Cup Final with Barcelona. He nurtured the sort of sophisticated football Taylor despised. He brought back Beardsley, ditched Palmer and gave us the 'Christmas tree'. The formation added two bands to the 4-4-2 as a way of getting more creative players into the line-up. It was also a sign that the ex-Crystal Palace, QPR and Tottenham boss had developed new ideas in Spain.

A joyful England played as hosts at Euro '96 – where the empty seats across the country showed that football fever wasn't yet feverish. The 4-1 Wembley win over the Netherlands was exhilarating and exciting, a rare thing for England. The ending was familiar – a semi-final defeat on penalties against the Germans, after Gareth Southgate's fateful miss. Venables resigned because he was facing court cases over his business dealings after a bitter dispute with Alan Sugar who had been with him at Spurs. It was a tremendous shame. Southgate reflected, 'Terry opened my eyes to things that no one else has. He has fantastic tactical awareness. Every senior player in that group went away having learnt a lot from him, which is an achievement.'

Dealing with the press is a challenge that England managers must rise to, such is the hysterical nature of the coverage. Two in a row lost their jobs for non-footballing reasons. Glenn Hoddle's team showed promise during the 1998 World Cup at which David Beckham's red card was the most memorable moment in a last-16 defeat against Argentina. Again, a penalty shoot-out defeat brought the end. We would have had more sympathy had Hoddle not revealed that he thought practising penalties was pointless. The newspapers had dogged him over his use of faith healer Eileen Drewery and it was views on reincarnation that proved to be his undoing. He told *Times* journalist Matt Dickinson, 'You and I have been physically given two hands and two legs and half-decent brains. Some people have not been born like that for a reason. The karma is working from another lifetime. I have nothing to hide about that. It is not only people with disabilities. What you sow you reap.' The fall-out saw Hoddle lose his job. It wasn't the last time an England manager was brought down by a newspaper.

Kevin Keegan led England to Euro 2000 amid hopes he could recreate with the national team something of his entertaining Newcastle side from a few years earlier. They did beat a poor Germany team in their second game, thanks to Shearer's header from Beckham's free-kick – but either side of that were two shambolic 3-2 defeats, to Portugal and Romania. Keegan was incessantly dubbed 'tactically naive' by the newspapers, and they had a point. England were 2-0 up against Portugal thanks to goals from Paul Scholes and Steve McManaman who both met crosses from the right. But the 4-4-2 with Scholes and Ince in midfield was overrun and Portugal turned on the style. The Germany win meant England would qualify for the quarter-finals if they drew with Romania. It was another wide-open game which stood at 2-2 until Phil Neville inexplicably conceded a penalty that sent the Romanians through. The Manchester United full-back shared the ritual pillorying with his manager.

Keegan quit after a World Cup qualifying defeat against the Germans in the rain-sodden final game at the old Wembley. England had veered from Taylor's direct football to Venables's sophistication and Keegan's naive enthusiasm with no sniff of a strategy. The next twist was to look overseas for a saviour. Once again, the nation was divided. Some people were furious that the founders of the game had come to this. Others were happy to accept that our shortcomings had left us in need of help. There were three continental managers in the Premier League at that time: Arsène Wenger at Arsenal, Liverpool's Gérard Houllier and Claudio Ranieri who had just joined Chelsea. The Englishman who finished highest was Peter Reid of Sunderland. When FA chief executive Adam Crozier announced the appointment of Swede Sven-Göran Eriksson he said, 'We mustn't kid ourselves about where we are right now.'

Not so golden generation

Eriksson had won Serie A with Lazio but had never managed in England. He had grown up watching English football on TV and had been influenced by the success English coaches Bobby Houghton and Roy Hodgson enjoyed in Sweden. He had won championships in Sweden, Portugal, and Italy but when he was asked in his first press conference whether he could name Sunderland's left-back he couldn't (it was Michael Gray). The morning after Eriksson's first match, an English Premier League manager caustically started his weekly media conference by saying, 'Four-four-two! He showed us English dummies a thing or two, didn't he?'

Eriksson was more inclined to traditional English football than most native-born coaches at that time. His best England game, a photo montage of which hangs on the wall at his house, was the 5-1 win over Germany in Munich. I watched it from the running track at the Olympic Stadium; it was exhilarating but I couldn't really explain how England won so convincingly. Eriksson concedes his side were lucky, especially with an awful miss from Sebastian Deisler shortly before Steven Gerrard's thumping shot made it 2-1.

England lined up 4-4-2 that night, although, as was often the case, the left-sided midfielder was a right-footer filling in

– Nick Barmby. It is extraordinary that a country where most youth and grassroots teams played 4-4-2 had so few high-quality left-footed midfielders. There was a big-man-small-man front pairing (Emile Heskey and Michael Owen), one of whom was expected to drop into midfield to link play. And there was a two-man central midfield of Gerrard and Paul Scholes. Eriksson describes Gerrard as a 'modern midfielder, box-to-box, who could do everything'. It was reminiscent of the glory era of English club football and unashamedly basic. Eriksson's main tactical concern was that his players got into a narrow 4-4-2 as soon as they lost possession and spread out when they had the ball.

That match helped England reach the 2002 World Cup but after that Eriksson's story is another one of near misses. They lost in the quarter-finals against ten-man Brazil, the eventual deserved champions. Euro 2004 and the 2006 World Cup both finished with penalty shoot-out defeats against Portugal in the quarters – both times Sporting Lisbon keeper Ricardo was England's nemesis.

In the 2004 game against Portugal, Owen gave England the lead after racing on to a massive clearance from keeper David James, and having conceded twice they equalised when Frank Lampard converted a John Terry nod-down at a corner – classic English goals. Wayne Rooney, who had scored four times in the group stage, was injured in that game and in 2006 he was sent off in the rematch in Gelsenkirchen. England held on for penalties, but the ending was familiar and painful as Ricardo saved from Lampard, Gerrard, and Jamie Carragher. Eriksson says his chief regret was not hiring a 'mental coach' to help England take spot-kicks.

Much of the debate during Eriksson's tenure was how to get the best out of the star midfielders of the so-called 'Golden Generation': Beckham, Gerrard, Frank Lampard, Scholes and Owen Hargreaves, all of whom finished their careers as Champions League winners. Eriksson stuck with 4-4-2 and in 2020 he picked his best England XI for Sky Sports: Joe Hart,

Gary Neville, Rio Ferdinand, Terry, Ashley Cole; Beckham, Gerrard, Lampard, Scholes; Owen, Rooney. Two things are worth noting: Hart didn't make his debut until after Eriksson had gone – the Swede makes no secret that he didn't rate England's goalkeepers. And given his time again he would still squeeze Scholes into a left-sided midfield role.

It could have been a different story: penalty shoot-outs are not lotteries but nor does losing one reveal fundamental problems in a country's football system. The truth was that England never looked like one of the best sides in the world, despite having some obviously talented players. Eriksson's side won seven of his 14 matches in major tournaments; they lost to Brazil, France – and twice to Portugal in shoot-outs.

Eriksson had a tetchy relationship with the newspapers who criticised his tactics on the back pages and his personal life on the front. It was this media intrusion that saw the FA's preferred successor walk away after the Swede's departure in 2006. Luiz Felipe Scolari had beaten Eriksson as Brazil boss in 2002 and then with Portugal in 2004 and 2006. He was initially keen to accept a long-term contract with the FA, only to change his mind when reporters, photographers and camera crews mobbed his house. Second choice was Steve McClaren, who had been part of Eriksson's coaching team and had just guided Middlesbrough to the UEFA Cup Final.

McClaren's 18-match spell was as grim as the weather on his last night. England failed to qualify for Euro 2008, losing their last two games against Russia and then Croatia at a rainy Wembley, while McClaren sheltered under a brolly. He put it down to making too many changes but also felt England lacked the strength in depth to ride out bad luck, 'We didn't have 25, 26 players – like England have now – who could compete technically, tactically, physically and mentally.'

Three English clubs qualified for the 2008 Champions League semi-finals: Manchester United, Chelsea and Liverpool. Ten Englishmen started the final and 13 played in the semis but perhaps the substitutes' benches back McClaren's argument

– increasingly rich Premier League clubs were shopping abroad
for their depth.

Given how many overseas coaches we've had in the Premier
League, it is odd that the two who managed England had no
experience here. Fabio Capello was one the managerial greats
having won Serie A four times and the Champions League with
AC Milan and La Liga with Real Madrid (he had also finished
top of Serie A with Juventus but that was in the *Calciopoli* era,
and they were stripped of the titles).

When he was hired by England, Capello claimed it was a
'dream come true' but if that was the case, he hadn't prepared for
his dream by becoming fluent in English. He claimed he would
be within a month but that was wishful thinking: he got by but
no more. He blames England's relative failure at the 2010 World
Cup on fatigue and bad luck.

The draw for the finals in South Africa could hardly have
been kinder, pitching Capello's side against the USA, Algeria,
and Slovenia. A blunder by Rob Green saw them draw with the
Americans before one of the worst games of football ever played
finished England 0 Algeria 0. Jermain Defoe's goal saw England
beat Slovenia but finishing second to the USA meant facing
Germany in Bloemfontein in the second round.

England's shortcomings were brutally exposed, but a
controversial moment became the main talking point. Germany
led 2-0 before Matt Upson pulled one back in the 37th minute.
Soon after that, Lampard's long-range shot hit the bottom of
the crossbar and bounced over the line. It was a travesty that
the officials didn't see it, or perhaps panicked. It was worse that
goal-line technology still wasn't used in 2010. Capello argues
that the momentum would have been with England going into
the second half and his side could have won the game. He is
kidding himself.

Thankfully some people in positions of influence weren't
blinded by outrage over the bad call – bear this in mind for
the next chapter. Germany were faster and better technically.
England had once again turned to a foreign manager and chosen

a fan of 4-4-2 who would use players out of the position rather than change formation.

Steven Gerrard was frequently used in wide positions where he was still good but less influential. He reflected on his England career for BT Sport, 'I don't think we had a manager who had a philosophy or a way of playing that worked in terms of constructing possession, of keeping the ball for long enough. Most of the time with England you picked the team, and you went out and tried to play. We played very individually. We also have to take responsibility ourselves. I felt I didn't hit my top performances playing for England consistently.'

Rio Ferdinand added, 'I don't think we had a manager who was – I don't know if this is the right word – brave enough to sort out our midfield. On paper we had the best midfield players in the world: Lampard, Gerrard, Beckham, Scholes, Hargreaves, [Michael] Carrick and even below that more players. We played a rigid 4-4-2. All these guys could have been interchangeable. Look at Spain and Germany now, they would have made sure their most creative guys would have been on the pitch.'

Capello became the next England manager to leave for non-performance reasons. He resigned in protest in February 2012 when the FA stripped John Terry of the captaincy after he was accused of racially abusing Anton Ferdinand in a Premier League game.

Roy Hodgson took over just before the Euros in Poland and Ukraine. England's group games were entertaining but the side lacked any sort of control, and they rode their luck to take Italy to penalties in the quarter-final where the outcome was depressingly predictable.

I doubt the rest of the world remembers much about England's contribution to the 2014 World Cup. They were ranked tenth by FIFA but looked a million miles away from being good enough and were eliminated before their third group game. That goalless draw with Costa Rica was the 11th in England's World Cup history. No one can accuse Hodgson of not naming attacking teams against Italy and Uruguay: Gerrard and Jordan Henderson were the midfield two in a 4-2-3-1; Raheem Sterling, Wayne Rooney and Danny Welbeck played behind Daniel Sturridge. But the play was tired and predictable. The Premier League had brought unprecedented wealth into English football, but domestic playing talent was sadly lacking.

Even mentioning 'the Iceland game' ruins the mood of a group of England fans. It rivalled the 1950 World Cup defeat against the USA as our worst – and this time nearly 17 million people watched the last-16 encounter in the 2016 Euros. Hodgson's side were grateful to be facing the rank outsiders after a lacklustre group performance had seen them finish second.

They took an early lead when Sterling was fouled, and Rooney smashed in the penalty. But they conceded from a long throw and went behind after a mistake by Hart. The last hour was purgatory for England fans as the players froze and ran out of ideas. Speaking to me for this book, Hodgson's assistant Ray Lewington rejected my offer to put it down to bad luck, 'No, I didn't think that. I thought some of it was the technical ability – and probably tactical. We could have done things better. I've learned from it and look back and think "we should have done this, we should have done that".'

I knew it wasn't luck; I was just being polite. The public and media were furious with the players who were accused of not caring. They became the focus of understandable irritation given the eye-watering salaries paid by Premier League clubs. I thought that missed the point. They were conquered by fear as much as by Iceland.

England's players were overrated because the Premier League was overrated in that period. Lewington agreed that there was a fundamental lack of quality, 'Gerrard and Lampard, Terry, Rio Ferdinand, and that lot were coming to the end of their careers, and we were putting in players who are now in the future in the England team. I always felt when we were playing the really top teams our technique was lacking. I think now that's been addressed and the new breed of players are every bit as good technically as the foreign players. I think we've really grown up.

Fair play to people like Trevor Brooking who got hold of the academies and said we've got to start teaching our kids technique and tactics and we're getting the players through who are more complete as players than we had.'

Tippy-tappy bollocks

Hodgson's departure after defeat to Iceland brought the FA back to a familiar junction. Should they appoint another foreign saviour, a pragmatist in the Ramsey tradition, or someone to lead England's transition to the brand of football played elsewhere in Europe and increasingly in the Premier League?

Important projects had already begun on the England coaching DNA and the Elite Player Performance Plan. The country's footballing development pathway was becoming clear and moving into a new era influenced by sophisticated continental football. The FA appointed arch-pragmatist Sam Allardyce. It would be hard to imagine anyone less in step with the direction of their coaching journey.

The year before, Allardyce spoke to the media after his West Ham side beat Hull 3-0 in a game that had been 0-0 at half-time. This is what he said:

'Changing the shape was the big thing and playing forward quicker. All this tippy-tappy stuff everyone keeps going on about as the right way to play football is all a load of bollocks sometimes. Getting the ball in the opposition's box as quickly as you can with quality and getting it forward and in behind the opposition is definitely sometimes the best way forward.'

The fate of the England men's national team and the wellbeing of the game down to the grassroots are not the same, but they are interlinked. In appointing Allardyce rather than promoting under-21 manager Gareth Southgate, the FA were saying that the most useful thing the England manager can do is win games, however it is done. Ramsey's scathing critics had accused him of ruining English football for decades – but the 1966 World Cup was the only one of England's first 32 major tournaments that we won. Allardyce strenuously rejects his portrayal as a dinosaur and we never got to find out what influence he would have had on the FA's vision because he was caught up in a sting operation by the *Daily Telegraph* and, even though he had broken no laws, he was forced out after one match and 67 days in charge.

If I'm honest, I didn't want Southgate as England manager because his only experience in club management was taking over the Middlesbrough team McClaren had led to the UEFA Cup Final and getting them relegated. I was too harsh. He was still a player and not fully qualified to coach when he got the Boro job and presided over a cut in budget. Since 2013 he had worked for the FA as under-21 manager and was part of the team developing the association's coaching strategy. In some ways he is the ideal England coach for the media age – diplomatic and likeable – but we haven't seen how he will fare in real adversity.

At the 2018 World Cup England reached the semi-final for the first time since 1990. For the first group game against Tunisia only four starters remained from the Iceland defeat two years earlier: Kyle Walker, Dele Alli, Harry Kane, and Raheem Sterling. Expectations were low ahead of the tournament and even if you agree that the quality of English player development is improving, it would be silly to suggest there was a fundamental leap forward in two years. Southgate's England rode their luck, as Robson's had in 1990 – as so many international teams do. Kane scored in injury time to beat Tunisia, Panama were accommodatingly awful and England lost to Belgium twice.

And there was the penalty shoot-out. We regard Venables and Southgate as successful England coaches, which is fair enough, but they're also the only two who've won matches on penalties. England drew with Colombia in Moscow in the last 16 and had Mateus Aribe not hit the bar and Jordan Pickford saved from Carlos Bacca, they would have gone out at the same stage as Hoddle's 1998 side. The quarter-final win over Sweden was their most accomplished performance but defeat followed in the semi against Croatia. England led through Kieran Trippier's free kick but a midfield of Alli, Jordan Henderson and Jesse Lingard was gradually dominated by the brilliant, experienced trio of Luka Modrić, Ivan Rakitić and Marcelo Brozović. Southgate's substitutions were essentially like-for-like until the 112th minute just after Mario Mandžukić had put Croatia 2-1 up.

Three years later at the delayed Euros played in 2021, Southgate was more cautious, and England went a step further. He was criticised for using two defensive midfielders in Declan Rice and Kalvin Phillips – although in the opening game against Croatia, Phillips was more advanced. The public wanted more of Phil Foden and Jack Grealish but England got through the group without conceding and then put in two of the best performances I've seen from the national team to beat Germany and Ukraine. I was at Wembley for the Germany game, and it was wonderful, partly because it was only the second football match I had been to since the Covid-19 pandemic began. The universal view of fans I spoke to was that England should attack more, unleash the new generation of talented players. They did enough to deserve the 2-0 win. The 4-0 victory over Ukraine was one of the most convincing England has ever enjoyed. They came from behind to beat an excellent Denmark team in the semi-final to set up only the second senior final for the nation that invented football.

As in the World Cup semi, England took an early lead through a full-back – this time Luke Shaw charged forward to meet a cross on the edge of the six-yard box. Again, I wanted England to play with more adventure but who knows whether that would have worked, and it was a set piece that was their undoing when Italy's Leonardo Bonucci smashed the ball in from a yard after a corner. Having guided the team with such serenity, Southgate massively over-thought the penalty shoot-out, bringing on Rashford and Jadon Sancho in the 120th minute. Rashford dragged his shot against the post, and Sancho's was saved. Pickford was close to becoming a hero with two saves, but another England substitute, 19-year-old Bukayo Saka, was also denied. A familiar old pain was back. Another old monster in new clothes also reared its ugly head that day, as legions of drunk and drugged-up supporters caused havoc in London and invaded Wembley Stadium. The online racial abuse aimed at the three players who didn't score their penalties was another reminder that our proud nation has its ample share of morons.

It was a bitter ending but that is how competitions finish for all but one country. Before and throughout the Euros I had more belief that England could compete with the best than I'd ever had. Our players were good enough. And they were young: the only squad members aged 30 or older were Walker, Henderson and Trippier. Rice and Mason Mount were 22, Sancho, Foden and Reece James 21, Saka 19 and Jude Bellingham turned 18 during the tournament.

When Greg Dyke became FA chairman in 2013, he set the target of winning the 2022 World Cup. Southgate and his players were very nearly ahead of schedule with a major tournament success, but it is unfair and unrealistic for a federation to set such a goal. Too much depends on fortune. Greece won Euro 2004. Johan Cruyff's Netherlands won nothing.

A realistic target is to go into major tournaments as favourites and hope for the breaks along the way. That was what Spain achieved in their glory era from 2008 to 2012. There were moments when those tournaments nearly went wrong for them, but we rightly regarded them as the best in the world.

I would argue that only France has a better crop of players in depth than England. Italy won the Euros but failed to qualify for the World Cups either side. Spain produced some wonderful performances in the latter stages of the Euros, but the current players are not the obvious world-beating talents of the previous generation. There are plenty of countries who can win the World Cup, but England is one of them. We are far from perfect, but we are in better shape than ten years ago. Let's see how we bounced back from the lows of 2007 to 2016.

2

Winning something with kids

REWIND TO Frank Lampard's non-goal in Bloemfontein, 2010. You have two options: 1. Take comfort and angrily blame the assistant referee's eyesight and FIFA for not having goal-line technology. Or: 2. Accept England were outplayed by Germany and set about improving playing standards in our country.

Option one has its merits. Goal-line tech was overdue and has improved the game with none of the downsides of VAR. And it is emotionally easier in the short term to put failure down to luck. Thankfully, this time English football took option two.

There was a youth development system in place, of course, and we will hear from some of the former pros who cherish their haphazard journeys into football. But Ged Roddy, the Premier League's director of youth, believed it was outdated and didn't match the demands of the day. Top-flight English clubs could afford players from anywhere and the gap between what academies were producing and what Premier League teams needed was too wide. Roddy's blueprint, remoulded in heated debate, became the Elite Player Performance Plan.

Roddy recalls, 'Probably the biggest challenge of the whole project was to change people's mindset and convince them that English players had the talent and were capable. Any of the other changes we wanted to initiate could not be made unless we achieved that first step. That took time and it was a long process.'[4]

---

4   Credit: Training Ground Guru

Academies would be graded according to published requirements and assigned a category. Category One academies would get more money and be able to recruit from lower-graded rivals at set fees. Clubs would be audited on the things such as how many of their graduates are professionals, standard of facilities, coaching, education, and welfare.

Category One training complexes are beautiful places if you like plush pitches and landscaped surrounds. I can't help contrasting them to council playing fields which veer from boggy to bobbly and back again in about a week. EPPP was well-funded – over £1bn has been spent on academies since its launch in 2012; some from club and owner investment which is made free of Financial Fair Play restrictions, and some from the creation of the Professional Game Youth Fund – a four per cent levy on transfer taxes. Professional football has not been as generous with the grassroots of the game.

The first contact I had with EPPP was working with Matt Jackson, the ex-Everton, Norwich and Wigan defender. He was Wigan's operations manager and was stressed about the workload from EPPP and questioning the wisdom of some of the minutiae.

Jackson said, 'We had a very old fashioned, underfunded, underperforming, under-resourced school of excellence which had only produced Leighton Baines – and he'd been released by Everton at 15. The EPPP project had been floating around without anyone really understanding what was coming and it was then upon us that in 18 months we'd be audited, and this fantastic academy with all these requirements would have to be in place.

'The chief executive asked me to come up with a plan. I quickly recruited Gregor Rioch who'd been through the audit process with Coventry and gave him no time at all. He did a fabulous job of getting the document ready to get through that first audit. It wasn't fun and people still talk about it being the bane of academy life because it's a severe process. It's forensic but that's what the FA and Premier League wanted.'

EPPP should be seen as part of the professionalisation of English football; the development of young players would no longer be a question of clubs or individual coaches figuring out their own system.

'It measured clubs and asked them to measure themselves and document their procedures,' Jackson said. 'It was brilliant at clubs like Wigan that had never given it any structured thought. It put parameters in place, and it was a massive, massive challenge. There was a lot of antipathy because it felt like a lot of interference for clubs who had brought players through their system previously without having to do any of these things and spend this money and recruit the staff required. Wigan were in the Premier League at the time, so I was in all the stakeholder meetings, and it was feisty. The Premier League were brilliant in welcoming opinions, and they got the full force of clubs who felt they'd been doing good things previously and didn't want this.'

Roddy describes the three-year audit cycle as a 'necessary evil' that meant EPPP could evolve. Jackson is now Wolverhampton Wanderers' strategic player marketing and loans manager. He rates EPPP as a big success, 'It's a very good idea, it certainly worked. The Premier League have been very good at remodelling some areas. We now have multiple excellent academies, places where players can go and develop safely and be looked after and, possibly more important for a system that churns so few people to the top of the pyramid, has a support network in place for the lads that don't make it and helps them think about what they're going to do outside of professional football.'

The injection of money and demands of EPPP have seen a rise of the number of coaches in academies from 250 in 2012/13 to 800 just in Premier League academies now.[5] Kids are divided into three phases, 'foundation' for under-nines to under-11s, 'youth development' from under-12 to under-16 and 'professional development' from under-17 to under-23.

———

5   The Athletic

Matt Whitehouse is the lead youth development phase coach at Coventry City. He also blogs about coaching. In 2013 he wrote a book called *The Way Forward: Solutions to England's Football Failings*.

A decade on, he is feeling positive, 'We've gone from being frustrated, disappointed, lacking success as a national team to being one of the best in the world. Our youth teams are winning tournaments, and it feels like, "Wow, we've got some talent coming through!"

'2010 to 2014 was a frustrating period. We had that disappointing World Cup with Capello, which always reflects on the youth system. Now we've started to see these young players emerging and in the last few years there have been more opportunities and minutes for players in the Premier League and success for the national team. Gareth Southgate has done a tremendous job because we've gone further than we had since 1990. There's a positive cycle; everyone is buzzing off it. In the ten years of me writing my blog there's been a massive difference.

'The infrastructure, the facilities are at a higher level, as are the quality of the coaches and players coming through. Globally the game has become faster, more highly technical and the players need to reflect that. There are still going to be players around the world who are better than ours, but the quality of our players is so much higher.

'EPPP allowed academies to reflect on what they were doing and bring some consistency. Getting the multi-disciplinary teams right, getting structures in place, making sure that clubs as whole have a stronger philosophy.

'In the past you might have had five full-time members of staff. Then you went up to 25, 50 full-time staff which allows you to do a lot more things such as individually tailored programmes, impressive sports science and other areas which have allowed the academies to become more professional.'

Saul Isaksson-Hurst spent ten years as an academy coach with Chelsea and Tottenham. He now works as an individual technical trainer with established players. He has helped set up academies in other countries – he was in Thailand when we spoke. He has an app called My Personal Football Coach and works as a consultant for Arsenal. Business is thriving, and so, he believes, is English football:

'We've gone from one of the worst development systems to one of the best in ten, 20 years. There are the FA courses, youth modules and so on but the EPPP really turned up the gears and started putting a lot more organisation and money in – and the fruits of that labour coming through.'

England named one of the youngest squads for the Euros in 2021, with an average age of 24.8. They had Declan Rice (22), Reece James, Phil Foden, Jadon Sancho (all 21), Bukayo Saka (19) and the remarkable Jude Bellingham who was just 17 and already a £25m Borussia Dortmund player.

Wales also had a young squad, many of whom had come through the English academy system such as Harry Wilson, Neco Williams, Dan James and Ethan Ampadu. Spain had the youngest squad. Belgium and Sweden were the oldest. Winners Italy were right in the middle.

Southgate keenly monitors the amount of on-field time English players get at their clubs – one indicator as to whether the academy system is working. In the beginning, the Premier League had lots of English players, which seemed an unremarkable notion then. In 1993/94, 367 Englishmen played a total of 629,964 minutes in the competition, for 22 teams.[6] That dropped to 608,474 the following year. After that there was a step-change with the reduction of the league to 20 clubs, but it was also noticeably less English with 475,154 minutes shared between 312 players. Match time for English players plummeted through the late 1990s and by 2002/03 there were only 207 Englishmen who shared 283,226 minutes. The trend bumped around until another decline in the 2010s, reaching a low point of 219,483 in 2015/16. The numbers were low again in 2018/19 when just 206 English players were on the pitch for 221,686 minutes.

---

6   fbref.com

Southgate spoke about his concern after only 54 English-qualified players started in a Premier League match round in 2018, 'We've got to arrest the slide. It isn't correct to say we're not developing good players. There's tremendous work going on at our academies. The big concern for me is that if this graph continues to fall away that we end up in ten years' time with an England manager who has got 15 per cent of the league to choose from. Why would that not happen? It is a big danger.'

He has got his wish, to an extent. One of Greg Dyke's long-term targets was for the Premier League to be made up of 45 per cent Englishmen. In the 2021/22 season, 400 foreigners played compared to 273 Englishmen which is 59 percent to 41 percent, not a massive shortfall.

The club from the big European leagues that gave most minutes to youth graduates in 2021/22 was the one with a policy of using only players from its own region, Athletic Club of Bilbao. Second was their Basque neighbour Real Sociedad, who used to have a Basque-only policy and now successfully strive to keep a genuinely local core. Another Spanish club, Celta Vigo, was third. The first English name on the list was Manchester United in 12th followed by Chelsea in 13th. The Basque clubs are instructive: if you have to produce young footballers good enough to play in the top division of a major European league, you can. In the Basque country everyone believes local kids become top flight footballers because they see them on the pitch every weekend. There is nothing physiologically different about Basques. The pathway is open, and the belief is real.[7]

The Premier League was mindful of creating opportunities for academy graduates and introduced rules restricting how many non-homegrown players clubs can register. Note that 'homegrown' and 'English' are not the same, as youngsters recruited from around Europe count, including the likes of Cesc Fàbregas and Paul Pogba – World Cup winners with Spain and France respectively. That situation will change with Brexit throwing up

---

7   football-observatory.com

challenges and opportunities. We will look later at how foreign talent changed the English game, mostly for the better, but it is understandable that England national team managers have lamented the lack of opportunity for English players.

Isaksson-Hurst is happy that the picture seems to be improving, 'When I was at Chelsea there was a lot of frustration. You thought, "We've got one of the best academies in world football and there's no pathway." Fortunately, that's changed in the last few years and Chelsea have embraced bringing players through. Arsenal, where I've worked recently, have got Bukayo Saka and Emile Smith Rowe and players of ability there – and Spurs have got a long track record. English clubs have changed massively from ten, 20 years ago and it's impossible not to see the high volume of talent coming through. It's still difficult because it's such a high line and a saturated market. Maybe that's why players are choosing to go abroad where there is less pressure, and you can get into the first-team environment quicker.'

It has been interesting to see the likes of Bellingham, Sancho, Reece Oxford and Jamie Bynoe-Gittens move to Germany as youngsters while Fikayo Tomori, Tammy Abraham, Chris Smalling and Kieran Trippier have played in Italy or Spain – but they are a small minority. Look at how many players of each nationality appeared in the 'big five' European leagues last season: Spanish 534, French 462, Italian 358, German 294, and English 288 – of whom 273 were in the Premier League. There were 107 Brazilians and 73 Argentines. The trend is in the right direction for England – up from 262 the previous season, while there were slightly fewer Brazilian and Argentines.[8]

England is not yet a major exporter of talented footballers; the financial incentive to stay is obvious. Matt Whitehouse believes clubs are becoming more conscious of creating opportunities:

'We've got Ryan Howley who made his Championship debut in April, aged 18, after being around the first team all season. He got Apprentice of the Year at the EFL awards, so he's had an

---

8 fbref.com

excellent year of progression, being supported by the first team, and playing for the under-23s. He's a young lad who's seen a pathway within the club. His challenge is to break into that first team consistently and it's up for the club to think whether he is ready. At 18, Jude Bellingham – one of the best players in the world – did that at Birmingham, almost out of necessity. They knew they had a talent and put him in and gave him games.

'The key thing is not making a debut at 17 or 18 but nurturing players in the following three or four years to achieve 300, 400 professional games. It's about getting the pathway right between 17 and 21, which means they're physically and mentally capable of succeeding. Too many players get their debuts, maybe play ten or 20 games and then they're out because they haven't been able to deal with it and haven't been prepared properly. You want players working between youth team, under-23s, first-team training, playing, being around it. The key is communication, that everyone is talking and knows what a player's development plan is.

'I've seen players at other clubs get thrown into the first team without anyone knowing who they are, just because they look all right, and they don't really manage them properly and they come back and lack confidence. At Coventry we discuss what's expected of that player and what his pathway is. Some players' journeys require loans to get minutes in senior football. Ryan has been at Coventry since he was eight and it's really helped him to become the player he is, but a loan might just help him get out of the comfort zone and experience different things. We've had lads who've gone up to Scotland to play for Ross County and Ayr and that's a great opportunity to experience a different league but continue their support.' When we spoke, Coventry were mid-table in the Championship, having faded out of the play-off race. Matt is realistic that managers in more pressurised situations are reluctant to turn to young players:

'In League Two the club brought through loads of young players because they had to. They couldn't afford to bring in players and these players got 20, 30 games and did really well. It's different in the Championship where you've got to be even better. It's no longer about necessity but quality. Our job as the academy is to produce even better players who can play Championship football.'

The stiffs

While Matt is confident that Coventry are on the right lines, I have spoken to plenty of people who believe we have a problem with the uncompetitive nature of football beneath first-team level. The top under-23 league – for clubs with Category One academies – is branded as Premier League 2. It replaced the under-21 Premier League in 2016/17, to give, as the Premier League website puts it, 'A greater focus on technicality, physicality and intensity to bring players as close to first-team experience as possible.' Teams can field a goalkeeper over the age limit and up to three 'over-age' outfield players.

Manchester City have won the last two Premier League 2 titles. They clinched last season's league by beating Leeds in front of 21,321 people but the crowds are nothing like that normally. City's oldest player was 20-year-old Cole Palmer. They started with five 19-year-olds, four who were 18 and one 17-year-old. Leeds' oldest player was 21-year-old Norwegian goalkeeper Kristoffer Klaesson and their youngest was 16-year-old Archie Gray, son of ex-Leeds player Andy Gray, grandson of Frank and great-nephew of Elland Road legend Eddie Gray.

They are very talented kids – but they are kids. All the ex-professionals I asked feared there was too big a gap between under-23 football and the Premier League.

Lee Hendrie came through Aston Villa's youth system in the 1990s and played for England under Glenn Hoddle. He explained, 'I don't like under-23 football if I'm honest. I like the fact that we had reserve-team football. Maybe some of the older pros didn't want to be playing in those games but I learned a lot from playing with them. You had to work hard to get into the reserves, and if you got in then it was more than likely that you were with players who were going to play for the first team at the weekend. It was exciting because it was the closest thing to playing first-team football.

'Call me old-school but if you're going to play with first-team lads, you're going to learn off them. You're coming up against, I don't know, Matt Le Tissier who was coming back from injury and the first thing you would do is look at the team sheet and see who you were against in midfield. The young lads in the under-23s won't get to play against the bigger players.'

Les Ferdinand was one of the first interviews I did for this book. I asked him a general question about what he would change in the game, and he jumped to this subject. 'I would throw the under-23 system right out of the window and go back to playing reserve football,' he said. 'On numerous, if not every, occasion I go to watch an under-23 game, they're all trying to do the same thing; all trying to play out from the back. They're trying to improve the technique of each and every player but then nine times out of ten the first-team managers don't believe the under-23s are competitive enough and the players need to go out on the loan to get experience.'

Ferdinand played in Football Combination, the reserve team for clubs in the south, Midlands, and Wales. It started in 1915 and folded in 2012. Reserve teams were colloquially referred to as 'the stiffs'.

Ferdinand said, 'I came through a system where if a first-team player didn't play on a Saturday, they played on a Tuesday in the Combination with what was called the reserves and you played regardless of who you were. It wasn't an under-23 game; it was for senior professionals. I learned more in that than I would have done playing a hundred under-23 games with none of that experience around me.'

It is hard to imagine a talented kid from London taking Ferdinand's route to the top now that so many more youngsters are in the orbit of professional clubs. He went from Southall to another non-league club, Hayes, before being spotted by QPR. His first match was in the Football Combination.

'I was working my notice from the wallpaper shop I worked for, and I turned up at QPR and Sammy Lee was the first person to greet me. He was coming back from an injury. There was Clive Walker, Gary Chivers, David Kerslake and a smattering of first-team players who hadn't played at the weekend. They were jumping on the coach, and we drove down to Southampton. It sticks in my mind like it was yesterday. Jimmy Case was on the opposition, and I thought to myself – wow, wow. These are guys I've been seeing week in week out play for their first team, even if they weren't at that moment. If that wasn't the right education for me back then, nothing was.

'We say under-23s now, but the guys can be anything from 18 to 22. They've played with the same guys from the age of eight or nine and all got into the under-23s – and they're still playing against the same fellas. Where's the progress? The individuals may have improved somewhat but they've played no men's football. That's why we loan them out. Something has got to change because it hasn't achieved what people were hoping it would.'

Matt Jackson joined Luton Town, who were then in the top division, part-time while he was studying for A-levels. He also remembers his tough reserve team baptism with fondness:

'It was open age, it was do-or-die. You'd have some senior pro who'd fallen out with the first-team manager. At Luton we had Steve Williams, the old Arsenal and Southampton midfielder who was brilliant for my development when I was 16 to 18. Most of us joined as YTS apprentices, although I did A-levels, so I wasn't part of the full-time programme. You had to be playing in the reserves at the end of that two years or it was very unlikely you were ever going to. Now we have players who've played under-18 football and never even played under-23 football and are a million miles away from being first-team players at the age of 19. That gap from youth football to affecting a first team has grown. We haven't got that part of the game sorted at all.'

Terry Gibson has been a coach at Fulham and now watches under-23 games as both commentator and scout.

He said, 'It looks like the clubs are just fulfilling a fixture, like they're obliged to play it. They don't play enough games in a year and the teams are always being swapped around because they have so many players eligible.

'When I was at Fulham it was under-21s and we were allowed over-age players. There were guys who never played for the first team, but they never played in those matches because it was almost beneath them. At best you could ask them to play in home games. We didn't agree with it, but it was the done thing. You wouldn't ask a 30-year-old at Fulham to travel to play Aston Villa's under-23s at their training ground on a Wednesday afternoon.

'I work for Man United TV, and I have a list of 40 names that might have played that season in those games and any 15 or 16 could be in the squad. They're not playing enough games and when they do play it's not in a structured system with the same players each week. No one is really concerned about the results over the season. It lacks competitive edge. The best players are out on loan or go through straight through. I never saw Marcus Rashford or Mason Greenwood playing for Man United under-23s.

'If you're 22 and in the under-23s at West Ham, Spurs or Arsenal you're in the wrong place. Your career should be somewhere else, playing regularly. These clubs have got so many players, they've got to try to get them some football somehow. The better ones go out on loan and their progression is either quicker or they're found out. You don't find out about players in the under-23s until after their careers should have been well up and running.'

Paul Mortimer was in Fulham's youth team before later playing for Charlton Athletic, Aston Villa, Crystal Palace, Brentford, and Bristol City. He is now a qualified counsellor and psychotherapist, and we will hear more from him later on that – but he is another sceptic when it comes to the under-23s:

'As a kid I bunked off school to make my debut. I didn't tell Fulham, but we were playing at Craven Cottage, and I played against players who'd come on for their first team at the weekend. I was an apprentice playing with players in the Football Combination and the mentality was different. I got my education being taught by first team players.

'By the time I came to play in the first team I was ready. Reserve-team football was competitive but now it's kids playing kids so when they step up to the first team, they look like a fish out of water. First-team squad players don't play in the reserves which is ridiculous. The players are conditioned to believe they don't have to.'

It would require a significant change of attitude to have today's players earning vast sums of money turning out on a Tuesday night with half a team of kids although such is the interest in football, I think you would get decent crowds. Ferdinand pins the demise of reserve teams on Arsène Wenger:

'Arsène Wenger did some amazing things when he came to this country in terms of changing professional footballers' mindsets – preparing for games and how you execute a game – but he saw seasoned professionals appearing in the reserves as a punishment. If his players hadn't been in the first team on a Saturday, he didn't want to "punish" them by playing them in the reserves.

'Kids are missing out because they're not getting the experience of senior pros who can guide, push and pull them and help them make the grade a bit quicker.'

This won't be news to the more thoughtful academy leaders. We have seen 30-somethings such as Olly Lancashire (Southampton), Jay Spearing (Liverpool) and Paul McShane (Manchester United) sign for clubs to bring experience to their development sides but it is a far cry from the lost world of reserve football.

Matt Jackson believes the lack of clearly navigable pathway to first team football could be a rare factor that works against the richer clubs:

'Manchester City will have youngsters turn them down because they can't guarantee opportunities. That's something other clubs will use against them. There'll be some club owners who would say we're spending an awful lot of money on our academy for very little output because bridging that gap from academy to first team is still the hardest thing. The average age of a Premier League debut is still 23 so that's a gap to fill for the 18-year-olds. We have an under-23 league in theory, but it's actually an under-19 league, so that spell gets filled with loans because we haven't got a competitive environment underneath first football.'

Kids for sale

Young players in the modern game might not have been roughed up by Jimmy Case or nutmegged by Matt Le Tissier, but they are bought, sold, and paid like senior professionals. Lee Hendrie fears it is unhealthy to pay so much to youngsters who might not have a first-team career:

'It's good they do their education, but we had to clean the changing room, make sure the boots were polished and shined and ready for matchday. That was learning your trade, giving you a hunger to be in that changing room. These days it's not like that. They get paid far too much money and some of the lads will start getting in trouble because they've earned so much.

'The majority don't make the grade and they have to go down the leagues and it's very different. They're not prepared for it. That's what worries me: in the modern-day, top-level game there's a huge gap to the National League. It's good that the boys go out on loans, but they're earning huge money and if it doesn't happen, where do they go? Some people can't deal with rejection and losing what they've had is when they might fall into bad times. It worries me.

'We were on, I think, £29.50 for our first year YTS and it went up to £32.50. If you were fortunate to get a first-year contract you'd be on, you know, £75 a week and a win bonus. The parents are sometimes at fault because they see the bright lights and think their son's going to be a footballer. It does worry me.'

Jadon Sancho did make it. He was from south London but joined Watford's academy aged seven and was later sent to boarding school by the club. His potential was spotted by the Premier League elite and around the time of his 15th birthday he was signed by Manchester City. EPPP rules allowed him to move for an initial fee of £66,000. Add-ons meant it could rise to £500,000 and a ten per cent sell-on fee eventually netted Watford another £800,000.

Sancho's reputation soared at City, and he was named as player of the tournament in the UEFA European Under-17 Championship in the summer of 2017 before he left for £8m to join Borussia Dortmund. The German club reportedly cut a deal with City fearful that advances from Tottenham and Arsenal might change Sancho's mind. They could have paid only compensation, worth around £170,000.

The Germans convinced him he would have a better chance of playing regularly with them than a top Premier League club. They had a point: he made 137 first-team appearances before returning to England with Manchester United aged 21. Dortmund banked a £73m fee minus City's sell-on clause. Sancho might have been attracted to Dortmund by the chance of first-team football, but he was handsomely paid; when he signed a new contract at the Bundesliga club his wages reportedly went up to £190,000 and a considerable pay rise followed his move to Old Trafford. Sancho isn't the only person who got rich – his agent was quids in too – and cases like his help ramp up the money offered to the best young footballers.

Matt Jackson says people in football are uncomfortable paying huge wages to kids who have no guarantee of matching Sancho's success. 'It's a huge issue,' he admits. 'The clubs have to pay the wages to protect themselves from players being tempted across borders via compensation. Celtic and Rangers can do it and obviously the German clubs, as we've seen, have been exploiting it. We've had the change in terms of international transfers for under-18s unless there are exceptional circumstances, so FIFA have taken steps to annul that side of things, but clubs feel they have to protect their assets. Agents are very good at exploiting weakness. There's a lack of understanding from families about player development. Why would you not want to be paid as much as possible? But if clubs are having to pay £100m for a first-team player whatever they invest between 15 and 18 they're going to get back in spades.'

Since Brexit, FIFA's ban on the transfer of players under 18 has applied to English clubs signing European players – which had previously been exempted because of EU law. When Nathan Aké signed for Chelsea from Feyenoord in 2010, the Dutch club's technical director Leo Beenhakker described English clubs as 'great white sharks'. Not that Feyenoord were minnows – Aké had joined them from Ado den Hag. Chelsea paid a reported £230,000 for the Dutch defender and later sold him for £20m to Bournemouth, who sold him to Manchester City for £41m.

'Brexit has changed things,' says Jackson. 'Players who were here have been allowed to stay but that was generally at bigger clubs with the best infrastructure anyway. If you look at Chelsea, Man United, Man City, their youth teams are still dotted with worldwide international players.'

The days of players like Aké, Fàbregas and Pogba being classed as 'homegrown' are probably coming to an end, now that Europeans can't come here for football reasons until they turn 18. FIFA's new loan restrictions will also significantly curb one aspect of clubs' business models. Clubs can only loan three players to or from any other single club. And we are now into a transitional period so from 2024 they will only be able to loan out six senior players. Some big clubs have dozens out on loan at any time. It might mean an end of extraordinary cases such as Lucas Piazon, the Brazilian who spent nine years nominally as a Chelsea player, making just one substitute appearance in the Premier League, an 8-0 win over Aston Villa, in which he had a penalty saved.

The block on importing 16- and 17-year-old Europeans has accelerated the inclination of big Premier League clubs to corner the market in young British and Irish talent, such as Manchester

City's £400,000 signing of 13-year-old Leke Drake from League Two club Stevenage.

Under EPPP, any club with Category One status has been able to raid rivals for players for small sums decided by a fixed compensation tariff. The lower the category of the academy losing the player, the lower the sums paid out. EPPP also saw the abolition of the rule that blocked the signing of players under 18 who lived more than a 90-minute drive from the club's training facilities, as long as they are 12 or older.

Premier League clubs have stepped up their domestic scouting networks and have a keen eye on Ireland, which has freedom of movement with the UK under an agreement that predates the EU. Clubs also took their last chance to snap up 16- and 17-year-old Europeans in 2020 before the Brexit rules came in. Football agent Craig Honeyman says EPPP has helped big clubs get the best youngsters:

'EPPP was the first step. You and I recall all those years ago when a 15-year-old Jermaine Pennant signed for Arsenal for £2.5m – that same deal would now cost just £400,000 or £500,000 because of the training compensation and fixed fees. The top clubs in this country hoover up talent to the extent that clubs are asking themselves what's the point? "Why do we have academies, only to lose our talent having trained them for four, five, six, seven, eight years before they go to a Chelsea, Man City, Man United, Arsenal?" Leeds were very active in their recruitment in recent years and they'll benefit in the next four or five years. They've taken a lot of talent from other clubs.

'We're seeing a massive scouting emphasis on Ireland where young players are getting spotted and coming on trials. Scottish, Irish, and young English players are at a premium.'

Manchester City's scorers when they clinched the Premier League 2 title are three different examples of academy recruitment. Cole Palmer, from nearby Wythenshawe, was scouted as an eight-year-old and trained by the club – which is probably the sort of thing most of us have in mind when we think of academies. Brazilian Kayky was bought from Fluminense for

£10m when he turned 18, and Liam Delap was signed from Derby County where his dad had been a player and later member of the academy coaching staff. Liam moved for an estimated £1m in 2019, announcing his transfer on Instagram:

'Buzzing to have signed for Man City, thanks to everyone for the 10 years I spent at @dcfcofficial.'

Harvey Elliott moved from Fulham to Liverpool in 2019, having already made his Premier League debut aged 16 years and 30 days. Fulham got a reported £4.3m with potential extras. Fulham signed Elliott from QPR, so they hadn't been solely responsible for his development. It is fair to note that the young players have worked hard and their parents have made sacrifices, so they are entitled to sign for whichever club they think best matches their needs.

The architect of EPPP, Ged Roddy, believes it is wrong that compensation levels have been allowed to stagnate as transfer fees have risen. He said, 'When we introduced compensation, typically a Premier League club would receive about £35m at the beginning of the season for its right to compete in the league. My understanding now is that the figure is closer to £135m. So, there has been an exponential increase in the wealth of the clubs at the top of the system, yet compensation hasn't moved and is now completely inadequate. I think the game should look at maybe retrospectively index-linking the compensation system to TV deals or, if not, re-introduce some element of jeopardy.'[9]

So, if the system was designed to allow the movement of players to the best academies, which are likely to be run by the richest clubs, why would others bother? Brentford don't. They closed their academy in 2016 and renamed their development squad Brentford B. They have successfully worked with their Danish partner club Midtjylland and picked up players released from academies.

The team plays friendly matches against senior, under-23, and academy teams with a squad of players aged from 17 to 21.

---

9   Credit: Training Ground Guru

Brentford say ten players have moved from the B team to the senior squad, although the Danish connection makes it an unusual case. When you consider where Brentford are, I see the wisdom of not spending a fortune to compete with Chelsea, Arsenal, Spurs and Fulham for young players they could lose for a low fee.

After looking at the first EPPP requirements, Matt Jackson's initial thought was that it wasn't worth Wigan's time and effort:

'My recommendation was that if you were looking at it purely from a financial perspective then absolutely not. You're making an investment into lads at nine, ten and all the way through, who always have a price tag. Around us we had a big four from Merseyside and Manchester – and Bolton and Blackburn who were very aggressive on that side of things. So, we had six clubs who would be able to take our players at prices that wouldn't cover their development costs.

'From a purely financial perspective we were better off setting up a B team like Huddersfield and Brentford. You can still invest but that huge infrastructure around EPPP wouldn't be required. They'd be that much closer to the first team. There would also be a multitude of players being released who'd been through the Category One clubs and if we had a scouting system in place to pick up the better players, that would be far more sustainable. I said that to [CEO] Jonathan Jackson at the time, but he wanted to back the youth of Wigan and have somewhere for them to play and develop in the academy.'

You can see why it would be emotive for the only professional club in a town to give up on the academy system, but a professional club could use its resources to support the grassroots pyramid in its area, getting more kids playing football on good pitches. Hopefully, exceptional players would still find their way into the system to get top quality coaching.

I think the biggest threat facing football is the decline in competitiveness. If EPPP is in essence about facilitating people like Matt Whitehouse and Saul Isaksson-Hurst to teach kids to improve their technique and help England produce a generation of wonderful players, then great. If a side-effect is to funnel the best players towards the clubs whose squads are already stuffed full, then that is a problem.

How's your control?

Old man story alert! When I was a kid, I played for hours on a school playing field opposite our house in Normanby, Middlesbrough. In my recollection it is packed full of kids playing football and cricket until dark. It didn't have any magical properties because I never got particularly good at either. Years after we moved away, I took a nostalgic detour down Lime Road and there wasn't a single kid on the field. It was surrounded by a metal fence, clearly designed to keep the schoolchildren safe during their break and lunchtimes. And who is against keeping kids safe?

That field, which features so strongly in my childhood memories and helped keep me fit and active, is now used for what, a few hours a week? The push towards control and safety is hard to resist. I have been a school governor for a long time and one of the first things I remember was a meeting about putting up a high metal fence. Effectively, we had no choice because Ofsted was failing schools for not segregating entrance areas from play areas. The headteacher hated the idea and imagined she would have to fend off angry parents, complaining their kids were being caged. The opposite happened. The only parents who expressed a view loved the fence. They were sending their kids to school afraid they were in danger.

I now live near a large park which often stands empty although never on a Saturday and Sunday. On matchdays, there are kids in kits with coaches, goals, and respect barriers. The car parks are rammed and contrary to what you read about youth football, the overwhelming majority of parents are good people supporting their kids. The odd coach, who can't handle the emotions of sport, goes red in the face but generally it is a positive environment. The kids are spending time running around with their friends until they get bundled back into the car and driven safely home to the Xbox or PlayStation.

English schools are criminally underfunded, but they are full of caring, intelligent, incredibly hard-working adults doing their utmost to give the students the best the system can offer. My school experience was far more chaotic. I remember going into an exam and being totally surprised by the content of the paper. Now everyone knows what narrow strand of knowledge, selected largely arbitrarily, will be the subject of examination. The kids will have been tested, coached in exam technique, and tested again. It starts in primary school, and it only ends when they leave the system. Schools compile data, pore through it, share it with governors, are assigned a place in a league table, and justify themselves to Ofsted inspectors. The students get through heaps of content, and their exam scores go up to such an extent that exam boards make the exams progressively harder. Everyone is a winner. Also note: the mental health support offered to increasingly stressed children is better than ever.

We know more about the human brain than before. A whole industry exists in how to understand your child and make them better people, superior to their peers. Football reflects society. We are obsessed with control and football clubs are more obsessed than most. Kids can be 'signed' to academies from eight, but clubs use various means of drawing them close before that, maybe with branded training sessions for which parents eagerly pay. Most football-loving kids are playing at grassroots levels and a network of scouts of variable ability are watching the best teams, usually looking for the fastest, most obviously skilful players.

From the under-nines they start their academy journey in the foundation stage and, if all goes to plan they progress through the age groups. It becomes a huge part of their life and demands significant sacrifices of parents although on the upside they probably get to spend a lot of time in the car with their budding footballer.

Lee Hendrie is one of many ex-pros who values his haphazard route to the Premier League:

'It was youth team level for us. We were allowed to play for our schools, our districts, our Sunday league sides, Saturday teams. They can't do that nowadays. When we were "school of excellence" – you could still play in different styles of football. Academies now are very regimented. I spoke to one of the boys and he said he was struggling in front of goal, and I said get a bag of balls and go out and practice to get the confidence and he said, "We're not allowed to do that no more."

'If we were struggling on crosses, we'd have, say, ten minutes of getting the ball out of your feet and putting it in the box. I used to like working on my touch. Now they have a training regime and it's all done on minutes and it's very on-point but if we wanted to spend half an hour extra, we'd get a bag of balls and practice. It's very regimented today.'

Paul Mortimer was a professional footballer, turned coach, turned therapist. He works with academies now and he is concerned:

'It's far more structured, and in my opinion, more limiting. When I was a youngster growing up, I never played 11-a-side until I was 13, 14. I played five-a-side and it taught me a lot, spatial awareness, understanding, anticipation, technical and tactical skills. Five-a-side is very quick, so you have to think quickly, you have to move quickly, your touch has to be correct, and you learn how to keep the ball. I was quick at a very young age. I trained as an associated schoolboy at Fulham but also at QPR, I played for my district, tried to play for my county, I didn't play for my school, I played for my Sunday side. I remember playing Saturday morning, Saturday afternoon, Sunday morning, Sunday afternoon, all the time, all the time. I played for a men's team at 15. I just loved to play football.

'Now the academy is the one place you can learn. I wouldn't have been the player I was if I hadn't played street football, Sunday morning football, men's football. If I'd just stuck with academy football, I think I would've been somewhat sanitised as a player, not really allowed to show my swagger and confidence.

'Lots of academy players are very similar. I counsel some and I deliver education, and all they know is academy football. I don't think that's a positive. Playing with your mates is where you can showcase your skills before you might have the confidence to show them at academy level. It's very difficult because that level is very much structured and pressurised.

'I coached at academy level and at 13, kids had to know set pieces. I always got into trouble with my bosses because I never did them, because at 13 I want them to show me what they can do. I want them to think for themselves but what we're doing is imposing on those young players what should happen when you want them to express themselves. They're being sent so many mixed messages, so you lose a lot of talented players because they're too frightened to showcase their skills.'

Recently I watched an under-eights side who were branded 'Elite'. The coaches called almost every pass and shot and reminded the boys to keep a disciplined defensive shape. 'Relax' is a coaching buzzword but the way they barked it out was anything but relaxing.

'I think the biggest single problem you have is when you call an eight-, nine- or ten-year-old a "player",' says Mortimer. 'Unfortunately, people in their heads change that to "pro" and they then have an expectation of this young person that they should be able to do certain things. We forget this is a child first and foremost. We call them "players" and there's an expectation of excellence, especially in our academy system where players are assets, not children. They have a financial number on them. No matter what anybody says, they do. They're not seen as children. They're somebody's child and that mindset has to change.'

10,000 hours

Around the time EPPP was launched there was a lot of talk that English players weren't getting enough technical training time compared to their contemporaries in Spain, Italy, France, and Germany. It was probably the peak of people believing in the abject nonsense of the 10,000-hour rule.

Malcolm Gladwell's book *Outliers*, published in 2008, has sold over a million copies and influenced a generation of educationalists, businesspeople, sports coaches and hothousing parents. Essentially, the argument runs that you can become world class at anything by putting in 10,000 hours of dedicated practice. Want to join the London Philharmonic Orchestra? Better start laying down those hours of concerted concert practice. Want to play cricket for England? Become a billionaire? Just practice and never give up. It is a clarion call to individual effort. It is up to you; put in the graft, collect your just desserts. It is an appealing, empowering, uplifting message. It is nonsense.

Beware of round numbers. Why would 10,000 hours be the cut-off point for both a violinist and a mixed martial artist? It was, as Anders Ericsson called it, a 'provocative generalisation'. Why should we listen to him? Because he was the man who did the research on which Gladwell based his best-selling book. The irony is that the 10,000-hour rule seized the imagination because it was quick and easy to get your head around; a sweet shortcut to success, as long as you are not the one doing three hours a day of violin practice.

If you want to read something sensible on the subject look at David Epstein's *The Sports Gene* in which he explains how, for example, the constitution of your eye influences how good you are at tracking a ball. Great musicians and sports stars have indeed put in long hours of practice, but no one measures the people who were kicked out of orchestras or self-selected themselves away from football because their long hours of hard work were getting them nowhere. Practising helps but if you are 5ft 2in then 10,000 hours of practice isn't going to make you a world-class basketball player. Sorry.

There is nothing in the 10,000-hour rule that couldn't be gleaned from the adage: practice makes perfect. Its main utility is to back up what the authority figure wants anyway. I want my players, students, kids to work hard and here is something that looks like science and is easily digestible. The danger is that the rule is used to pile pressure on to young people, creating rifts in relationships, mental and physical breakdown. Please don't make your child do 10,000 hours of bare-knuckle boxing.

A central tenet of the EPPP was giving more coaching hours to promising footballers. That is fine, as long as you understand the potential downsides. Matt Whitehouse acknowledges that the 10,000-rule is still influential:

'The 10,000-hour rule gets thrown around and it may not necessarily be true, but it does give you a region of what players need in terms of their history of development. If they're only getting 6,000 hours of development at 16, are they ready to be able to play in the first team yet? They might still need a few more years of high-level training. That means more training, more travel, more commitment so if clubs are trying to get more hours in earlier for players that means you've got seven-, eight-, nine-year-olds doing three or four sessions a week. Personally, I think multi-sport development is important because that gives physical literacy that isn't just football based.'

Indeed, a 2018 study by the American Academy of Pediatrics compared athletes younger than 18 who specialised in one sport with generalists and concluded that, 'Athletes with high specialisation were at an increased risk of sustaining an overuse injury compared with athletes with low and moderate specialisation. Athletes with moderate specialisation were at a higher risk of injury compared with athletes with low specialisation. Sport specialisation is associated with an increased risk of overuse musculoskeletal injuries.'

Whitehouse says academies are in danger of being one-track, 'We're having so much football training and if your levels aren't there, people say, "I don't think you're committed." That makes me think a combination of grassroots football and other sports isn't a bad thing for the lads early on.

'The foundation stage in academies is a really positive thing for lots of lads but there's an element that it's all football. There's a lot of commitment for parents in terms of travelling, with energy prices going up and the standard of living becoming harder. Travelling for hours to away fixtures when you could be playing locally is probably not beneficial. Travelling three or four hours for a 60-, 80-minute game seems excessive when they have to focus on education as well.

'Kids who play racket sports, swimming, martial arts, have a stronger physical capability long term. Lots of players who've succeeded did multi-sports early on. The ones who specialised early almost get to a point where their bodies aren't able to adapt because they've only done one sport. The academies could offer more multi-sport opportunities. As you get older you might specialise and commit to an elite programme but maybe at early ages not so much.'

Matt Jackson was an outstanding general sportsman before he became a Premier League footballer and made over 500 league appearances. He thinks the long hours of football training carries another risk – churning out players who do the same things:

'I think it's one of the downfalls of the system. We now produce outstanding technical players, because of the contact time we have but it becomes a massive part of their life all the way through. There are development centres at four, five and six years of age now, although it's not structured at that age.

'You'll have heard about 10,000 hours to achieve academic excellence or elite performance and that underpinned a lot of the thinking around the EPPP. The contact time means you can look at every area of development – they're multi-skilled, have excellent ball manipulation skills throughout – but we do tend to produce very similar players. It is far more technical than we've ever been, and that's reflected in the way the national side plays.

'When EPPP started we had a unique style that didn't always work and certainly hadn't had success. We're now far more aligned with what's seen as the old continental model with very good technical players. They're physically developed as well because everything is measured and tested but we don't get multi-talented sportsmen now. Players get immersed into the football system and I think it's a big problem.

'The better-funded academies provide other sporting opportunities as part of their training, but I played county basketball and badminton. I played cricket and had an athletics season. Players aren't allowed to play outside of the club situation. We had schools and district and county sides, but you also played a lot of different sports. It brought out different sorts of skills and you saw different types of players existing in the professional game, although now everyone is a fantastic athlete and excellent technically.'

It is an interesting dilemma: the intense focus on football has helped to produce the sort of technical players that only a few years ago we associated with Spain or Germany. But is it itself a limiting factor?

Of course, most kids in the academy system won't become professional players which is widely acknowledged, but not, according to Paul Mortimer, truly understood:

'The environment has conditioned them that the only thing that matters is on the training pitch. I say to the kids, "How old are players when they finish?" And they say 25, 28, 30, 33. I say, "When is your next training session? That could be the end, your very next tackle." I ask them if they're ready for what comes next. They don't know what you mean, they've devoted all their time to football. Football has conditioned them that football is the only thing.'

The Premier League isn't deaf to this. It states that one of its aims is to provide 'world-class education via inspirational and innovative teaching, which develops educationally rounded people through the delivery of a holistic approach'. It has its own education department 'to support the technical, tactical, physical, mental, lifestyle and welfare development of all academy players'. Big clubs will send the most promising youngsters to expensive private schools. But Mortimer sees the downside of single-mindedness, 'I counsel players who are coming towards the end of their careers: 500 games, legend at their club and they started to hallucinate and take drugs because the end was coming, and they can't do anything else. They're frightened of trying to do anything else because football is all they know. That mindset we have to change.

'On the walls of one training complex, they've got photos of academy graduates that have gone on to be players, but you have to show the ones that went on to be accountants and lawyers. We have to show them the truth: it's a pyramid – there are loads at the bottom and very few at the top. But we don't.'

Former Manchester City academy player Jeremy Wisten took his own life in 2020 after being released by the club. An inquest in November 2021 was told that he didn't believe he received the 'right support' from City after leaving. This is not an unrecognised problem within the professional game. Part of Matt Jackson's job at Wolves is managing the wellbeing of players the club doesn't want to keep:

'It's the most important thing. The welfare of the players who aren't making it to the professional game is as high as it has ever been. There have been a number of high-profile suicides of young men who've been released from academies and while nothing matches the pain of the families, it's also the club's worse nightmare. There's an awareness that we have to care for the young men leaving the system.'

I asked whether football was a nicer world than it was when he was a player. Jackson said, 'It's still ruthless in terms of dreams being shattered, and it will always have that for it to remain an elite environment. But it's now excellent in supporting all elements of adolescent life of the young footballer. It's also good for the top players in determining what their injuries are, what psychological problems they may have and how they can deal with life issues that aren't necessarily in their control. It's definitely a more supportive environment. There's a far better diversity of people which is good for the development of everybody in the game, and that's ethnicity, sex, and even sexuality. There's an awful lot of what wouldn't have been a part of my professional life growing up.'

Working in a different part of the system, Mortimer puts the emphasis on how far there is still to travel:

'I've spoken to a lot of players and asked what they're like when they've played poorly and lost. They all say, "I'm not talking to anyone, I'm moody." I say, "Why? You're penalising your family. You're penalising everyone else with your anger."

'It sounds weird, but we have to move towards the person and away from the footballer, understand the person more and help them evaluate themselves as a human being. That way they'll understand the ups and downs of football. Because when things are going well, players can still struggle. They can't handle the pressure of performance.'

I can't imagine there are many people better than Paul Mortimer to talk to young footballers about their wellbeing – Premier League player, coach, with years of training in counselling after his career switch. The danger is, as with schools and workplaces, that we've created a system that hothouses people, sometimes from a heartbreakingly young age, piles pressure on them and then offers mental health support. We have to find a way to give kids the coaching they need to become excellent technical players without making their childhood miserable. One road that academies might be tempted down is recruiting kids not based on their physical or technical ability but on perceived coachability, which would be a different mistake.

Coachability

> 'Your child's success or lack of success in sports does not indicate what kind of parent you are. But having an athlete that is coachable, respectful, a great team-mate, mentally tough, resilient and tries their best IS a direct reflection on your parenting.'

If you search Google images for 'coachable kids' you get the quote above displayed at a sports ground, and a host of articles about why we need to be good learners. We are back into the controlled environment: who doesn't want kids to be respectful, a great team-mate, mentally tough and resilient? Don't get me wrong: it is a good thing to be eager to learn. The problem comes when we start using coachability as a filter rather than a quality to aspire to. I have seen it specifically listed as a quality that a sports organisation was seeking in young players. It ties in with the culture of the 10,000-hour rule. If it is all about hard work and we don't recognise intrinsic, or if you prefer, God-given, ability then why not just recruit nice kids with two sound parents who always get them to training on time?

Answer: because that is not diversity. Diversity is not a tick-box exercise. It is not the same as 'not discriminating' – we have to make sure there are no blocked pathways for kids with talent or potential, whatever their background.

Matt Whitehouse says it is a real problem, 'Academies want to recruit players who are coachable which means conformist, not too many issues, who listen. They're nice lads and nice players. Then there are lads who have a bit of edge and maybe aren't easy to work with, who can be confrontational to coaches, maybe a bit physical in training. In the safeguarding and welfare world of academies those players can be seen as a problem whereas they actually tend to be the ones who've got that little bit about them who can progress through the levels.'

He cites Jude Bellingham who left his local club, Stourbridge, to join Birmingham City's academy aged eight, was playing in the under-18s aged 14 and the under-23s when he was 15. He made his senior debut aged 16 years and 38 days and played 41 matches in the Championship before he was sold to Borussia Dortmund for an initial £25m, becoming the most expensive 17-year-old in football history. He made his England debut aged 17 years and 136 days. In 2021/22 he won more tackles than anyone else at Dortmund and was the most fouled player in the Bundesliga.

Bellingham has resilience, but Whitehouse says he wasn't classically coachable, 'I saw Jude come through the levels as a youth player watching him in Midlands football and he had that edge at times, that horribleness in him. People were saying, "He's got a bit about him." He was such a good player he backed it up with performances, but I tell you he wasn't easy to work with. Coaches would say you had to be really smart with how you work with him, but he's at the top level now as an 18-year-old because he's had that bite in him, that aggression.'

Ten years ago, I would have questioned whether players like Xavi Hernandez or Andrés Iniesta would have successfully come through the English youth system but now Whitehouse has a different concern:

'Luis Suárez would have really struggled in academies here because he was hard to manage, you know. At Ajax as a young player, he was all over the place, pushing and pulling people like you see him do. Academies here probably would have thought he was a "bad 'un", and maybe not right for this environment but he's a world-class forward, one of the best ever.

'At Coventry, we try to have lots of player-led stuff, but we refocus around competition a lot, I know I do, because the competitiveness has to be ingrained. Winning shouldn't be a bad thing. It's just how you deal with it – focusing on the process not just outcomes, making sure players are fully invested in getting better and don't quit because the results are bad.'

Paul Mortimer says the academy environment with its taxing demands on the time of players and parents had led to a change in the background of the kids in the system. I asked him whether football had ceased to be dominated by working-class people.

He replied, 'Without a doubt. When I was a kid, my parents never came to football. I had to take two buses and a train or get a lift from somebody else. If you look at the average academy game now, both parents are there, two-car families, middle-class. I coached at levels where a lot of the players were quite affluent. Football was a working-class white man's game. That's what it was. It's not anymore, it literally isn't. The footballers were working class as well. Now if you look at the disparity between the average man in the street and the footballer's wage it's ridiculous. Players used to go home on the bus or train with the fans. That doesn't happen anymore.'

If I am arguing for genuine diversity, then I should acknowledge that it is a positive that better-off kids are no longer effectively excluded from football. The trick is finding the balance. Mortimer also thinks coaches err towards easily managed kids:

'The individual is often seen as a troublemaker. I look at a "troublemaker" and I see authority figures struggling to understand that person. It's easier to label those people so they can be moved on, rather than trying to really understand them. They must learn the way you want them to learn. So, we build a group of players who are very similar. I go to watch some academy football, but I can't watch it, I really can't because there are no stand-out players or if there is a standout player, it's because they are athletically gifted, very rarely technically individually gifted.

'I don't like it because I don't see individual talents who have swagger, confidence, arrogance – in a positive way. You have to conform to the ethos of the academy environment. I've worked in it and I'm still around it now – and it always makes me feel slightly uncomfortable if I'm honest.

'Every time we label a child it says more about you, that you can't understand that child and how they learn. It's a huge problem in our schooling system and in life in general; we label people without understanding what's going on for them. We tend to label and that impacts and inhibits development rather than enhancing and elevating it because we don't know how to do that. Sometimes we have to take a step back and review our practices.'

In defence of people working in the education system, this wasn't new stuff to me. In my experience, they are aware of the problem and work hard to accommodate everyone, but Paul is right, the system demands each generation of children is shepherded through a series of examinations on strictly limited resources – and individuals are in danger of being lost.

This chimes with Stewart Robson's observation on the limitations of young players, 'They're all very nice technically. They're all able to manipulate the ball, they're all able to find a pass, a simple pass, they all have the basics. They're much better technically than they were years ago but they're losing the ability to go past people, losing the ability to turn with the ball, losing the ability to run past people at pace and get crosses in.

'There's a fear of giving the ball away so we play safe. All the drills, and movements they do will be passing movements rather than coaching individual brilliance so you're going to get a lot of players being much of a muchness. I'll use an example, the Harry Winkses of the world, who is like many other midfielders, you know, a good footballer but is he any better than anybody else? Gareth Southgate has picked, I don't know, hundreds of different players to play for England but it doesn't change what the team looks like or how they perform. They're all very similar.

'At the European Championship the best player, even though he had been playing poorly for Man City was Raheem Sterling because he can run past people with the ball, and I'm not saying he's a great dribbler but at the Euros he changed England's fortunes because he ran with the ball and there aren't enough players who are good at running with the ball.'

No leaders, no wonder

If you type 'no leaders' into Google, you will get a stream of stories along the lines of 'Former Manchester United star X says the current team lacks leaders'. The yearning for leaders is often a yearning for a superhero to appear and solve any manner of problems. It is understandable – football remains a chaotic sport and having strong characters take responsibility at critical moments is massively important, if hard to quantify. Football clubs are pouring resources into measuring as many aspects of the game as they can. The inherent danger in measuring things is that we stop valuing what can't measure.

For Terry Gibson there is no mystery, 'We micromanage players. Very few of them moan about anything. I moaned about doing 12-mile runs – every single time. We were tougher to manage because players were allowed to have an opinion. I could do my own warm-up for a game of football – I didn't need someone there. You see them out with the rubber bands now, and I wonder as a sports science coach how far you could push them to make them look foolish before anyone would say, "Why are we doing this?"

'When I was playing the manager might say, "You're a marker, you're a marker, you're in the wall," and players worked it out for themselves from there. If a substitute came on, the captain would tell him who to mark. There might be a player struggling with an opponent and he might ask his mate to swap. They would take responsibility. We can't on one hand give players no responsibility and then moan about them not being leaders.'

That Gareth Southgate is considered the picture of a modern leader shows how much things have changed. In the Euro '96 semi-final, Tony Adams was England's captain and Stuart Pearce, Paul Ince and Alan Shearer were more obvious examples of what we then saw as leaders than the quietly spoken Southgate. I'm not complaining; I think his thoughtfulness and willingness to learn are better qualities than the sergeant major chest-thumping model that Adams represented.

Paul Mortimer puts that change down to the influx of foreign players:

'There's a lot more emotion in the game so a leader might look completely different. Jordan Henderson's a leader but he's not a fist-waving, kick everyone kind of leader, is he? How he talks and presents himself is very different from Tony Adams.

'In this country we'd look at Adams, Bryan Robson, Steve Bruce. The foreign influence comes in and leaders are different. I'm a man of the 1980s and I go for men like Franco Baresi and Paolo Maldini who were leaders. AC Milan was my team. They didn't kick people or wave their fists, none of that, they just led. It was in them.

'Physically, everyone is much of a muchness, it's all scientific. You don't see a man mountain who everyone is going to be physically intimidated by. The modern footballer is an athletic person, a thoroughbred, so leadership has to come from elsewhere.

'The modern leader in football isn't just on the pitch, it's off the pitch. It's social media, let's not discount the importance of that. Leaders are often popular and social media is a popularity contest, literally. Marcus Rashford is a leader off the pitch, not on the pitch.

'Raheem Sterling is a leader, on the pitch as well. The public and press don't like him as much as they should because they don't value what he's saying. Among the black and ethnic minority people in football he's a God because he speaks for them in a way that we haven't been able to speak.

'Football clubs are brands, and the captain is important. Man United is an example of how their leader, their captain is struggling. I know Harry Maguire, you'd like him. He's a very level-headed lad but something emotionally has gone wrong at that club. It's one you need to erect a fence around and not go anywhere near for five years.

'Leadership is a great example of how football has changed. It's not Captain Marvel careering into tackles anymore. They have to be eloquent and articulate. People will ask their opinions. I just can't imagine Bryan Robson or Tony Adams talking about current affairs. The modern leader needs so many more strings to their bow other than being able to kick a ball in a straight line.'

3

The England DNA

MATT CROCKER was almost apologetic that Southampton FC's training complex was a mere 37 acres. It looked big enough to me but apparently Leicester City have 140 acres. There were perfect pitches as far as I could see and a huge dome housing an artificial pitch; the days of Premier League training schedules being shaped by wind and rain are gone. As he showed me around, Matt told me a story of his mate who took a team on a tour of Spain and was shocked that their opponents were obsessed with winning. He wonders out loud whether we have strayed too far away from focusing on results and how a team of young Brits would get on if you told them to win at all costs.

I had invited myself to Southampton to ask Matt about his role in the development of the England DNA, the project that attempted to define and roll out a clear playing and coaching philosophy throughout the various England teams, and into grassroots football. Direct football was out. The FA would strive to produce technically excellent footballers and its teams would play an intelligent possession-based game.

'I never want it to come across that in 2013 this revolution happened,' said Crocker. He stresses that I shouldn't paint him as a visionary, 'There had been some really good coaching and coaches in England. Dan Ashworth [then the FA's director of elite development, now Newcastle United's technical director of football] did a lot of hard work in convincing the powers-that-be that we had to invest in all our national teams, which was no mean feat, and that we had to get a sense of connection and togetherness in how we played.

'The development of St George's Park was massive but so was Dan's role and the work Ged Roddy had done with the EPPP. The time was right. I don't want it to come across as I'm slating people in the past because there have been some inspirational people. We piggy-backed off a lot of work.

'You're one individual and football is so powerful that change is difficult. You often hear, "It's always been this way," so you ask why. It was so deeply ingrained from grassroots football to coach education to a national programme, it was difficult, but it was a great ride for six years.'

I asked Crocker about following in the footsteps of the much-maligned Charles Hughes. He laughed but answered diplomatically:

'Charles Hughes and his book, yeah. I think there are fundamental differences in how we play but he created a DNA. His experience would have told him that at that time to be successful we would have to play a certain way. Nobody knows the answer, sometimes you put your finger in the air and get everyone behind a unified plan.

'We realised with the EPPP came an improvement in players' technical ability because of the volume of work they were doing. Historically I think they were having two-hour sessions a week. Now kids are having four, five, six times that. Then there's the day-release programme where you can take kids out of school and backfill their education at another time. It gave us such an increase in technical coaching hours.'

Watching that infamous 1973 World Cup qualifier against Poland, the most disappointing England player, to my eye, was Tony Currie of Sheffield United. Received wisdom held that he was a maverick whose talent was suppressed by a system that overvalued grafters. Perhaps the simple fact was, players like him weren't good enough to have a system built around them; the tricks and skills didn't work often enough. Is the lesson of the professionalised era of EPPP and England DNA that if you want stylish football that is easy on the eye, but still able to win matches, you need a system churning out technical players in droves? A key paradox of English football is that few people advocate for direct football but lots of teams and coaches default to it. Crocker believes that the 'years of hurt' had opened English footballing minds.

'Having not been successful for 30-odd years it was time to do something different. We got all the experienced national coaches in a room, a real diverse range, and decided what to go with. A lot of it was how the clubs were playing. We were talking about playing from the back and being more patient with the ball. It's not saying we don't play forward. If there's an opportunity to get the ball forward into feet and play between the lines, we definitely wanted to do that.'

In other words, the time was right to throw Hughes's legacy out of the window once and for all.

Crocker is a Welshman who describes his stint at Cardiff City as the best apprenticeship ever, trying to meet the demands of the controversial Sam Hammam. He then had his first spell at Southampton until 2013 when Ashworth offered him 'a blank piece of paper' with the FA's DNA project, giving him the task of aligning the national teams with coach education.

He said, 'I guess it was our blueprint for football. In the past, each England age group team had a head coach who would select players and dictate the style of play. There were fantastic coaches, so no disrespect there, but there wasn't much consistency with how those teams played.

'We said these are the types of players in certain positions that we're looking for, this is what performance support looks like, these are the sort of games we're going to play, and this is how we're going to coach. Then obviously we linked that into how it can influence coach education and future generations of coaches, who'll be working with those players. In an international programme you're lucky to get 50, 60 days a year with the players so you need a robust education programme that enables coaches to be aligned with what we're doing.

'It literally started with a flip chart, a blank piece of paper. We asked what an England team looks like when it's got the ball, when it hasn't got the ball, in those moments of transition. What should you see? If there's a red team and a blue team, you should be able within two minutes to say, "That's the England team." That's whether you're watching the under-15s, the senior men's team, the women's team, whatever. There should be that strong sense of identity and playing style. We spent a lot of time on that.'

One of the England age-group coaches at the time was John Peacock, whose under-17s had become European champions in 2010. Five of that squad went on to become England internationals with Ross Barkley winning more caps (33) than the others combined. Conor Coady, Jack Butland, Sam Johnstone and Nathaniel Chalobah all played for England while Saido Berahino represented Burundi and Benik Afobe was capped by DR Congo. Connor Wickham was the player of the tournament. The conversion rate of youth caps to senior caps compares favourably with the Spain team they beat in the final. Peacock led another set of under-17s to the European title in 2014, from which Joe Gomez (11), Dominic Solanke (one) and Lewis Cook (one) are currently the only other full internationals.

'John had been in the programme for many years,' Crocker recalls. 'He was brilliant at telling the story of what had gone on before. If it was only a bunch of new guys in a room throwing ideas around when you came to implement them, you would hear, "We've done this before." John was a brilliant common-sense check but was really positive about trying to impact and influence the changes we wanted to make.

'At the other end of the spectrum, Dan Micciche was young, forward-thinking, creative, right out-of-the-box coach. Trying to get those two to align in the middle and getting something that we could leave the room with took a hell of a long time.'

Another key figure was Dave Reddin, who had been the fitness coach for England's rugby union team when they won the 2003 World Cup, before becoming head of performance services for the British Olympic Association.

'Dave had experiences from other industries and sports, so he was brilliant at connecting us with England rugby and cricket who were doing some great culture work which football had never really seen. We wanted to decide at the beginning what our identity was and how we were going to connect the players to a strong identity and a culture,' said Crocker.

'You would hear stories, historically, about players, not turning up for England but turning up for their team days later. So how do we make sure there's that emotional connection, that sense of pride? That started not with the senior team but with the under-15s – the first camp, the first day.

'We spent a lot of time working on identity and then connecting that to what we would call rituals, I suppose, storytelling. So, the under-16s would go to play Brazil in Brazil, the first time we'd been back there for years, and rather than saying, "We're playing Brazil, off we go," there was a big piece of work taking the players to Wembley, telling them about John Barnes's goal in the Maracanã, and the history about players in England and in Brazil. We were such a diverse team from so many different cultures we spent a hell of a lot of time on that rather than just turning up to play.'

You might have noticed the 'legacy numbers' on sports shirts. It is a recent innovation in football, and they have to be tucked away to meet FIFA regulations. The idea is to connect current players to the generations in whose footsteps they walk. Harry Kane is England's 1,207th senior men's international, Bukayo Saka is 1,253. They were assigned retrospectively as well: Stanley Matthews was given 603, Bobby Moore 804, Kevin Keegan 887, and Paul Gascoigne 1,006. Those players might seem to belong to the same tradition but Luton Town's 6ft 3in centre-forward Mick Harford was 1,002, John Fashanu was 1,014 and perhaps the most-maligned England player of all, Carlton Palmer, a favourite of Graham Taylor, was England's 1,041st male international.

If the DNA project works in the long term, presumably, we won't see players like Harford, Fashanu and Palmer in the future.

'If we're going to play a certain style, we had to be clear that we would pick players who could do what we're asking them to do,' Crocker confirms. 'If we want to play a patient, progressive game where we keep the ball for longer, there's no point in picking, no disrespect, a big, physical side that weren't as technically gifted. We had to sacrifice results for playing what some would call smaller players, and we built a player profile around specifically what we were looking for. We trained the scouts to identify those players, we were really clear on what an England player in a certain position looked like.

'It can be complicated because if our under-17s are playing say, Slovenia, with no disrespect to Slovenia, we're going to have a lot of the ball, and we then need a full-back who's attacking and good on the ball. But if you're playing France or Spain, you need a player who can do both. You might not have the ball for a long time so you might have to sacrifice some of those forward abilities. We didn't want to sacrifice too much and just have the defenders and play two banks of four, park the bus and try to play on the counter attack, we wanted to try to out-possession Spain. I remember the first time we did that – I think it was the World Cup under-17s final. I think we had 58, 59 per cent possession against Spain which was unheard of. That was probably the first time I felt we were gathering some momentum.

'We did an interview once with a set of coaches, I won't name names, but one of them said, "You'll never out-possession Spain." We didn't give him the job because we wanted to rip up all those old stereotypes, of what English teams and English players are capable of. We wanted to make sure there were no barriers.'

That 2017 FIFA U-17 World Cup was played in India and England were 2-0 down in the final before coming back to win 5-2, with Phil Foden the outstanding player. Also in the starting XI were Curtis Anderson, George McEachran, Marc Guéhi, Jonathan Panzo, Tashan Oakley-Booth, Rhian Brewster (who won the Golden Boot), Callum Hudson-Odoi, captain Joel Latibeaudiere, Steven Sessegnon, and Morgan Gibbs-White. Conor Gallagher and Emile Smith Rowe were on the bench.

Borussia Dortmund asked for Jadon Sancho not to play. There is always a drop-off from international youth teams but that is a good rate of retention into top level football. Largely the same set of players lost the same year's UEFA European Under-17 Championship Final to Spain on penalties. Spain had Ferran Torres, Hugo Guillamón and Juan Miranda, who are now La Liga regulars, while the player who scored both of their goals, Sergio Gómez, left Barcelona for Dortmund and then moved to Anderlecht. I would say England have had a better rate of conversion. We failed to qualify for the 2019 edition and the 2021 tournament was postponed.

Welshman Steve Cooper was the England coach for that 2017 tournament, and later moved on to Swansea City before getting Nottingham Forest back into the Premier League. Unlike previous Forest management regimes, he has been keen to embrace the club's history inviting the Brian Clough generation of Garry Birtles and John McGovern to chat about their experiences and the work he is doing at the City Ground.

'We wanted to change, and I want to say this in a respectful way,' Crocker said, 'from the approach of, "I'm the coach. I know everything. Listen to me and I'm going to tell you how to play." We wanted more of, "Oh my God, we have some amazing players that we need to listen to and engage."'

Matt Whitehouse's concerns outlined in the previous chapter suggest this is not a battle that has been decisively won.

'It's really difficult for a traditional coach to get their head around,' admits Crocker, 'because you have to show a sense of vulnerability if you're not always the one in charge and you're not the one with the knowledge. We're empowering the players to step up and have these responsibilities. There was a lot of toing and froing over whether it was right. It was a difficult thing to work through, but we made some fundamental changes to coaching and came up with our 12 fundamentals some of which are really basic. Some of them are like, "In a training session have a minimum of 80 per cent rolling ball." That means shut your mouth, and let the kids play. Where did we get that figure from? We plucked it out of the air; there was no science behind it. We thought, "Let's put a figure on it and see how we go."

'Of all the things coaches want to talk about it's the 80/20. I've heard coaches say, "I've got my assistant standing on the line making sure I don't stop it for more than 30 seconds." I remember Dan Micciche introducing in his sessions that if he stopped and talked for more than 30 seconds or a minute, the kids could just carry on playing. The lads would spot the ball and play again. Little things like that weren't for every coach, but we were trying to empower the players – telling them it's not about us, it's about you.

'We introduced, controversially, around 2015, a specialist coaching model. So, we didn't have a head coach and an assistant, we had a head coach and an in-possession coach and an out-of-possession coach. We asked those guys to look at games through a specific lens such as, "What do my team do when we've got the ball and what can my team do to affect the opposition when they've got it, what are the weaknesses in the opposition that we can exploit?"

'I remember going to St George's Park to explain the concept to 30, 40 youth development leads, so academy coaches, heads of development across Premier League and Football League clubs and it was marmite, it really split the room. A third of the room were like, "Great, the FA's trying to do something different." At the opposite end you had 30 per cent saying, "That's ridiculous, football doesn't work like that." And you had some in the middle saying, "Let's see how it goes."

'When I look back, some of the big wins we had were because we started to help the players not just to become better players for England, but they started to see that we could help them with their individual development and become better players.

'Some of our specialist coaches, Aaron Danks [now an assistant coach at Aston Villa] and Lee Skirms, were on their laptops finding clips and pulling players individually and saying, "Have a look at this" – players would be gathering around talking about training clips and match clips. I think that was the first sense that the players got engaged.'

The out-of-possession coach for the 2017 U-17 World Cup win was Ian Foster, who played mainly for Kidderminster Harriers before moving to Ireland to start his coaching career. By 2022, he was in charge of England's under-19s, who became European champions, beating Israel in the final. Most of his squad were with top Premier League clubs augmented by Ronnie Edwards of Peterborough, Alex Scott of Bristol City and Daniel Jebbison of Sheffield United who have benefited from more senior playing time. In common with most teams, they had some hairy moments while trying to play from their goalkeeper, but they mixed up their style well and were a notable threat from set pieces. They will be among the favourites at the U-20 World Cup in 2023.

I first came across the England DNA on my FA Level One coaching course. I had a great week in the July sunshine in Basingstoke. The Hampshire FA offered an intense course, whereas all the others anywhere near me required me to be available on weekend afternoons and Wednesday nights, and I worked in the football media. The written work was the least arduous I had done in decades, but the time spent with the tutors and other grassroots coaches was well spent. There was a healthy mix of grassroots dads and young people looking for a career.

One thing that jarred was the language. DNA is deoxyribonucleic acid, essentially genetic instructions for the development, functioning, growth, and reproduction of all known organisms. It is not something you have meetings about and change. My question was whether the real DNA of English football is fast-paced with low emphasis on possession, valuing physicality and bravery over technicality and tactics. I put it to Matt Crocker that the FA's project wasn't about preserving, it was about moving on. It was probably the question he was least comfortable answering:

'John Peacock and Gareth Southgate were in the room, and they have a deep-rooted sense of what historically has worked and what hasn't worked. Through storytelling they were able to navigate and enable us to keep certain elements, that sense of pride and bulldog spirit, that resilience – but there were also flaws in terms of stereotypes. You know, can we keep it for more than five passes? At moments of pressure will we always crumble: Wayne Rooney kicking out, the Beckham red card, those instances, so many of those, I guess, failures in key moments. We were careful to not allow that to dictate our future.'

I asked about the timeframe over which the DNA project would be judged because, in my opinion, football works in too short cycles; managers are sacked after a few bad results or a poor tournament.

Matt replied, 'That's a good question, but I don't know because I'm not that clever to work things out. I do know that there was a significant change in the success of young England players through teams winning but more importantly, if you look at Gareth's teams now, they're full of amazingly technical players who are efficient movers and clever players and have got amazing technical attributes.

'I don't think this is a silver bullet. We played our part alongside the introduction of the EPPP, better facilities, more aligned coaching programmes at clubs, more varied games programmes. Now it's not just the so-called big clubs, who are able to take their academy kids on tours abroad, everyone is able to give that exposure at a young age.

'If I'm a 12-year-old and I'm always being told, "Spanish players are brilliant," and even though I've never come across a Spanish kid, I start to believe it and when I do play against a Spanish team, I've lost the game before it's started.

'I remember the World Cup-winning under-17s going on their first ever camp to Italy, [when] we first started to introduce the DNA. It was a blinding camp, two weeks with a game every three days – competition, all the strongest teams: Brazil, USA, Italy. We said we were going to focus purely on identity. I remember Dan Micciche putting the objectives for the tournament up: 1. Live the DNA. 2. Show good character.

3. Win the game – but not at the expense of one and two. I really believe all that work, from under-15 to under-17 came through in that World Cup final where we're 2-1 down at half-time and Steve Cooper told me how the players wrote the game plan themselves at half-time. That's how much it had shifted in two and a half years.

'I am proud to think I was one of many individuals who played a small part in improving some of those young players. Would some of them have got through the system if we hadn't done this? Yes, but maybe it wouldn't have been as straightforward because some of those stereotypes around Spanish players – and the nations that were so-called better than us – still existed. I think we did change the perception and it wasn't a one-off. Now people are saying, "England has great young players." We had them anyway but maybe no one was talking about them, and we didn't align ourselves to the fact.'

Has the DNA worked?

The England squads for the World Cup and European Championship tell us we are punching our weight, which wasn't the case a decade or so ago, despite the riches of the Premier League. Saul Isaksson-Hurst says the combination of EPPP in the academies and the England DNA created the conditions for ongoing success:

'It's a perfect storm of both organisations having a root and branch restructuring. It has been driven by the professionalism and investment by academies and the improvement of staff. That's supported by the younger age groups teams and the work that England have done, modernising the way they play.'

Lee Hendrie rates England's young players as highly as any other nation's but sees a lack of desire in some of the best of the group to get international experience through under-age competitions:

'I'm very optimistic. England are in a category where we should be competing with the best. Germany are also strong at both international and league level but I feel we've taken it to a another stage. The Spanish are trying to bring youngsters in under Luis Enrique. They look really good but we're not a million miles away.

'The thing that worries me is the attitude of some of the lads who've been in the full squad at a young age, and then playing under-21 level doesn't mean enough to them. The under-21s have suffered in the past few years at competition level, they've been really poor and we're talking about players who should be doing a lot better.

'I don't know whether Gareth has got that message across to the lads that they might be in under-21s, but I want to know what you're capable of. I think England are a strong squad, they should be dominating the under-21 stage. That affects the first team. We've got a lot of young players and I think he's got a real balance so yes, I'm really optimistic.'

He is right that England's under-21s have struggled to make an impression on the European Championship, although they were semi-finalists in 2017 and runners-up in 2009. In 2017, Aidy Boothroyd's squad contained Jordan Pickford, Ben Chilwell, Nathaniel Chalobah, Jack Grealish, James Ward-Prowse, Demarai Gray, Nathan Redmond, and Tammy Abraham, the latter two of whom missed penalties in England's elimination by Germany.

The gold standard for success at youth level being translated into senior football was Spain, whose 1999–2007 under-age squads fed their world-beating achievements from 2008 to 2012. Their 2010 World Cup-winning squad was packed with highly decorated youth graduates: 1999 U-20 World Cup winners Iker Casillas, Xavi, and Carlos Marchena, 2002 European Under-19 Championship winner Fernando Torres, European Under-19 Championship winner and 2003 U-20 World Cup runner-up Andrés Iniesta, 2004 European Under-19 Championship winners Sergio Ramos and Raúl Albiol, 2006 European Under-19 Championship winners Juan Mata and Gerard Piqué, and 2007 European Under-19 Championship winner Javi Martinez. Others who won the 2008 and 2012 Euros either side of the

World Cup, adding to international titles won at youth level, were Juanfran, Álvaro Arbeloa, Rubén de la Red, and Sergio Garcia.

Hendrie says, 'That Spanish youth success to when they won the World Cup a few years later jumps off the page. Some of these English lads who are playing under-21 level who maybe don't want to be there should remember that's your pathway to the full squad, so show us what you're capable of doing.

'When we were with the under-21s we had a hunger, and the squad was very good but now I'm watching some of these lads now and wondering whether they really want to be there. Do they want show to Gareth I'm here, good enough for the full squad?

'I know there was the Sancho generation, but you have to do that again and again. You dominate youth football like the Spanish did. If you're not in the full squad, you're obviously not doing what you should be, so this is where you learn about playing for your country. We should be dominating youth football because we have potentially got the best youngsters in the world.'

Matt Jackson was an England under-21 international under Lawrie McMenemy. I asked him whether the English development structure can be described as world-beating.

He said, 'It isn't in that we haven't delivered trophies. We are as well-prepared, as well-structured, and well-funded as anybody else in the world. We have to balance that with knowing that every single major tournament we go to, someone who is vastly under-resourced compared to us produces performances that make you think they're not far off. Throwing money at it and becoming as streamlined as possible helps but it doesn't guarantee you winning international tournaments. It's going to be a big breakthrough when we win one and I think another could follow quickly.'

This comes back to the problem with extrinsic targets of the sort that Greg Dyke set – essentially, win the World Cup or you're a failure. Shit happens. Brilliantly prepared and coached sides lose football matches, even if they have spent more time in the cryogenic chamber than their opponents. Jackson throws in the issue of media-created pressure:

'For all that the EPPP does, it doesn't deal with what the national press is going to look like during a tournament. Players can be prepared and resilient, but we've seen what the country does to the national team in international tournaments, and it might be a decisive factor in why we haven't won anything for a long time.'

I will close this section with a more sceptical voice. Stewart Robson was a highly promising England youth international in the Charles Hughes era and made his first-team debut for Arsenal aged 17. He was called up to the senior England squad but missed out on his debut because of injury. Now he is an expert co-commentator with ESPN and BT Sport. He isn't a typical 'football man' and isn't afraid of upsetting people in the game.

'I don't think there is a DNA for England at the moment,' he said. 'They'll go with the flow. Gareth Southgate will look at Jürgen Klopp, look at Guardiola, look a bit at what the Spanish are doing, look what the French are doing and take a bit of that and a bit of this. The only time we have had a DNA, where somebody said, "This is how we should play!" was under Charles Hughes. Unfortunately, he got it wrong, but all the coaching courses were done off the back of that book and all those papers he wrote. He was the only person who actually came up with a philosophy of how England should play. Everybody else has done their own little thing but they've played with it a little bit.'

Robson recognises that England have lots of good players but doubts whether Southgate has provided the leadership required, despite his largely positive public image and results:

'I don't think he is a particularly good coach. When he was in charge of England development and oversaw some of the coaching, he was very wishy-washy with his strategies and his philosophy. He kept saying, "I'll go round the clubs and listen to what everybody else says and then take a general poll." No, you're meant to be the technical director, you've got to be an innovator. He's not an innovator.

'He has done very, very well. He has made the players feel happy, he's dealt with the press brilliantly, he has made the fans like England again, the players enjoy turning up, there's a nice culture there. He's done all those things but he's not an innovator or a good coach and it's been proved when things have started to go wrong. We saw that in both the final against Italy in the European Championship and in the World Cup semi-final against Croatia. I'm not sure what he was trying to do. It was obvious he was trying to make changes or do something different, but he didn't.

'He talks in cliches and riddles. What he should have had with him is a top-class coach. I'm sure Steve Holland is a good coach but he's not going to be one of the key innovators who's going to change England's fortunes. He's going to carry out nice training sessions, keep it fairly simple and England will play the way they play. We're not going to see anything vastly different.'

England's poor Nations League performances in the summer of 2022 put a dent in Southgate's relationship with the fans and gave succour to his critics but I'm not reading too much into that. I believe England have an excellent squad of players, with limitations, especially in central defence. Jordan Henderson, Trent Alexander-Arnold, Phil Foden, Raheem Sterling, Mason Mount, John Stones, Ben Chilwell, Reece James, Kieran Trippier, Harry Kane and perhaps Joe Gomez are all at least possibles for the World Cup squad and have all played in a Champions League final. English football has more strength in depth than a decade ago. We have been to a World Cup semi-final and lost the Euros only on penalties. So, if Stewart Robson is right and the driving force wasn't the FA or the English coaching fraternity, where have our ideas come from?

4

Economic migrants

ONE OF the last things Johan Cruyff said about English football was that it had too many foreign players. Ironic, given that the Dutchman's philosophy now runs so deep in our game. He was the greatest advocate for the intelligent, technical footballer although he was no tactician. Albert Ferrer said Cruyff's Barcelona Dream Team concentrated almost entirely on attacking philosophy and skills. They didn't even plan set pieces.

If football philosophy has schools, then Pep Guardiola, Erik ten Hag and Graham Potter would belong to the Cruyff School. The brilliant but cantankerous Dutchman was the leader of the Ajax and Netherlands sides that bucked the trend towards physicality to bring beauty to European football in the 1970s. Or so the legend runs. The footnote should add that those Dutch sides had a nasty streak and his Barça team had Ronald Koeman hitting long diagonals for Hristo Stoichkov. Cruyff was rooted in the real world. In 2015, his assessment for *De Telegraaf* was that English football had to chase out many of its overseas players.

'Clubs should make agreements to play with at least five or six English players,' he wrote. He acknowledged that the UK was then subject to EU freedom of movement laws so he suggested a gentleman's agreement or, he predicted, 'The problem of a weaker English national team will not be solved anytime soon.

'As long as there are too many foreign players, the domestic talents will find it hard to break through. There is hardly any competition and players who are not featuring in the first team have to hope on playing in an occasional friendly.

'I can't find any structure in their youth development. If you look at how many technical coaches Ajax are employing, it is hard to understand how far behind a traditional football country like England is. And this is even more strange considering the fact that every British golfer has three of four coaches and that there are many specialised coaches in rugby too.'

I guess he didn't know about the EPPP and the surge in investment in English academies. We took his advice though. Greg Dyke had made the same case when he joined the FA in 2013, describing the English game as 'a tanker which needs to be turned'. That was the thinking behind restricting Premier League clubs to registering only 17 non-homegrown players in their squads. That has unquestionably influenced the increase in playing minutes for English players in recent seasons, although to nowhere near the numbers of the 1990s.

The influx of foreign talent into English football was a confluence of two factors: the increased TV money from 1992 and the Bosman ruling in 1995. In the early days of the Football League there was no restriction on signing foreigners and there were footballers here and there who had come to the country for reasons other than taking up the game. Once again Herbert Chapman's determination to seek marginal gains changed everything. The Arsenal manager wanted to sign Austrian international keeper Rudi Hiden in 1931 but the Players' Union objected, and the authorities brought in a requirement that footballers had to have been resident in the UK for two years before they could play. This did allow for the likes of former German prisoner of war Bert Trautmann to star in goal for Manchester City. He played the 1956 FA Cup Final with a broken vertebra in his neck, days after he was named the Football Writers' Association Player of the Year.

The barrier to importing players was lifted at the insistence of the European Economic Community in 1978. This led to a small, generally well-received, wave of foreign stars arriving, paradoxically mainly from outside the EEC. Argentine World Cup winners Ossie Ardiles and Ricky Villa joined Tottenham. Birmingham and Sheffield United also went to Argentina for Alberto Tarantini and Alex Sabella. Middlesbrough, Southampton, and Chelsea signed the Yugoslavs Božo Janković, Ivan Golac and Petar Borota respectively.

Arnold Muhren and later Frans Thijssen signed for Ipswich. Manchester City got Kazimierz Deyna, who was regarded as Poland's greatest ever player until the emergence of Robert Lewandowski. Deyna's goals were crucial in City's relegation battle in 1978/79. A sign of the times was that his transfer fee was partly paid in photocopying equipment which was of more use to his Polish army side than English currency.

English clubs didn't have the money to buy the very best. Trevor Francis's £1m move from Birmingham City to Nottingham Forest in 1979 was a sensation here but Giuseppe Savoldi and Paolo Rossi had both already moved between Italian clubs for more. Cruyff cost Barcelona the equivalent of £922,000 in 1973. In fact, no English clubs were involved in the world transfer record after Jackie Sewell moved from Notts County to Sheffield Wednesday in 1951, until Newcastle bought Alan Shearer for £15m in 1996.

Between 1978 and the mid-1990s clubs were wary of signing players from abroad who might struggle to recreate their form in England. Deyna was a prime example – he was a world-class star but his spell in England was blighted by injury and homesickness. English clubs were augmented by signings from Wales, Ireland, Northern Ireland and, especially, Scotland. From 1978 to 1985 every English team in a European Cup final played with at least three Scots. Ipswich, Tottenham, Arsenal, and Everton all played in UEFA Cup or Cup Winners' Cup finals with at least one Scot.

When the first weekend of the new Premier League kicked off in 1992, there were only 13 overseas players, four of whom were goalkeepers: Peter Schmeichel (Manchester United and Denmark), Craig Forrest (Ipswich Town and Canada), Hans Segers (Wimbledon, non-international Dutch), Jan Stejskal (QPR and Czechoslovakia). The outfielders were John Jensen (Arsenal and Denmark), Anders Limpar (Arsenal and Sweden), Robert Warzycha (Everton and Poland), Gunnar Halle (Oldham and Norway), Ronny Rosenthal (Liverpool and Israel), Michel Vonk (Manchester City and non-international Dutch), Ronald Nilsson (Sheffield Wednesday and Sweden). Andrei Kanchelskis of Manchester United had been a USSR international and in 1992 played for the CIS before opting for Russia. The most influential of the lot was France's Eric Cantona – who won the last Football League with Leeds and moved to Manchester United that November.

The Bosman ruling was delivered on 15 December 1995, and that weekend's Premier League fixtures saw eight games on the Saturday and one each on Sunday and Monday. I count 257 players getting on to the pitch, of which 169 were English. There were 17 Scots, 13 Welsh and six Northern Irish.

Ireland was the European country most represented, although many of those were English-born. There were five Norwegians, three Dutchmen, three Danes and two Germans. The only Frenchmen were Cantona and David Ginola, the only Brazilian was Juninho, the Belgian was Philippe Albert, and the Italian was Andrea Silenzi of Nottingham Forest.

There was Georgia's Georgi Kinklazde, Ghana's Tony Yeboah and Zimbabwe's Peter Ndovlu. Dwight Yorke, from Trinidad and Tobago, had signed for Aston Villa in 1990 after Graham Taylor spotted him during a West Indies tour. The foreign players were few in number and are fondly remembered.

They weren't the best in the world: that year's Ballon d'Or was won by George Weah who had moved from Paris Saint-Germain to AC Milan that year. Second-placed Jürgen Klinsmann was the nearest the Premier League could claim – the German had left Tottenham after a successful one-season stay in 1994/95. The highest ranked Premier League player at the time of the Bosman ruling was Yeboah, who finished joint 23rd. The foreign influx wasn't in full flow, but nor were the locals making a splash – the only Englishmen listed, Alan Shearer and Ian Wright, got a single vote each.

The Bosman ruling changed everything; as Alex Ferguson put it, 'All hell broke loose.' The European Court of Justice ruled that Belgian midfielder Jean-Marc Bosman had had his rights restricted by RFC Liege when his contract ended. The club put him on reduced wages and refused to sell him unless potential buyers met their valuation. A Belgian court awarded him a free transfer, but he took his case to the ECJ where, too late to save his career, the judges ruled that EU freedom of labour laws meant that out-of-contract footballers should not be subject to transfer fees. It was a massive switch of power from clubs to players and agents. In 1994 Chris Sutton had signed for Blackburn on a reported £10,000 a week; seven years later when Sol Campbell left Tottenham for Arsenal, he was paid £100,000 a week. Football also had to recognise that EU citizens were entitled to work in any member state. Players from outside of the EU, such as Juninho and Kinkladze, would still need work permits but Swedes, Italians, Spaniards, and Norwegians were as free to play here as any Briton.

Premier League clubs hit the transfer market. From those Ballon d'Or contenders Gianfranco Zola and Gianluca Vialli joined Chelsea in 1996, Marc Overmars moved to Arsenal in 1997, Marcel Desailly followed Zola and Vialli in 1998 and Davor Šuker signed on at Highbury in 1999. In fact, 12 of those nominees played in England before they retired. Weah was probably the most disappointing, signing for Chelsea on loan aged 33 and then Manchester City. The great Liberian is a perfect example of post-Bosman profligacy. He had little enthusiasm for coming back to England after his spell at Chelsea, but City offered him £30,000 a week and a two-year deal shortly before his 34th birthday. He fell out with manager Joe Royle, who he called 'dishonest', and City were relegated.

If we take a match round from December of the year after the Bosman ruling (the corresponding weekend was disrupted so I've jumped to a round between Boxing Day and New Year's Day), I count 246 players used of whom 131 were English – I don't know why fewer subs were used.

Wales and Ireland were a player down, Northern Ireland two down but Scotland the same. There were now 12 Norwegians and four Italians. The new arrivals included stars such as Zola, Dennis Bergkamp, Ruud Gullit, Patrik Berger and Fabrizio Ravanelli – but also Sheffield Wednesday's Orlando Trustfull.

The first wave of post-Bosman arrivals improved the standard. There was a belief that Northern Europeans would adapt more easily. Certainly, Spain right-back Ferrer experienced a culture shock when he joined Chelsea in 1998:

'I could see a big difference because I was coming from Barcelona where it was all about working with the ball and basically not running at all. I landed at Chelsea, and I had Vialli as a manager (and I had Claudio Ranieri, two Italian managers) and the first thing they said to me was run a series of 1,000 metres and we'll see about your time. It was all very physical, and I didn't understand. It was difficult because I'm a sprinter. I was very pacy but for a sprinter with short legs to be running a series of 1,000 metres was very complicated, so I lost a bit of my speed. I realised why, in my first game, no one ball passed the ball for 20 minutes; it was like boom, boom, boom, boom and I was like "What's that?"

'It took me honestly three or four games to get used to this sort of football. Fortunately for me I went to a club where most of the players were European and played a very similar sort of football to Barcelona, but it was more physical than I expected, more direct and the players were very strong. All the games were very open, up-and-down games – attacking, defending. In Spain it was more under control, more tactical and that was a big difference for me.'

Ferrer's first opponents were Coventry City, who beat Chelsea 2-1 with goals from Darren Huckerby and Dion Dublin. That Chelsea team of August 1998 contained two England players, Graeme Le Saux and Dennis Wise, three Italians, two French centre-backs, a Dutchman, a Nigerian, a Uruguayan and Spaniard Ferrer.

On Boxing Day 1999, Vialli named the first line-up for a Premier League game that contained no British players. Chelsea were away to Southampton, with Wise and Sutton injured. The players didn't realise the significance until they ran out from the tunnel and were greeted by a phalanx of photographers. They won with two goals from Norwegian striker Tore André Flo. Southampton, who fielded seven Englishmen, got a consolation from substitute Kevin Davies. Chelsea's non-English XI ended when Jon Harley came on as a 74th minute substitute.

Vialli's selection made history, but Chelsea's players didn't think it was a big deal at the time. They were used to a squad of different nationalities who spoke to each other in English; for them that was life in the Premier League. Midfielder Gus Poyet said later, 'If we had been on the losing side, I think there would have been a lot more criticism. We would have been killed. You win and everything is fine, had we lost, it would have been a different matter.'

Note the pragmatism of English football, as articulated by the Uruguayan: if you win, nothing else matters. Clubs had few qualms about diluting the Englishness of their teams; if there was a mass of talented footballers available for lower fees then why not?

Well, perhaps because there was a quite high failure rate. Diego Forlán made 112 appearances for Uruguay and was the player of the tournament and top goalscorer at the 2010 World Cup. He was a brilliant forward, but it is hard to sell his spell in England as a success. He joined Manchester United from Argentine club Independiente for £6.9m in 2002 and scored 17 goals in 98 appearances. I was at Anfield the day he wrote himself into United folklore by scoring both goals in a 2-1 win against Liverpool. Supporters still sing about it, 'He came from Uruguay, he made the Scousers cry.' I asked him how he adapted to English football as he tried to make an impact at United:

'When I arrived at Manchester United, they were the best players in the world. It was physical but it was also technical.

With Manchester United it was difficult because they play like a Spanish team but were also physical with the best players.

'I felt there was more difference when I was playing in the Premier League against Newcastle, Aston Villa, and other teams away from home. You could see, with the fans, with everybody, it was more up and down, more physical. But if your team had the quality of players, you knew there was a time in the game when they would make a difference with the quality and technique.'

He left United for Spain where he scored 59 goals in 128 games for Villarreal then 96 in 196 for Atlético Madrid, including both in the UEFA Cup Final win over Fulham in 2010. His Villarreal side faced Everton in a Champions League play-off in 2005, after the Merseysiders had finished fourth under David Moyes. Forlán said the English side couldn't match the Spanish style, as Villarreal won both legs:

'I felt the difference when I went to Villarreal, and we played Everton in the qualifying for the Champions League. We knew at Everton it was going to be tough and physical, and it was. But we got a good result, and we knew that coming back home we were going to play more with the ball, and they were going to suffer.'

Forlán no longer sees the same stark difference in styles as in the mid-2000s, with the Premier League having adjusted most:

'I think that you have more international coaches and international players, and you can see, say, Liverpool playing the same way as maybe teams in Spain and Italy. It's more similar, but it depends on the quality of the coaches. I think everybody's physical of course because you can see Sergio Ramos and other players how tough they are, but they have good technique. Also, you can see them in the Premier League and in Italy, but I think it's more similar now and it's not as different as it was back in the day.'

Andrea Orlandi is now a successful agent and pundit. From 2007 to 2015 he played in the English game, initially for Swansea in League One, winning two promotions to reach the Premier League before leaving for Brighton & Hove Albion and later

Blackpool in the Championship. He was in Espanyol's academy but was released for a very old-fashioned English reason of not being physical enough. He moved to a private academy then to Alavés. Then came a slightly incongruous loan move to Barcelona, who needed a left-sided midfielder for their B team. He made one La Liga appearance for the Catalan giants, shortly before they won the 2006 Champions League.

'It was only one game but for me it was enough,' Orlandi recalls with a smile, 'One game for Barcelona, I'm really proud of it.'

Interestingly, he didn't join Swansea for the money, and grew to love playing in the English league:

'Barcelona made me an offer to sign permanently but we couldn't do it with Alavés, and Roberto Martínez called me and asked me to come to Swansea. I didn't know anything about Swansea, the club, or the city. I didn't even know Swansea was in Wales. They were in League One, but Roberto convinced me it was the right move. I had other offers, including from Greece that were financially better, but I thought the English league would be better for me because of the way I was made, I just wanted to play.

'It was a bit shocking at first coming from Barcelona with the best facilities in the world. On my first day, they gave me a bag with my kit and told me to get changed. Basically, there was no training ground, there was just a pitch and the players put their boots on in the car park and started training. It was a culture shock, but it was good for me, it kept my feet on the ground. It took me a while to adapt but once I did, I loved it.

'Roberto told me the first six months will probably be a struggle but once you get over that you will probably want to play here for the rest of your life and that was exactly what happened. The first few months I wasn't sure if it was the right decision, I was in and out and then I got a knee injury – but after that I thought "wow, this is where I want to be". The atmosphere at the games: there was passion, there was intensity, there was absolutely everything.'

I asked Orlandi how he adapted to the style of the English league in the mid-2000s. He admitted he was helped by playing for the right managers:

'The main thing is to get up to speed. I remember my first game was against Leeds at Elland Road, I came on when we were losing 1-0 and I was going to control my first ball in English football. Someone pushed me from behind and while I was still eating the grass, they scored their second goal and my team-mates were looking at me thinking, "What are you doing?" I thought, "OK, welcome to England. I'll have to wake up."

'I wasn't at the level in terms of intensity, the speed of the game. I was technically very good, but I had to get a few kilos on my body and speed my game up. But I'm pretty sure Spanish midfielders are suitable for English football because once you get that, it's such an enjoyable game because you find spaces. It's an open game, and I was fortunate enough to play with clubs with a style that suited me.

'I would never have come to the UK if Roberto wasn't Swansea manager and it was difficult for me to find a club afterwards because British coaches would look at me and say, "He can't tackle, he can't head, he's not a box-to-box. He's not a midfielder. What is he?" So, I played under Roberto, Paulo Sousa, Brendan Rodgers and then at Brighton under Gus Poyet and Óscar García. These kind of managers gave me the chance to play in the UK. At Blackpool I had Lee Clark for the last few months of the season and at the beginning he couldn't really see me as his player but by the end of the season I was his captain.

'The main thing for a player is to get your breath back because the game is so intense that you make one effort after another and another and you can't really breathe. It takes a while to adapt but once you do for a midfielder it's such an enjoyable style of football. The hardest position for a player coming from abroad is striker – if you're not up for it. You're going to get elbows everywhere; you're going to be challenged and kicked. If you don't want that then don't come to the UK because you're not going to enjoy it.'

Part of Orlandi's job now is helping players move between leagues. He admits it is easier for foreign players to move to England than the other way around:

'It is harder for British players to go abroad. In England they have everything. They have a training style they've been used to, they have financial security, they've got, if not the best, then one of the best leagues in the world so why would you leave your home country?

'I think it's quite easy to spot the players in La Liga who are suitable for the Premier League. They need to have the physical attributes to start with, then you look at the mentality because they need to be intelligent and open enough to adapt to another league. I was given time but there's usually no time – look at Saúl Ñíguez, his loan move to Chelsea [from Atlético Madrid for 2021/22] didn't work because he was still adapting and there's no patience.

'Marc Cucurella is the perfect example. We knew he was going to be the perfect fit for the UK and for Brighton especially. I think it's easier to see players who are going to be suitable for the Premier League rather than the other way round. I was very surprised at how well Kieran Trippier adapted to Spain. I thought he would have struggled but he was impressive.'

The migration of players is the obvious reason that the countries' styles have converged but there are others. Foreign managers followed the players to England, while TV and electronic communications made the world a smaller place. Whatever doubts existed about throwing the doors of English football open to the world, the people who experienced the transition closest were generally the most welcoming.

Lee Hendrie made his Premier League debut for Aston Villa eight days after the Bosman ruling in December 1995:

'I had John Gregory as my manager, and we were one of the only clubs with an all-English side at one stage. It was a big change, there were lots of foreign players coming and it was quite strange at the start. The foreign boys segregated themselves, they had their own clique, which you could understand.

'Eventually we had the likes of Olof Mellberg and Marcus Allbäck, there were lots of foreign boys. They were coming into an English set-up and some of the lads struggled to speak English: Juan Pablo Ángel, Nobby Solano, people like that.'

Despite problems with transition, Hendrie said the imports brought a new level of professionalism:

'It was fantastic because these guys with their approach to life and the sport were completely different. They wanted to work hard, stay out [on the training pitch] and do extra stuff. Not many people were like that in the English game. That was the difference, they wanted to do things correctly.

'I always looked to the guys who wanted to be at the top of their game, working on getting better, and I found the foreign boys brought that into our changing room. They were very passionate about what they did. I'm not saying we weren't, but they were passionate about their personal performances, and that started to shine through.'

Hendrie played with Alpay Özalan, who was living proof that foreign players didn't only bring technical skill and tactical appreciation to England. He was a classic signing of the era; bought from Fenerbahce on the evidence of an excellent performance at Euro 2000. It seemed like good business at first, but Alpay became unsettled when Villa refused to sell him after he had been named in the team of the tournament at the 2002 World Cup. He was eventually forced out after sparking a tunnel brawl at the end of a match with England in 2003.

'I remember Alpay when they brought him over from Turkey and he was an absolute different level in terms of passion, I mean, he could have a fight in a phone box, but he was that passionate – that was his mentality,' said Hendrie.

'The Swedish boys were more relaxed, whereas Juan Pablo Ángel was fiery when he had to be. We had lots of different characters with different attributes, and I thought it was a really positive thing for our changing room.

'You don't want to lose sight of what your game is, but the foreign boys look at coming to the Premier League as a massive opportunity whereas sometimes the English boys take it for granted.'

In the 1993/94 season 367 Englishmen played a total of 629,946 minutes in the Premier League; in 2002/03 those numbers had fallen to 207 players and 283,226 minutes[10] – nine years on and just 56.4 per cent of English players had survived (or had been replaced by countrymen). The pitch time had fallen by more than half. Matt Jackson was at Everton until 1996; in his last Premier League appearance for the club, he was one of ten Brits in the starting XI, the only exception being Swedish winger Anders Limpar. He was sold to Norwich in the second tier and later to Wigan in the third tier. He was twice promoted at Wigan and played his final top-level match in 2007. I asked him whether he saw the mass arrival of overseas players as a block on his ambitions or as importing excellence into the English game.

He replied, 'The second one, 100 per cent. As a player you strive to always be the best. A criticism levelled at players is that they reach a level and don't care anymore because they're all millionaires. But players spend their entire life having to be better than the cohort around them to move through the system then into a first team, and to continue in that first team.

'Players have that edge. You get competitive games of footgolf, cards, dominoes, whatever because it burns very brightly within them. If you opened the domestic game to the entire world, players would have to find a way to exist in that system.

'Arsène Wenger coming into Arsenal was a sea change. Prior to that there was a drinking culture, everyone was doing pretty much the same thing. Diets were average to say the least but everyone was doing the same so that was the leveller – ability then determined who the best teams were. Wenger came to Arsenal and brought a more scientific approach and we saw rapid development of players we were already aware of – Tony Adams, Steve Bould, Lee Dixon, Ray Parlour. Those players talk about

---

10 fbref.com

having to transform their lives; you saw how quickly they moved on. Add in the foreign quality, then we as footballers knew very quickly that we'd have to change or be embarrassed.'

Paul Mortimer's last Premier League appearance was for Charlton at home to Tottenham, in April 1999. It was 1-1 when he was substituted, and Spurs went on to win 4-1 with the last two goals scored by José Dominguez and David Ginola. Mortimer is another former Premier League player who thinks the foreign signings were a positive, but he isn't without reservations:

'I thought it was brilliant; look at the impact of Eric Cantona at Manchester United. The reason why foreign players came in was because we overvalued and overpriced our English guys. Everyone knows it. On the whole foreign players have been very good but there have been some terrible ones who've come over here for the money – because the money has been fantastic.

'I do think there had to be a quota because in England, as in Spain and in Italy, the homegrown players need a pathway. Nowhere in English football should there have been a team without any English players because underneath that first team, young players look and think, "I have no chance now." We want the best over here. We don't just want foreign players who are on a par with our players because that just stifles the pathway for English players.'

Les Ferdinand is a rare example of an English footballer who played in Turkey – having a year on loan at Besiktas.

He says, 'I signed for QPR at 19 so I didn't go through the apprenticeship stage that most players do. I went straight in as a professional. Although I had the robustness from playing men's non-league football at a young age, my technique and game understanding needed work. I joined QPR around March time and managed to make a couple of substitute appearances. The next year I was getting my body adapted to professional football and that took its toll, and I had a few injuries. The year after I went to Turkey, and I always call it my footballing apprenticeship. It taught me how to be a professional footballer. I had a great manager in Gordon Milne who put his arm around me and said to me, "Listen, you've got loads of ability. I can't understand why you're not playing for QPR." Turkish people had a high regard for English football so there was great expectation on my shoulders, and I don't think I let them down.

'Our football now is a lot more cosmopolitan than when I went to Turkey. Not only do we have lots of foreign players but foreign managers too. They're bringing their ideas and blending it in with what we have in this country. I'm not sure there was a foreign manager in our league when I went to Turkey, so it was very, very different – but for me, being able to get away from my surroundings and concentrate 100 per cent on football was probably the making of me as a footballer and as a man.'

Ferdinand played his first match in the new Premier League a few weeks into its debut season. The only non-Brit in his QPR side was goalkeeper Jan Stejskal. His last appearance in a radically transformed English top flight was in a Bolton side alongside Fernando Hierro and Jay-Jay Okocha in December 2004. He says the arrival of top talent was a good thing but wonders whether we made too many compromises:

'One hundred per cent; you wouldn't look at those players coming to the Premier League and weakening it in any way shape or form. It's probably the influx of foreign managers and foreign ideas that has changed the way we think. I'll always say that we needed to improve the technique of the players in this country, but I didn't think we needed to lose our identity and I think that's what we did.

'It was the FA's perspective, if you go back over the years, that if Spain won the World Cup or the Euros, we follow what Spain had done from their youth teams upwards. If Germany won the Euros or the World Cup, we'd follow what Germany did. If France did it, etc. We were always adapting to the European country that had been successful.'

El Mister

Is it not extraordinary that no English manager has ever won the Premier League? That is 30 years in which the competition hasn't been won by a coach from the country in which it is played. Only two Englishman have even come second - Ron Atkinson with Villa in 1992-93 and Kevin Keegan with Newcastle in 1995-96. Who would have thought that would be a high point for English coaching?

The Premier League has been won by managers from Scotland, France, Portugal, Spain, Chile, Germany, and Italy. Managers from 23 different football nations have been appointed by Premier League clubs. Scotsman Alex Ferguson dominated the early and middle years of the competition with 13 titles. Why Scotland used to produce so many good managers is a discussion for another day. I am guilty of a minor 1992 reset because Howard Wilkinson's Leeds won the last edition of the Football League, although that was itself an outlier.

There are English managers in the competition – Brighton's Graham Potter was the highest-placed finisher for 2021/22 in ninth place. All three relegated teams were led by Englishmen: Mike Jackson at Burnley, Roy Hodgson at Watford, and Dean Smith at Norwich. All of them were appointed during the campaign with their teams in obvious danger. The same was true of Frank Lampard who finished 16th with Everton. In 2020/21 the bottom five places were occupied by English coaches. In 2018/19 Neil Warnock (Cardiff) and Scott Parker (Fulham) went down with Huddersfield's Jan Siewert, a German who had been at Borussia Dortmund's reserve team.

Harry Redknapp is the Englishman with the most wins – 236 from 642 games. Sam Allardyce is the manager with most Premier League clubs – eight. English managers do get Premier League jobs, just not generally ones with potential for great success. Of recent appointments at the time of writing only Eddie Howe at Newcastle and Steven Gerrard at Aston Villa were Englishmen put in charge of ambitious projects.

Of the overseas bosses to win the title, only Claudio Ranieri can be said to have pulled off a miracle, at Leicester in 2016. Arsène Wenger undoubtedly did a wonderful job in the first half of his career at Arsenal, professionalising that club and by extension the league in general. Jürgen Klopp has brilliantly revitalised Liverpool, restoring them to the top echelons of the world game. José Mourinho, Pep Guardiola, Roberto Mancini, Antonio Conte, and Carlo Ancelotti were all title winners elsewhere in Europe, Manuel Pellegrini had won titles in Argentina and Ecuador although not in Spain with Villarreal or Real Madrid before he was appointed by Manchester City. Lampard was a rare Englishmen who got a job with a title contender, but that was exceptional as he was a club legend returning while Chelsea had a transfer ban. The trend is that top positions go to foreigners with track records of winning other big European leagues.

Only six Englishmen have managed in the Champions League. Redknapp and Bobby Robson achieved straightforward qualifications with Spurs and Newcastle. Lampard guided Chelsea to fourth place in the Premier League and won a Champions League group before he was sacked, and Thomas Tuchel took the team on to win the competition. The other three were almost accidental: Ray Harford (Blackburn) and Craig Shakespeare (Leicester) were internal replacements for title-winning managers and Gary Neville was one of the strangest ever managerial appointments, given that he had no experience when he took over at Valencia, who had finished fourth in La Liga under Nuno Espírito Santo.

Long-serving English managers have at times let off broadsides at their contemporaries from abroad. Sean Dyche, who spent a decade in charge of Burnley, parodied the adulation Klopp received at Liverpool, 'Jürgen Klopp came in and played sort of a 4-4-2 and said let's run really hard and press, people thought it was incredible. "Wasn't Sean Dyche doing that years ago?"

'Antonio Conte came in at Chelsea and he got commended for bringing a hard, fast, new leadership to Chelsea, which involved doing 800m runs, 400m runs and 200m runs. Come to my training and see Sean Dyche doing that and you'd say, "Dinosaur! A young English dinosaur manager. Hasn't got a clue." So, is it perception or is it fact? I have no problem with it. It's the reality I say.'

In 2019, Allardyce vented his frustration at foreign managers, and perhaps foreigners in general, during an appearance on Bein Sports:

'We get sucked into the fact that they all do better than we do, and they all bring their kids up better than we do and they all play football better than we do, everyone goes on about it so we all must have to change to what they do.

'Too many of us now are, "You've got to put your centre-halves both sides of the 18-yard box, you've got to play out no matter what," and realistically most goals in the Premier League come from you making mistakes and giving the ball away in your own half not by good play.'

Terry Gibson is a classic example of an English ex-footballer who passed all the examinations available and got a start in coaching with Barnet, Wycombe, Northern Ireland, and Fulham before moving into media work. He is adamant that the lack of homegrown coaches is not a reflection on the standard of education:

'Foreign coaches come and do our courses. All my coaching courses have had people from all over the world. There are fewer opportunities for English coaches, so we have to be better. Have we got people who are the best? Probably not. Have they had the opportunities? Probably not.

'The clubs are owned by foreign people and a lot of the players are foreign, so if the best foreign coaches are available, it's understandable. It does make for one of the most powerful leagues in the world, the richest league in the world, so we can't complain. It's enjoyable to watch and there's no doubt we've had the best coaches come to the Premier League because the finances are there to pay them and to get the players they want. The best managers in the world want to come to the Premier League at some stage in their career, that is clearly proven now.'

Sue Smith has a UEFA B coaching licence but also works in the media. She has grown accustomed to English clubs seeking overseas management:

'I was surprised Eddie Howe got the Newcastle job – not because I don't rate him, but I just thought they'd go abroad. It would be great to see an English manager managing Liverpool or Manchester City but the best managers at the moment are Klopp and Pep. Maybe once you get an English manager at that level, we might start seeing younger managers coming through.

'The FA has done a great job at getting more women coaching in the WSL. They're very much promoting that, and it's good to have Emma Hayes winning lots of things [with Chelsea Women]. She's had the backing from the club, but it's great to have a confident female role model. It helps more younger coaches want to get involved. I don't think there are problems with English managers. I just don't think they're given the opportunities they deserve.'

Smith named Brighton's Graham Potter as an English manager who has the talent to progress:

'If Graham Potter was foreign, would he have got a top-six job? He's brilliant, the way he gets his team playing is attractive. I know the end bit probably needs work, but when it works, they're brilliant. On the ball, off the ball, everyone knows what's expected, he changes things during a game, tactically or by personnel. He obviously hasn't got the funding to bring in a £100m striker but what he does with the players who are there, how he coaches them, how he can get the best of them, he's a really good manager. He gets linked with big jobs but never gets one.'

Potter's pathway to the Premier League wasn't typically English. He was a full-back who played more matches for York City than his other clubs, a list which included Stoke City, Southampton and West Bromwich Albion. He started his managerial career with Östersunds in the Swedish fourth tier, leading them all the way to the Europa League knock-out phase where they beat Arsenal in the second leg in London, although they were eliminated. That got him the job at Swansea where his style of play as much as results saw Brighton move for him in 2019.

English managers used to spread the football gospel around the world. Three of Barcelona's first four managers were English, and that is not unusual. Italians sometimes refer to a coach as 'Mister', a recognition of the role's English provenance. As late as the 1980s Howard Kendall, Ron Atkinson and Terry Venables managed Spanish clubs, as did Welshman John Toshack who won La Liga with Real Madrid. Venables did the same with Barcelona and led them to the European Cup Final. He was undeniably one of football's innovators.

In 1985 Venables described his work to Hugh McIlvanney, 'It wasn't easy. Apart from the obvious difficulties of altering the formation, the playing system and the attitudes of the team, I had to do it without the knowledge of the language. Mind you, those restrictions may have encouraged me to concentrate on essentials, to simplify what I was getting across to the fellas.

'There were many changes I worked for, such as what we call pressing the ball, which means hustling the opponent in possession with three or four players at one time and trying to rob him in parts of the field where we could counter attack fast and effectively – instead of falling back and only winning the ball when their whole team is in front of you. If you can win it halfway through their team you have only maybe five guys to get past to reach goal. It sounds childishly simple but when you can get the chaps doing it, life becomes a lot easier out there.'

It sounds remarkably like *gegenpressing* doesn't it? He should have given it a fancy name. Other teams had pressed before – Jonathan Wilson describes Viktor Maslov's Dynamo Kyiv doing so in the 1960s; the hugely successful Ernst Happel, who won the European Cup with Feyenoord and Hamburg and reached the final with Brugge, was a pressing manager, as was Cruyff's old boss Rinus Michels.

Stewart Robson laments the lack of English coaches at the forefront of tactical thinking – with notable exceptions of Venables, John Cartwright and Malcolm Allison:

'I think that has always been the case. Coaches copy success but don't know why it's done. So, Pep Guardiola at Bayern

Munich and Manchester City likes his full-backs to come infield, across the pitch and become the holding midfield player which allows the other midfield players to go higher up the pitch and a lot of teams do that now – because that's what Guardiola does. Before that when [José] Mourinho was successful, they played 4-3-3 and the two wingers didn't always come back all the way, they stayed in a position where if they won the ball, they could counter attack – so all teams did that for a while. You're looking for innovative coaches in England rather than looking at what other coaches from abroad do.'

The obvious question was why. Robson continued, 'I don't think we understand tactics. We're not brought up with tactics as youngsters and people just copy what they've been told. People say things like, "We've got to hold a high line," but they don't know the philosophy or the mechanics, they just say it. I've worked with coaches in England who say things but don't know why. If you asked them why all they'd say is, "Well, that's what you do." People say "squeeze up" but you can only squeeze up when nobody is touching the ball. So, while the ball is in the air or travelling from one player to the next, a back four can squeeze up but as soon as the ball is about a yard from the next player, you've got to drop off again because they might hit the ball straight in behind you. Not many people understand the mechanics of it.

'I've seen coaches work and they do what they think they should be doing but there's no innovation. The innovators were people like Arrigo Sacchi when he played 4-4-2 brilliantly, if you ever watch his videos, he knows exactly what he's trying to do. He was almost inventing the way it should be done.'

Maybe there is something to be said for kids playing oft-maligned football video and computer games that contain more tactical nuance than I have ever heard in the English media. I had never heard the expression '*segundo volante*' to describe a specific midfield role until my son asked me what it was while he was playing *FIFA*. In English football we don't describe a position as a 'three-quarter' but if you've played *Football Manager* you will know what a '*trequarista*' does. A '*mezzala*' is basically a number eight – although I would hazard a guess that most English fans don't associate 'eight' with a specific tactical role. A football commentator friend of mine joked that if he ever uses the expression 'false nine' he is being held at gunpoint. I suggested he should start talking about the half-space but be sure to say it in German.

There is a line to be considered here. The work of a *mezzala* isn't unheard of in English football so it can be said to fall into the category of new language for old concepts that Sue Smith described in the introduction. Using expressions without understanding why, for example, you might want players operating in the *halbraum* – becomes copy and paste coaching or commentating – but not having the language to match concepts can hold back our thinking. If all our language for positions applies only to the 4-4-2 it is hard to explain nuanced tactics. We mustn't limit ourselves because we're sniffy about using different concepts.

Ged Roddy acknowledged the system hasn't created a stream of English coaches getting big jobs but he was hopeful, 'My fervent belief is that the next leap forward will be the establishment of homegrown coaches in senior roles in our game. When you look at the German system, the first wave of beneficiaries of their changes were great young players coming through and there was a lag before their coaches came through, almost ten years.

'Now you look at those German coaches and you see them at the very top of the game. My hope is that in the next ten years our English coaches will have the same opportunities and pathway to the top.'

Saul Isaksson-Hurst is also hopeful that we're in the early days of an English coaching boom. 'As a footballing culture we're still in our infancy. We had Sam Allardyce as England boss relatively recently. There aren't enough English coaches like Graham Potter coming through because until relatively recently the English FA were telling coaches to stick it in the mixer and we all played 4-4-2. As a culture, we've come a long way and it's going to take time for a young generation of coaches to come through. You can argue that a lot of the young guys aren't getting the opportunities quickly enough, but I've seen in the Category One academies' under-18s and under-23s there is some phenomenal coaching talent such as Dan Micciche and Kevin Betsy, some of the best coaches I've ever seen in the world, and it'll be their turn soon.'

Indeed, soon after we spoke Betsy was appointed as Crawley Town's manager – it is a long way from League Two to the top, but we will see. Hopefully Saul is right and that having widened the base of the pyramid of coaches and started talking about the tactics and intricacies of football we will start to see the emergence of the English Jürgen Klopp, Pep Guardiola, Thomas Tuchel and Julian Nagelsmann.

Brexit

Stay with me. I'll try to keep it brief, but Brexit is reshaping the English football landscape. Matt Jackson, Wolves' strategic player marketing and loans manager, has had plenty to read.

'It's huge, because the lower-league clubs can no longer go to the continent for cheap alternatives to domestic players,' he said.

Clubs signing non-British or Irish players now need a Governing Body Endorsement, which doesn't follow the old procedure for non-EU players. Under the agreement between the Premier League and FA, approved by the Home Office, there are still two processes: a points-based system earning a GBE and an Exceptions Panel for those players who don't generate enough points. The points system is now more complicated with extra criteria added. International appearances still count but club games are now factored in. And the level of competition matters; essentially, anyone playing more or less a full season for a club in one of the top leagues will qualify.

Another group of 'youth players' has been created to allow clubs to sign 'exceptional' 18- and 19-year-olds who don't have enough appearances. They can earn points in league matches, even if they stay on the bench, for first-team cup matches and for playing in development teams in either domestic or international competitions. Again, the ranking of the club's league matters. International appearances at youth level, between under-17 and under-23, are now included, with countries' ranking and the level of competition is considered.

Jackson believes it will push up prices for British and Irish talent, 'It hasn't stopped clubs bringing players in, but it has made it elitist. It takes out the layer of cheap alternative signings, so you'll have to scout far more competitively, and it'll push prices for domestic players up. You might think they're overpaid now but clubs are going to have to work harder to keep hold of their best assets.

'Technically, it should be good for the English game. Top-level clubs can still recruit internationally but through the four leagues there might be more domestic players who are also better, even if they aren't at elite level.

'Clubs will often have a domestic number two goalkeeper because they won't need to influence the starting 11 but gives you an extra slot for an international player. It's a start. As when EPPP started, clubs will find the best way to use the relegations to their own advantage. It's an ongoing circle of closing loopholes, bringing in new legislation and sculpting it to what the FA, Premier League and FIFA are trying to achieve.'

I asked agent Craig Honeyman if the Brexit changes will make the Premier League more English and he gave me a flat 'no', 'It will impact the Football League more. I think the Football League will turn into a thoroughbred training ground for players who then move on to Premier League clubs.

'The Premier League will still have vast numbers of foreign players continuing, international players and we'll see more South Americans. Previously you couldn't have taken a Messi or a Ronaldinho but now you can and that will be a big difference. Clubs are widening their net into South America and the USA.'

Ray Lewington was split between the desire for English clubs to sign the best players while leaving open the route for local talent:

'I think the Premier League will find a way. It's so tough now for English players coming through to be up to standard. I'm a little bit torn. I don't think we should say, "You have to play four or five players from wherever," but at the same time you need to make it easier for some of our players. If they've been given a chance and they're not good enough, that's fine. Premier League clubs can literally scout anywhere in the world and if you've got the whole world's football community to select your players from then homegrown youngsters are going to find it very hard. I think there's a compromise there. I don't know how to do it, but I do think the Premier League will get around it.'

The Brexiteer

Paul Embery is a passionate advocate of Brexit. He is a fireman and trade unionist turned author and TV presenter. His book *Despised: Why the Modern Left Loathes the Working Class*, has sold well, tapping into the notion that traditional working-class concerns about belonging and identity have been disregarded as the educated elite has become more liberal. As a kid he played for Senrab, the East London Sunday League club that incredibly boasts among its old boys Ray Lewington, Jermain Defoe, Ray Wilkins, Sol Campbell, John Terry, Lee Bowyer, Ledley King, Ezri Konsa, and a string of other successful footballers including internationals for Ireland, Nigeria, Antigua & Barbuda, Turkey, Algerian and Jamaica.

Paul said, 'I come from a football family; my uncle played professionally. I played for Millwall as schoolboy. I went to most of their home games at the old Den but I'm a Wolves fan for some reason. I grew up in Dagenham, but I remember watching *Match of the Day* before Wolves had their car crash era – they had people like Emlyn Hughes and Andy Gray, and I really liked the old gold and black. My brother supports Ipswich, my dad supports Bolton and his brother West Brom – there's no logic. We all should support West Ham but none of us do.'

I contacted Paul because I wanted to know how his political and cultural analysis applies to football, how

127

nationalistic is it reasonable to be when we are watching and playing sport.

'When you look at the World Cup or Euros, there is a broad coming together from all sections of society where people feel an affinity for the country and a desire for their country to do well. Football can cross class divides, racial divides, religious divides etc,' he says.

'I saw a photograph recently of Aston Villa winning the league in 1982. They played away at Arsenal, and you can see black faces and white faces and that struck me as an example of people from different racial backgrounds coming together through football. That happens through the national team which is a good thing.

'You have to guard against the aggressive, hooligan element who embarrass the country and wrap themselves in the St George's flag and want to fight every foreigner, but we've improved on that. Football can be a good form of patriotism without any hostility.'

He didn't know about Athletic Bilbao's Basque-only recruitment policy. They don't genuinely compete to win La Liga anymore, but they have never been relegated and have an extraordinary conveyor belt of local talent. I asked Paul how English should we want English clubs to be.

'I think it's important to have some sort of national identity within your domestic league. The danger is that it just becomes a branch of an international league without its own identity. I think it's important that any kind of national approach isn't hostile to others. Having pride in your own country, in your own domestic football league shouldn't mean hooliganism or hostility but I don't see anything harmful in saying broadly it should be made up of homegrown players but not to the extreme of saying we don't want any foreign influence at all. People coming in from overseas contribute too.'

And what did he think of the post-Brexit plans for football transfers? 'I guess it would mean we don't have a stream of average players coming in under freedom of movement laws.

One of the problems of that has been choking off our own talent and forcing them to play at a lower level. It's always struck me as illogical that we were subject to an agreement that if you're part of a particular economic block you have the right to come here whereas someone from outside that block with the same qualifications would have more hoops to jump through. Football is similar, and that harmonisation is probably a good thing.'

Was he worried the new rules will make life easier still for the bigger, richer clubs? 'I guess that's a danger but that taps into the broader debate about immigration policy. It's sensible to say we want the brightest and the best, whether that's in engineering or football, and I guess that does mean in some circumstances that the businesses that are able to attract the best will be able to do so and others won't. The alternative is to have a looser, freeform approach but there are dangers with that.

'There is an issue with the wealth inequality in football. It strikes me that the galloping chasm between the Premier League and everybody else is getting wider and wider and we've only got a handful of teams who are going to get anywhere close to winning the Premier League. It's rare for a team to do well in their first season in the Premier League and there are questions about how you level things up, but I don't see any real alternative to the broad Brexit system that's been proposed.'

One of the underlying causes of support for Brexit was politicians not appreciating the emotional aspect of immigration policy. I think a country with an ageing population will be economically better off if it welcomes workers from abroad, especially those educated at another country's expense. But for a lot of Brexit supporters the balance sheet was less important than their sense of fractured community and untethered identity. Football reflects society. Fans sing, 'He's one of our own,' even if they know he's not as talented as his South American team-mate.

We come again to the duality in the soul of English football. Do we pull up the drawbridge or throw open the doors? Answer: we do both while wrestling with our conscience. Outsiders brought *rondos* and *rabonas*, they brought fresh ideas and intellectual energy – something English football has sadly lacked. We have always played too safe. There was an anti-intellectualism in the notion of the 'football man'. It didn't help that former grammar school teacher Charles Hughes got his hands on the country's youth coaching and insisted on a style of play based on flawed understanding. Add in the exploitative nature of upper-class owner versus working-class player relationships for much of the game's existence and it is understandable that players were wary of interference from anyone who supposed himself better or cleverer. But that led to a refusal to challenge orthodoxies. So, we turned to foreigners. Catalan journalist and broadcaster Guillem Balagué has been taking notes.

A Catalonian homage

Guillem's plan was to come to England for three months in 1991, improve his 'terrible' English and leave. Instead, he stayed for decades, hopping between England and Spain as he wrote books, columns, broke transfer stories and became of the most famous faces on Britain's leading sports channel. In 1996 an old college friend asked him to cover that summer's European Championship for Spanish magazine *Don Balón*. That was his toe in the door of football and a year later he rang Sky Sports producer Dave Lawrence asking to write a report on the channel's coverage of La Liga. Dave invited him to London, he joined Sky's La Liga team and never looked back.

For Guillem, English football thrives most when it is open-minded:

'The biggest transformation is that people in English football have started to look abroad for answers. In 1991 you wouldn't even think of watching, paying for or following foreign football. There was the Italian football on Channel 4 [1992–2002] which had a lot of followers but there was no coaching influence from it. It was just funny to follow foreign teams.

'Little by little it changed. It had to do with the arrival of Klinsmann a little, Zola a little, Rafa Benítez too. People started to look for answers. Rafa signed after a Valencia-Liverpool game because the directors of Liverpool thought, "Wow, this guy!" and the players were impressed as well. Wenger felt like an adopted Englishman, but he did also offer completely different answers.

'Two things that define the Britishness that I know and admire: 1. The humbleness to realise that you're not getting enough here, and 2. the ability to go out and find the people who can help you. That's the Britain I admire. You have to go through a lot of humbleness for a country defined by its conquest of half a world to say actually, we just don't have enough answers here.'

My first full season commentating on Spanish football for Sky Sports was Frank Rijkaard's last as Barcelona manager before he was replaced by Pep Guardiola. It was thrilling to watch that Guardiola team ripping up opponents, bamboozling them with passing and movement. Spain won the European Championship in 2008 but it was Barcelona who truly lit the imagination. They started the first season slowly under Guardiola and got only 87 points in La Liga, but 105 goals told the story: possession and positional football but with a thrilling cutting edge. They beat Athletic Bilbao 4-1 to win the Copa del Rey and capped it all off with a mesmerising 2-0 victory over Manchester United in the Champions League Final in Rome. They weren't just a brilliant team; they were changing perceptions of how football could be played. Xavi, Andrés Iniesta, and Lionel Messi effectively ended an era where big players had dominated. Opponents tried to bully them only to spend 90 minutes chasing the ball.

Guillem is not alone in connecting the extra investment in youth coaching via the EPPP and the England DNA with the surge in interest in Spanish football:

'A bunch of things were happening at the same time – a perfect storm that meant that a new generation of coaches went beyond the level one courses that you get. I'm UEFA B [qualified] and what you get is a bit limited, but they started reading books and it was the likes of Graham Hunter, Phil Ball and myself telling how it works in Spain, going beyond the personalities and controversies of British media, and getting into tactics.

'I've heard from so many coaches that their reference point was Pep Guardiola's book, *Another Way of Winning*. I'm talking 15 years ago, there were open eyes and open ears to really try to understand what makes Spanish football culture.'

Before I started commentating for Sky, I used to travel to cover games for the Italian world feed – a supply of commentary and features in English that comes as part of the TV package for international broadcasters. The Italian feature producers aimed for a level of tactical analysis that we simply didn't get in England then. It didn't work terribly well because my Italian extended to buying train tickets and pizza and the translations often didn't make a great deal of sense.

Guillem says the foreign influence on English football was about more than the nationality of the players and managers:

'The critical thing is that you failed and failed again and failed again and there were brave people who looked for different solutions. They went to Spain, because that was successful, they went to Germany and to Belgium. It's important to say that it wasn't just importing talent. There was money and foreign coaches and players coming but, for me, it starts with the mental framework of accepting that this had been a failure and that change was needed.

'In England and Germany, it wasn't easy. We [Spain] are a country that's very happy to open up to the rest of the world and we had South Americans, Yugoslav, French coaches and we have learned from all of them. We never said that ours is the only way, which is something that you hear often at many levels of society in Germany and in Britain. But there was a time when that door opened and they said, "Let's go and learn out there." Players came, coaches came, Sky Sports gave Spanish football great prominence, general publishers started publishing books on foreign cultures and players.

'I have to be eternally thankful because I don't know any other country in Europe that gives foreign football as much prominence and importance and changes people's lives as Britain. Obviously, in the Far East where there is no huge league, and people look at the Premier League as a reference but in Europe, the influence of foreign football is unmatched in Britain.

'In Spain, we admire the Premier League, but it's a minority thing. In Britain there are people who regarded Spanish football as their league, and they went to Spain to watch games. They brought their British culture to the way they lived Spanish football. There were Saturday and Sunday evening games on Sky, and you started wondering how Spanish football won things, and was also attractive. Then you start buying the books and getting into coaching and the culture of your country has opened its mind to all that. It was normal that this started to influence decision making and coaching courses. It was wonderful to be part of it, very enjoyable.'

When I did my FA level one course, I cited Iniesta as an example of why players should learn to dribble past opponents, not just pass around them, and the tutors and my fellow students knew exactly what I meant. Ten years earlier English people knew who famous foreign footballers were, but they were less likely to have understood a reference to playing style and tactics.

Guillem became director of football at Biggleswade United in 2014, a Bedfordshire club, now in the Spartan South Midlands League. They have a Spanish coach called Cristian Colas who has a UEFA pro licence and is in his second spell with the club. They try to play in the tradition of Guardiola and Barcelona, but it hasn't been straightforward. 'The pitch doesn't allow it,' Guillem admits ruefully.

I asked whether the notion of a short-passing, positional game being in the English football DNA is wishful thinking on the part of the FA.

Guillem replied, 'We've had English guys in their early 30s who were all about Pep Guardiola and had read all the books and everything but as soon as we drew a game, we went back to hitting the channels and back to long balls. They don't really believe in it, but they want to be part of what's happening and take bits from it. The amount of people, at all levels, who have asked me to please give them access to Pep Guardiola's training sessions and I am like, "Why? He is preparing a team for Saturday. What does he have to do with what you do with your team in step five or Championship or League One? What would you get out of it?"

'What's happening with Pep is a deep, culturally rooted thing that has to do with cultures mixing and with what Pep is passionate about and what he has learned. That is not the experience of an English coach – it cannot be. They don't know anything about Johan Cruyff, they are just hearing about it. So, my hope, with the culture of changes, that it makes you think differently and as a consequence you end up putting things together in a different way that is a revolution. A lot of people just stay on the surface of Spanish football culture.

'I hope what you are getting is that the DNA of English football is the ability to learn and grow through that. You cannot say the DNA is building from the back or that when you attack, you have three defenders at the back or going through patiently through the middle. You're absolutely right, it's not in the make-up.'

Guillem believes that the person who best understands how to marry the deep traditions of the English and Spanish games is indeed Pep Guardiola:

'If you want to see what the DNA of English football should be look at Pep because he has done that mixture. That's the Pep of now with quick transitions, with keeping the ball and controlling games but at times letting it flow and losing control and taking advantage of it. A lot of things he's doing now has to do with English football and what he has learned. Remember, at Barcelona he used to say that after we recover the ball it is 15 passes before we attack? The idea was that we were all in our positions and then we go. Now when City get the ball it's a quick transition otherwise, they face a defence that's very tight.

'He is adapting. Pep Guardiola doesn't play like Pep Guardiola anymore. He plays like Joseph Guardiola, the

Englishman with a bit of German. That's what English football should be: learning. And how beautiful it is that you can learn from [Mauricio] Pochettino and Guardiola and all these people who have been in the Premier League. It is the perfect PhD for coaches if they want to learn and if they look in the right place.'

Speaking of PhDs, let's have a look at another growing influence on English football.

5

Don't shoot

GRAHAM POTTER provoked a mixture of hilarity and despair when he hinted that Brighton fans were putting his players off by urging them to shoot during their 0-0 Premier League draw with bottom side Norwich in April 2022.

'The build-up suggests we're getting there,' he told the media afterwards. 'Of course, the longer you go, you can hear the crowd, "Shoot, shoot, shoot," and that sometimes is a challenge for the players because sometimes there's an opportunity to shoot – sometimes it's a chance for the block and then the transition. And sometimes maybe one more pass gets you in a better position but, if you miss the pass, you should have shot.'

Brighton's 'expected goals' (xG) for that match was 2.9. They had 30 shots, of which four were on target. In their next two games they beat Arsenal and Tottenham with xG ratings of 0.5 and 0.7. It is perfectly fine if you have no idea what all this means. There are a different xG models designed by companies using data compiled by tracking years of real-life matches to work out the likelihood of a goal being scored from various positions. It is imperfect but has been successfully used, not least by professional gamblers. The guys who watch the matches and input the data get a small fee; the real genius is in the interpretation.

Brighton's chairman is Tony Bloom, a professional sports bettor, poker player and entrepreneur. Under his stewardship the club has risen from League One and built a new stadium after years of delays and frustration. They finished ninth in the real

Premier League table in 2021/22 but only 18th in the percentage-of-shots-on-target table. Potter out!

If you are still bamboozled, the last bit was a joke. There is still only one table that matters, no matter how many astrophysicists and data scientists are employed by Premier League clubs. But make no mistake, football and data are coming together, rapidly. A 2014 article in *When Saturday Comes* described *Match of the Day* showing players' heat maps as 'giving football's new snake oil a national audience'.

In 2017 Jeff Stelling made himself the football data community's *bête noire* by calling out Arsène Wenger's use of xG stats to defend his Arsenal side's performance in a defeat against Manchester City.

'The daftest thing he said after that game,' Stelling said on Sky Sports, 'he quoted expected goals, you know the little stat you see? He's the first person I've ever heard take any notice of expected goals which has to be the most useless stat in the history of football. What does it tell you? The game has finished 3-1, why do you show expected goals?'

For what it is worth I think heat maps are a useful tool for coaches – for example for showing kids the sort of area a top player might cover while operating in a certain position. I also think Stelling had a point. OK, xG is not useless but it was ludicrous of Wenger to offer it up as mitigation or a consolation to Arsenal fans after a defeat.

The book *Moneyball* came out in 2003 and while it lit the imagination of sports fans, football's sceptics pointed out that baseball is a far easier game to break down into data because of its stop-start nature. But technology has moved on and Premier League clubs have pots of spare cash. Liverpool employed neuroscientists to help them develop their strategy for penalty shoot outs and won both domestic cups in 2021/22 on penalties. Did the science win it for them? No idea. The sample size is two matches but the stakes in penalty shoot-outs are astronomically high, and Liverpool have so much money it seems worth a punt. If nothing else, being told that a neuroscientist has selected you personally to take a penalty is a nice confidence boost in a moment of great tension.

What do the old pros think of football's analysis revolution? Tony Gale isn't a fan, 'There aren't enough coaches on the grass and there are too many in the classroom for me. Get the coaches back on the grass where they should be. There's too much analysis. One of my favourite sayings is there's "paralysis by analysis".'

Garry Birtles sees it as clubs seeking out every advantage, 'You have to go with the modern flow and analyse how you must analyse because that's the times. It's like music, it changes and some stuff from the '80s is not so good, but some is really good. If you get stuck in the past, it's wrong because things evolve. I speak to Nigel Clough at Mansfield, and they do that all the time – go through past games and work on things that they got wrong, and the players sit and watch it. It's not just at the top level, it's everywhere now. That's got to be right if the technology is there.'

Jon McKenzie is a Leeds fan, podcaster and self-styled 'tactics commie'. When we spoke, he was the head of content for Analytics FC and as he put it had his 'hands in the weeds of the data'. He has since transferred to The Athletic. His background wasn't mathematics or physics – he studied philosophy and theology at St Andrews and Cambridge Universities but when he finished his PhD he was out of love with academia and went into journalism, later joining Analytics FC, a data company that had grown out of a blog and a podcast. It developed a data scouting platform that clubs could subscribe to rather than have their own data team. They now do more consultancy services because so many clubs have their own data departments.

Jon gave me an example of their work – helping Kevin De Bruyne get his market value from Manchester City:

'He went into contract negotiations without an agent for various reasons. In his first meeting they basically sold him a low-ball contract and he thought they were trying to jerk him around. He came to us and said, "I want you to produce a report that shows the level I'm at compared to comparable players within

European football, show the impact I could have on Manchester City winning the Champions League, compare me to other players who have that sort of impact and then do some salary work so we have a benchmark." We did that and he managed to get the contract he wanted.

'Previously, data companies were doing one-size-fits-all data analysis. You would look at one metric or a few metrics and look at everyone in world football and find an outlier and say, "This guy looks really good," or, "This guy looks really bad." But now, because footballers, clubs and agents have so much money, they ask for bespoke reports that wouldn't be done without people paying.

'Héctor Bellerín came to us, and he wasn't interested in money at all. He was looking for a loan deal out of Arsenal because wanted to play in the World Cup. He said, "I want to find a club who would suit me stylistically and raise my chances with the Spanish national team." We were able to build some models, ran some Monte Carlo simulations that showed if he went to, say Villarreal, whether there would be more or less chance of him getting the right-back slot starting or back up for Spain and compare that to other clubs.

'Analytics FC works with everyone: players, agents, owners. There's an acquisition service to do due diligence for anyone who's looking for a club. You can find them a club, tell them what they should be looking out for, take a financial autopsy whatever.

'There's a coach identification. Clubs subscribe and it gives them a good sense of what's going on in the market. It will help them find similar coaches, style-wise, to coaches they already have and give them an idea of who to keep an eye on.'

I wanted to know how far we have travelled in terms of understanding the beautiful free-flowing game of football through analysing data.

Jon said, 'I don't think we'll ever be able to break everything down into its constituent parts and say with certainty that anything will happen in any given scenario. A lot of the upside of using data in football is workflow. It allows you to do things more efficiently so the majority of the data work has been done in recruitment. There's so much money in football now that if you get your recruitment decisions right, you're making palpable financial savings. If you're buying a player for £20m and you know he's more likely to fit into your system than another player, or he's not going to have as many injuries as another player then you're making big savings. Clubs are usually happy to throw money into a data recruitment department and those guys make the workflow easier.

'You're looking for a certain profile of player so you build a statistical profile and compare players across the board, and it will throw out a long list. You break that down into a manageable shortlist and give it to your traditional scouting department. Most clubs now will have a policy that both sides, data recruitment and traditional scouting departments have to agree before a club buys a player. A lot of stuff is still intangible and unquantifiable. The data department always has to be one way of finding gains – but not all of the gain.'

A perfect example of the growing reputation of data analysis in football is Liverpool's 'transfer committee' which went from being a laughing stock when Brendan Rodgers was the club's manager to holding reverential status now. Traditional scouts and big-brained analysts with PhDs in theoretical physics and astronomy work to Jürgen Klopp's playing philosophy and team plans. A club that paid £35m for Andy Carroll only to appoint a manager who wanted to play possession football has been transformed into an exemplar of wise trading, spotting the potential of Mohammed Salah and Andy Robertson when others didn't. One of the failings of the Premier League era, in my opinion, was the waste of vast sums of money on transfers and salaries of players who either weren't good enough, were ill-suited to the clubs they joined, or weren't able to integrate.

'A lot of it is club dependent,' Jon says. 'The comparison is going to be between clubs like Liverpool and Manchester City, increasingly now, and Manchester United who really haven't done things very efficiently. Everyone at Liverpool works to a model.

They have a very high hit rate. Manchester United have lacked that overarching model beyond being a large corporate brand that generates money through franchising, which obviously works off the pitch. On the pitch it's been buying marquee players without much thought. You can't look at what's happened at Liverpool in the last seven years and not realise that doing things in a smart data way is going to benefit you.

'People like to talk about *Moneyball* and bastardise the phrase and the concept but in baseball it remains the case that you can get financial gain by approaching recruitment in a certain way. In football if you spend more money on wages, you'll be more likely to win. It doesn't really seem that's going to change. So, a lot of these clubs that have "wasted" a lot of money are still doing largely OK. If you're a mega corporate company who can afford to take those hits, then you're pretty much guaranteed to stay roughly around the top. Manchester United have been catastrophically bad since 2013 but they've never dropped below seventh or eighth in league. If you're that big you're guaranteed not to fail. I think things might be changing now. We're at a stage where a lot of clubs are cutting off the fat and it feels as though football itself is getting to a point where you can't really expand the bubble any further. Once you've sold clubs to global states there's not really a bigger buyer out there.'

We were speaking before Erik ten Hag had started his job at Manchester United, who were on their way to finishing sixth in the Premier League at the end of Ralf Rangnick's baffling spell as interim manager. Brentford were about to finish 13th in their first Premier League season, a remarkable effort for a club that had finished 14th in League Two in 2008 with an average attendance of 4,469. They really kicked on after 2014 after being bought by Matthew Benham, an Oxford University physics graduate who became a banker, then a professional gambler. His company Smartodds pays a team of people to watch matches and collate data which is then analysed and sold on to professional gamblers and to inform Brentford's transfer dealing. They are extremely secretive about the detail. Benham has made a series of clever decisions but as Jon McKenzie points out, there is no magic:

'Brentford are an interesting company because they do everything smartly, but so much of their model is based on this idea of making these smart decisions, that if they make a mistake, it can set them back for a couple of seasons.

'They're held up as an example of a club doing the right things but, in the Championship, Matthew Benham was still having to dump a load of his own cash on it for the running costs. If you're a club running everything according to these sorts of models with an eye to being sensible, you're still probably going to be making a loss until you hit the big time. You're still walking a tightrope; there's no one out there running away with things just because they're running the processes properly.'

If it was easy everyone would be doing it. In March 2021, the BBC website featured Barnsley in an article about the data revolution, citing the South Yorkshire club as a success, not unreasonable given that they were chasing promotion the Premier League under coach Valérien Ismaël. It quoted Chien Lee, the founder and chairman of NewCity Capital, the private investment firm that is the biggest shareholder in the club, one of five the company had invested into in Europe.

Lee said, 'Since we bought Barnsley three years ago, we have been heavily using data. We use it mainly to identify talented young players and coaches as well. It is proving very successful. We are looking for players and coaches that play the style that we want, and that is very much a passing game.'

Barnsley missed out on promotion that season and lost Ismaël – whose style involved energetic pressing and, by modern standards, direct play. In 2021/22 they had three different managers including Poya Asbaghi, a 36-year-old Iranian-Swede with no experience of English football. They were relegated, finishing bottom of the Championship with 30 points. Their French partner club AS Nancy also finished bottom and were relegated from Ligue 2. *Moneyball* is not an instruction manual.

Back to Potter's concern that anxious Brighton fans, ignorant of the efficacy of working the ball into optimal shooting positions, are doing more harm than good. There has been a drop-off in long-range shooting at top clubs as they analyse more data. Of course, as with all statistical innovations, this might have happened anyway. A friend of mine at five-a-side, when his side was losing, would shout, 'Shoot more, lads!' In my exhausted state I might respond, 'There's no f---ing point shooting from the other end of the pitch, is there?' If only I could have shown him the data.

So how has our greater understanding of analytics changed what happens on the football pitch? Jon McKenzie explains, 'Whenever you're doing any sort of analysis, and it doesn't need to be data, it could be tactical, you're going to have a better understanding as we increase our knowledge base. There's still a long way to go. Football is what we call in the industry stochastic, which means it has patterns which are repeatable but there's still a lot of randomness and chaos so you're always trying to find those threads with which you can paint a picture without being led down a blind alley.

'When people say data or stats they really mean on-ball events such as a player making a pass or taking a shot, a tackle, or an aerial duel. Obviously, a lot of what happens in football is the off-the-ball stuff and as things stand it's difficult to measure that. It's hard to analyse centre-backs for example mainly because it's hard to know what good centre-backs do in defensive situations, particularly in terms of positioning.

'The industry is now working towards working with what's called tracking data which is essentially logging the position of all 22 players and the ball, relative to one another. The idea is that once we've got that data, we can start running models which say actually, "These centre-backs for Liverpool are really good because in these sorts of defensive transitions they're never more than X distance apart," or it may say, "This centre-back pushes forward in this scenario which allows the defence to be better structured." We're not really there at the moment. There are

143

clubs using it. Liverpool, unsurprisingly, will be starting to use tracking data but that's the next step in the evolution.'

On a Tuesday night in January 2021, Leicester beat Chelsea to go top of the Premier League. One of the scorers, James Maddison, spoke to Sky Sports and credited the club's analyst, Jack Lyons, for helping to improve his goal scoring statistics.

Maddison said, 'I'm working on my game, improving. We played Sheffield United earlier in the season and I always watch the games back and Jamie Carragher said in commentary, "James Maddison needs to get his numbers up if he's going to be challenging for the England spots." Me, the gaffer, and Jack the analyst – he'll be buzzing that I mentioned him – sat down and looked at where I can get more goals.'

Maddison's next sentence shows how football analysis is not an exact science, explaining he was 'kind of almost smelling where the ball is going to drop'.

Of course, in football the richest clubs buy the best of everything. Leicester were three points above Manchester City who had two games in hand. That week Manchester City hired Laurie Shaw, a PhD in computational astrophysics, former hedge fund analyst and government advisor, as their lead AI scientist. At the end of the season, they were champions again, 20 points better off than Leicester. The next season the gap was 41 points with the Foxes finishing eighth. I have put those events side by side for the convenience of my narrative, but we do just that with the comings and goings of players, drawing conclusions that might not be merited. Fundamentally Manchester City had been able to assemble a better squad because they had more money. It is hard to assess from the outside whose analysts are better.

Given that any advantages gained from innovation are fleeting before the money raises its voice again, how do small clubs compete in this new world? Answer: the best way they can. Daniel Hutchings worked as a match analyst for Barnet and Stevenage before moving to Canada to join Cavalry FC. He got a Football Studies degree from Southampton University before getting his first job at Barnet.

'You struggle to have a life outside of football,' he told me. 'It's such a cycle. A few days before a game we'll go through the opposition analysis and paint a picture of what we want the game to look like, where the key dangers are and how we're going to counter. What we look at post-game is dictated by what we talked about before.

'Players' attention span is quite limited, so we try to keep the information as clear as possible, without boring them because after 15, 20 minutes they start to lose attention. A large part of it is deciding what key information to give them without overloading them. We'll present something to the players as a team and some individual bits on anything they can improve. For example, last weekend we saw an opportunity for one of our strikers. He kept getting one v one with the full-back but then playing backwards so we sat down and showed him. Hopefully he'll try to change that. Then we start looking at the next game, although I'll have been looking at the opposition beforehand. At Stevenage I think we had 60 games including pre-season.

'Recruitment can part of our job, but it depends on the club. We watch a lot of games. Before we play a team, we try to watch three or four of their games, so we see a lot of football.'

I asked Daniel how we can gauge the effectiveness of analysis. 'We like to think we make at least a little difference! You can look at stats and they can be really helpful, and they can be the opposite because they lack context. You see that on TV with, say, ball possession or xG. Stats can be manipulated to support or counter the same argument. Ultimately, we'll work out if we're making a difference by results. There are so many variables, there's no way of knowing.'

It was an honest answer. We don't know how much this changes the game because there is no controlled experiment. The clubs with the biggest analysis teams are usually the clubs with the biggest budgets so their facilities, medical setup, coaches and players are generally better too.

'Some managers aren't big on analysis, so my attention gets diverted to working with individual players. You can see it in individual performances, it's about finer details, that extra one percent to make a difference in results,' said Daniel.

'Looking at clubs like Brentford who completely delved into the stats side shows there's space for it in football. I'm a bit of a realist; there needs to be a conversation about context. After every game we get data reports from different stat companies and if I'm honest, we ignore 90 per cent of it. Our job is to delve in and determine what's relevant.'

Does this ultra-professionalism make football less fun? The modern era has seen clubs take the burning love we have for football, its excitement and thrilling competition and commodify it. Has that become an obsession that makes the game less appealing? Is football eating itself? Handily, Jon McKenzie is an expert in data analysis who studied philosophy and theology:

'I think in the past there was more space for drama, now as football has professionalised, clubs are hyperaware they have to win at all costs, and you encourage your players not to be affected as much by things that are on the pitch. You don't necessarily see players jumping in for big challenges, losing their rag and getting into one another's faces. For me that's all part of the professionalisation, the realisation that if you act and play in certain ways, you're more likely to win.

'I'm going to be honest, hand on heart about the impact of being more savvy, it has had an impact on my fandom. It changes the way we view the game. I don't have quite the same innocence I had when I started supporting Leeds.'

We spoke when Marcelo Bielsa had been recently replaced by Jesse Marsch, who did manage to keep Leeds up but at a cost.

Jon said, 'There's this phenomenon of us sacking our old manager, and the results justifying it but a lot of the fanbase are feeling pretty empty because the football is just not as attractive. I feel as if I watch football with an analytic eye. You lose that immersive experience where you're not bothered about how the goals are scored, you're just bothered that they are.

'A lot of what we experience with modernism is loss. A lot of football fans are caught between the desire to win – and the desire for the aesthetic to be a certain way, and often they're in contradiction. At Elland Road, fans will shout "shoot" when a player is 30 yards out but if Leeds are to win, they've got to be taking shots from better positions.

'With VAR people say, "I just want decisions to be right," but they don't think of the corollary of what those bigger picture things are. No one thought the imposition of VAR would change the way we view the game, they just thought you'd bring in video referees and you'd get more correct decisions. But the gain in terms of getting more correct decisions has been experienced by the fans as loss.

'The same thing is true with the professionalisation of football using analysis. The gains make your side more likely to win but that comes at a cost – a sense of loss. I don't think that's just a nostalgic view. What's the Philip Larkin line, "Never such innocence again," – I feel that's where a lot of us are at. Maybe as you grow older, you'll always experience that loss of the football you watched in your childhood, but I think that's been accelerated now because the analytics world is telling you that you were doing things wrong.'

6

The English style of play

'WHEN DID the style of play outweigh the result? It's a brainwash by all what's happening outside of football. It's a brainwash that we should only play this way.'

Sam Allardyce spoke to the Oxford Union, in 2020, explaining to some of the brightest young minds in the country why he has been unfairly traduced in the consciousness of the English football public.

'The diversity of the Premier League is the reason we have the world's best football league, the world's best, there's no doubt about that. To say we only play by playing the ball out from the back and nothing else, it brainwashes everyone into trying to play that way and if you haven't got the players capable of playing like that you'll fail and even if you say, "I'm trying to play the right way," you will lose too many matches and lose your job.'

I don't understand why managers with so much money in the bank are so afraid of the sack. With no financial worries, you can set up your team whichever way you believe is best. Allardyce has had more Premier League clubs than any other manager. His ability to quickly organise a team made him appealing to clubs in crisis, but his brand of football often alienated fans in the long run. His name is associated with the notion of old-fashioned football, dull and pragmatic. He rejects and resents the notion:

'We all have the responsibility to play and entertain and win and the more we win the more we are able to increase the quality of player but for me how you play should never overtake the importance of the result.

'The fans will be very forgiving if you win a football match and haven't played very well. Fans won't be forgiving if you out-play, out-pass the opposition but lose three on the trot. We've already seen a massive amount of goals from the opposition doing a high press and taking the ball off those centre-halves and putting the ball in the back of the net. That's not entertaining; that is just stupidity.

'I find it an incredible change that the style of play is outweighing results. It ended up costing me the Everton job. I took Everton from 16th, 15th to eighth but I was sacked on the style of play. I've never known that in the history of the game.'

Everton weren't a long-ball team by the standards of the 2017/18 Premier League but nor were they entertaining. They scored 27 goals in Allardyce's 24 games, as they rose from 13th (a minor memory error) to eighth. They were 19th in the whole season's table in terms of shots, crosses, and dribbles that led to chances. They were third in tackles won, top in both pressures and fouls. Since he left, Everton have finished eighth again, then 12th, tenth, and 16th. Allardyce got one more job, suffering his first Premier League relegation with West Bromwich Albion in 2021. José Mourinho described Allardyce's style as '19th-century football'. It was a typically elegant if meaningless insult. Allardyce countered against his critics, 'When they hit a 50-yard ball it was a cultural pass; when we did it, it was a hopeful hoof.'

Burnley's sacking of Sean Dyche in April 2022 looked like the end of an era. His side had figured consistently highly in the charts for long passes attempted with a low rate of completion, being 'bettered' by Neil Warnock's Cardiff in 2018/19 and Allardyce (and Slaven Bilić) at West Brom in 2020/21. There is no 'long-ball' side left in the Premier League. Liverpool made the highest number of long passes in 2021/22: 4,525 attempted, but a hit rate of 68.5 per cent suggests they are not hitting and hoping. Manchester City were second (4,223 at 74.2 per cent completion), Wolves were third and Burnley fourth – the first side with a completion rate of less than 50 per cent. Teams still hit some long passes, but they do so more accurately.[11]

Tony Gale argues the move away from direct football was necessary for the English game to compete internationally, 'Some ex-players are not too pleased about the way we play out from the back, but it has to be done. You have to take more risks. Naturally, you don't do it on bad surfaces but there are risks to be taken. The risks are great, and the rewards are even greater. You look after the ball better.

'Imagine if we'd given licence to people like Glenn Hoddle, instead of criticising him all the time for what he couldn't do instead of what he could do. We were very quick to have a go at the people like Hoddle, Alan Hudson, Tony Currie – it was all about what they couldn't do. Some of the players who were picked in front of them – you used to think, "Cor blimey!" I won't mention the names because that's not very nice.'

The former Fulham, West Ham and Blackburn defender believes the direct style of football was the root cause of England's repeated international failures for decades after 1966:

'It was too crash-bang-wallop and too cautious. It was low-risk football. The ones who nearly got it right were Terry Venables and Hoddle, playing out from the back. In England we didn't play international-style football. We never played out from the back and that was our root problem; it's no coincidence that now we've got better as an international team.'

Gale describes a contrast between the styles of the successful club teams of his era who won European competitions playing more sophisticated football and the national team:

'We went through a spell when we weren't playing enough European-type football. Our sides did when they went to Europe but, funnily enough, on the international stage, players that I knew, who'd won everything, weren't playing enough football out from the back. We weren't brave enough.'

---

11 fbref.com – 'A long pass is over 30 yards, a short pass 5-15 yards, a medium pass 15-30 yards'

Technical coach Saul Isaksson-Hurst witnessed a shift in philosophy in the academy system:

'In my early days in academy football we were playing big category one London clubs and they had under-nines, tens, 11s sticking it in the mixer, smashing it in the channels, long-ball game if you want to call it that, route one, and smashing people, the old-style English football and they thought that was an acceptable way for youth footballers to play.

'Thank God Gareth Southgate pulled the England national team into the modern world. The modern game dictates you need technically excellent players and a plan to play modern football which is based on playing out from the back, playing through the thirds and being able to dominate one v one particularly.'

Isaksson-Hurst has no time for nostalgia and says the old English style simply doesn't work:

'The game has moved on ... you can talk about the '70s and '80s when English teams had a lot of success but look at more recent history and we've been diabolical. The players and teams we've produced haven't been good enough and we've been wildly off the mark compared to our European counterparts and people around the world. We had to look at the way we develop players and play the game and we've done that now, and we're now competing in tournaments which we hadn't done for God knows how long.

'English football has always traditionally been very direct, route one, what the FA until fairly recently had been promoting in their courses ... get the ball forward very quickly, it's a hot potato. My philosophy is based on the antithesis of that, we're challenging players, forcing players to stay on the ball and make decisions on the ball whereas previously it was "get it forward quick" with the crowd getting antsy, rather than producing technicians all over the park like the modern game requires. Whether you're a right-back, a centre-back, a centre midfielder or a striker you need to be able to stay on the ball and dominate the one v one duel. Even goalies need to be that these days; that's how far the game's gone.

'We've improved massively. Southgate talks about the desire to control possession, to control the ball in the middle of the park. It's a key element to the modern game. As Pep Guardiola says, if you've got the ball, the other team can't score. The problem with 4-4-2 is that other teams play with three in the middle. I'm not saying it's impossible because there are ways around it but the most successful teams in the world and the top managers are using variations of 4-3-3, 3-5-2 or another way of getting an overload in the middle of the park. It's a lot easier to control possession that way. In academy football why wouldn't you teach kids to try to control the ball? It's a lot easier to teach kids to run after second balls than have the quality to try to control the ball which is the world class skill.'

Coventry's Matt Whitehouse accepts there is a significant gap between academy coaches and paying fans:

'Culturally in England, fans don't want to see playing out from the back. They want high energy, high tempo, creating chances. Fans get bored seeing the possession, probing kind of game. With managers we're seeing a divide with the young generation coming through like Russell Martin who really wants to play a progressive style at MK Dons then Swansea and old-school managers, who still get jobs because they're effective.

'These managers get results, and it's a results game. If a chairman decides we really need to get somebody to get some points and that sort of football is what they're used to, then you see that. The hope is that you'll see that coaches who believe in the quality of football succeed in first teams. I think there are more academy coaches moving into first team environments now which is positive.

'It's not just style, it's philosophy and culture, nurturing young players, developing them, not just thinking about winning. You're starting to see that come into first teams as well because ultimately, they're still young lads developing their game. If coaches can help them push on, you'll develop better players which will win games anyway.

'There are still going to be managers who believe in direct football but there's definitely a change now in the first-team world with more progressive football and when those managers do well it will become more pronounced.

'In the next five, ten years you'll see even more of that progression because so many of the young coaches are coming through academies. Even ex-players are going into academies now before they coach in first teams, so they're understanding the long-term philosophy.'

Lee Hendrie played for Aston Villa in the Premier League between 1995 and 2006. He is now a co-commentator for Sky Sports and thinks he would have preferred playing in today's football:

'These days it's more fitness-based and more technical. That's where my game was quite strong. My fitness levels were quite good, I always worked hard on being the fittest, trying to maintain that and work on my technique. I think to play in the sort of games they play now would suit my game a hell of a lot better, just because I was more of a flair player.

'Challenges could be quite aggressive, and you had to be firm. I had to adapt to being kicked, be strong, be aggressive myself at times. That was down to sheer frustration because I wanted to play football all the time, that's why I'd prefer to play in this age. There's more football played and it's more about being an athlete.

'Off the field there's a lot more to it, more meetings, sitting down and going through the process of games, how we're going to approach games, how to change tactics, more fine details that the top managers are now putting in as their spin. It wasn't like that for us.

'We'd do our set plays, go through team shape and things like that but not much throughout the week.'

Where did this shift in style come from? The EPPP piled resources into youth coaching and mandated a level of professionalism, but the philosophy is imported, as Matt Whitehouse acknowledges:

'Around that 2010 to 2012 period Barcelona were playing some of the best football ever seen, certainly by our generation, and it inspired a lot of players and coaches who wanted to play like that rather than the old English fashion. Now you've got a lot more teams who play out from the back as normal whereas in that time it was seen as too risky. Guardiola's football made people say, "I want us to play like that and have more Messis, Xavis, Iniestas."

'Small players had been neglected in academies and from that you start to look at late developers and players born in the late part of the year, June, July, August. Do they get neglected? Were we playing in a way that helps these players develop? The style of football will determine the sort of players who come through. If you want to play an "up and at 'em" physical game, you're going to need physical players. If you're going to play a more tactical, technical game then you're going to need technical players.

'Wenger started to bring that in at Arsenal from around 2006 with Cesc Fàbregas and players like that but I think Guardiola's Barcelona, because of the success they had, along with the Spain national team, inspired a generation of coaches.'

But it is not a straightforward process. Taylor Collard is an Englishman in Spain, working as a player development coach for a club in Barcelona. 'There are so many youth teams, and the level is so high,' he told me. 'What's been a big insight is how they get into the smallest details.

'I had a placement at Preston North End, and it was the bigger details, "This is how we play when this is happening." You might have a nine-v-nine, UEFA B style, how to create chances from the left side.

'Here they look at the smallest details within the games, "You didn't position your body in the right place at this time, to enable this pass which would have enabled our play." It's more about the principles and how we structure play.

'The big scenario they focus on is playing out from the back. Every team I've seen play here will have the centre-back stand with the goalkeeper and receive the ball with a two-yard pass and maybe go out to the *laterales* and play from there.'

Taylor is a fluent Spanish speaker and notes the difference in the language of football with less emphasis on pitch geography:

'A centre-back plays in the centre, at the back. But *pivote*, for example, doesn't translate. It's not just a position, it's what he does. If we have a kid come in to play *pivote* he knows what to do, he understands the branch of vocabulary that comes off the position. He knows he'll play central but that he needs to dip into the left and right channels when the centre-back has the ball. He knows how he needs to support the left-winger or right-winger when he has the ball.

'We have a *punta* – in our team we play it as a striker. The literal translation is point – but it's not a position on the pitch, it doesn't mean a centre-forward, it means point of the attack. We go to you as the point of the attack, and then perhaps back to the *laterales* and back to the *pivote* or *avancado* if you're playing with those two in midfield. The *avancado* is a freer role.

'We play lots of different formations. The kids are tactically on it, they all know the ins and out of formations although coaches prioritise play development – can you play football?'

We are changing our style in England, but we are nowhere near a widespread understanding the role of a *pivote* – which makes it tough for coaches to import Spanish-style football wholesale. Lee Hendrie advocates for the modern, continental style but accepts it has its downsides:

'Towards the end of my career, I played at Tamworth. We were in the Conference, and we played against West Bromwich Albion academy in a pre-season. They wanted to play football from the back, across from the left to the right and back. It looked pretty, and it was nice when it comes off, but we beat them 3-0 because we were aggressive, we played the ball forward, got it into the right areas.

'I was always taught playing in midfield, your first thought should be can I play forward? Can you play it into someone's feet? Can you join in? My thought was, if someone is tight to me, I can spin it into Dwight Yorke or Dion Dublin. I wanted to play it forward because if I gave it away, we were still in our formation.

'We talk about the 4-4-2, but it's rare you see a rigid formation these days. I remember playing from the left in a 3-5-2 and thinking, "I'm going to go to that right hand side when the ball's over there because the full-back won't know whether to come with me." That's why I would love to play in the style of this era – I used to run all over the place, but I would get myself back into the formation.'

Ray Lewington has spent more than 40 years in professional football as a player, manager, and coach. He has seen the game change faster than fans might want:

'All Premier League teams play now so undoubtedly the game has changed. If you go and watch a Championship game, it's almost a throwback. There are a lot more tackles allowed, and it's a lot more direct. A lot of people I know, not in football but my friends, some who don't even like football, watch it and say it looks like old-fashioned football because there's that ruggedness.

'The Brits love that. The analogy is with a boxing match – if you've got a technical boxer who picks people off, the Brits would rather have someone who goes in there and takes ten punches for every five he throws. They love a fighter, they love a trier, that all or nothing attitude that we were always known for: roll your sleeves up, get stuck in, all that. You don't get that in a Premier League game now. It's much more tactical.

'It's very quickly sliding into a non-contact game now which I think would be really sad. We have to be really careful of it being sanitised. It's pure tactical and that's the impact of foreign coaches. There are virtually no English coaches, virtually all of them have come from abroad which has been fantastic because we needed shaking up because our national side would never compete with the top Europeans if we just played our island mentality game.

'Now, with the influence of foreign coaches we're very much playing a European possession-based game. Take a team like Brighton who are absolutely fantastic from box to box. Although he's an English coach [Brighton boss Graham Potter] he's been influenced by foreign coaches. I think it's a good thing without doubt and you look at the quality of our young British players coming through – all of them can play in tight areas whereas English players never could. We were big pitch players – we hit long balls and we had to run. Nowadays they play between the lines and lads are taught to play in tight areas. We have become, I would say, as good as any European country with our young players coming through.'

Does that mean English football has lost its distinctiveness? 'We're getting closer and closer, and I think that's a bad thing to be honest. My one criticism of English football is that we've always followed the leader. If Spain win the World Cup, then for the next four years it's always, "What do Spain do," and everything was moved over to the Spanish way. Then Germany win the next World Cup and we all switch again.

'I think we're now beginning to get an identity of our own and we're not copying anyone because we're virtually all becoming the same anyway but we're actually doing it our way and we're going to go with it. But there's no doubt about it you could be watching any game and not know who you're watching. You'd be hard-pressed to say, "That's a German game, that's a Spanish game and that's an English game."'

I spoke to the interviewees separately, so they didn't know if their views agreed with the others, and none of the points of criticism that follow are aimed at other contributors. Les Ferdinand, who watches more Championship football in his role as QPR's director of football than some of the other contributors, feels exasperated seeing teams adopt a style of play they're not suited to:

'Even in the Championship with every single team you'll see the goalkeeper putting the ball down at his feet and playing through the centre-halves. You've got to play to the strengths of what you've got and what you've built. There's no point in giving the ball to centre-halves and wanting to play out from the back if they don't have that capability. You see teams on umpteen occasions trying to play out from the back and you're thinking they just don't have the personnel to do it but they're following suit because that seems to be the in-thing; everyone's got to play out from the back.

'Pep Guardiola's got some of the best players in the country and they're able to do that because their movement and their ability to control and pass the ball is better than most other teams.'

According to FBREF.com's data, Premier League players are passing the ball more than they were five years ago – and increasingly that passing is backwards and sideways. The total of passing yards in 2017/18 was 5,317,200, of which 37 per cent was towards the opposition goal. In 2021/22 the figures were 5,687,128 of which 32.5 per cent was progressive.

Five years previously, seven teams had successful long passing statistics at 50 per cent or lower (Crystal Palace, Everton, Stoke, West Ham, Newcastle, West Brom, Burnley) and could perhaps be loosely termed 'direct'. In 2021/22 only three teams were at 50 per cent or lower for inaccurate passes of over 30 yards (Watford, Everton, and Burnley), two of which went down.

I hadn't checked those stats before I asked Southampton's Matt Crocker whether we had reached a point where teams were being too patient.

He replied, 'Really interesting question. A lot of our national coaches and scouts would have this conversation: are we seeing the same sort of football? You go and watch the academy games and, you know, the goalkeeper gets the ball and the full-backs spread, the ball goes to the centre-back, and back to the keeper, to the full-back – you know the patterns of play are consistent but are there teams doing things differently? It's a difficult one.

'There's a fine balance. If you're doing something and it's offering success and growing the players' confidence, then keep doing that. However, if you're doing it and you're getting pressed the hell out of and losing the ball and it's in the back of the net and those kids' heads are dropping and dropping then as coaches and players you're going to have to think of new solutions. Maybe rather playing through you go round or over, there are other ways of playing out from the back. It's not just a five-yard pass, it can be a keeper with a five-iron into a number ten who takes it down on his chest and brings midfielders in and off you go – that's playing out from the back. Playing out from the back is not the keeper shelling it as hard as he can as far as he can and hoping for the best.'

So, can a DNA for a club or a country involve playing with a big, fast centre-forward? 'Absolutely. It might not be the style I want to play but is that an effective way to get results if you've got players like that – absolutely! Not every team is going to have exactly the same coaching philosophy and style, especially at first team level where you've got to win games. If you had two 6ft 4in centre-backs and two 6ft 4in centre-forwards who weren't very good with their feet, it wouldn't be the best plan to start playing through the thirds. Play to your strengths. You need something that says, "This is what we're going to stick to for a sustained period of time." A problem we've got with English football is that a manager comes in, brings a big entourage of staff, six months later a new manager comes in, rips it all up and starts again.

'We need a robust framework as a club that says, "This is how we are on the pitch and this is how we are off the pitch," and bring in managers to support and supplement that by a couple of per cent every time – not to rip it up and start again because you're changing staff, performance staff, the types of players you're bringing in, and changing your academy. That's not sustainable especially if you're a club like ours.'

So, there you have it, youth team coaches, from the horse's mouth, the man who designed the England DNA says you can play direct football, if you have a sustainable plan. Saul Isaksson-Hurst was less forgiving. Again, it's only fair to point out that I've chosen to present their opinions next to each other:

'I still see people in academy football playing route one direct stuff, smashing it in the channels and they say, "It's good, it prepares them for this or that." Maybe I've been spoiled because of the clubs I've worked at but at Arsenal, Chelsea, Tottenham our remit was to produce Champions League players and to produce players to play the highest level requires an extreme amount of technical work. It's easier to teach someone to put it in the mixer or smash it into the channels than produce someone who can receive the ball under pressure, evade pressure, turn, and play forward under pressure.'

Even for weaker teams? 'You still want to try to play the right way. If you're a small club and you're going to play Chelsea academy it's always going to be tough and, especially in the development phase, it doesn't really matter about the results. You've got to find a way to play around the pressure and you'll work hard off the ball and you're not expecting to dominate possession but you're still expecting to have some quality moments on the ball.'

Taylor Collard has had plenty of conversations with Spanish coaches who want to know about the latest developments in England:

'I tell them we're just copying to be honest. We take the best of what we've seen and try to implement that in an English way. I tell them it's not just kick it, lump it. Although I think at lower levels English teams are still lumping it.

'We joke about it. We're in a match and maybe a couple of goals down and the coach would say to me, "What would the English do here?" I say we would probably find the biggest player and go long.

'They've been so welcoming to me and curious about how we do it. They want to talk about players, tactics, the littlest details. They want to talk about why Man City want Pep Guardiola, but Gareth Southgate plays three at the back against Scotland.'

Matt Whitehouse sees a potential danger in English football being stuck on the tiki-taka track:

'There have got to be coaches who have a different approach because that's how you might have to win a game – adaptable football. Are you able to play longer? Are you able to go round your opponent and cross the ball? Are you able to go through them with possession? Can you counter attack? Are you able to adjust? Are you able to have flexible formations or are you rigid and regimented? The beauty of academy football is that you can develop players who are adaptable and can play interchangeably, which means you can change style quite freely.

'I think that's where the game is headed because you're seeing players who can play in multiple positions; multifunctional footballers who can play everywhere. I think the academy system can develop players like that. Obviously, the amount of time they spend with players means they can be given that large skillset. At first-team level then you'll have players like James Milner who has the skills to play any position at the top level. That's a hell of an achievement at his age and what he has achieved.

'My hope is that it doesn't just become stagnant, boring, everyone does the same, and that as coaches and players we can adapt to the opposition and find weaknesses and attack weaknesses. I think the game could be even more tactically focused, in that sense. I'm thinking Bill Belichick in the NFL who doesn't have one style with the [New England] Patriots, he adjusts every week depending on the opposition. His ability to coach the players means that you'll never get the same thing twice because they're so adaptable. I can see our game moving towards that kind of approach.'

New laws, old tactics

Stewart Robson is less optimistic. He told me the Premier League was thriving but even at the highest level of the English game there is a lack of imagination and innovation:

'Crowds are turning up and there's obviously a lot of enthusiasm about the Premier League but tactically I would say we've gone backwards. The laws have changed, and we've seen so many penalties given because the ball is in the box so why don't teams get the ball in the box quicker and more often? That's where you're going to score and where you're going to get penalties.

'It's not just crosses. Roll balls into front players in and around the box because you're winning penalties. Any challenge, if it hits somebody on the hand, it's a penalty. I'm not saying throw it in willy-nilly, but you've got to find a way of getting the ball into the box with more quality, more often. I see this lots: for 70 minutes teams pass it around the back, and they go square, and they can't unlock the defence, then they say to themselves, "We've got to unlock the game now." So, for the last ten minutes they start throwing crosses into the box, start getting it forward with more urgency and they create chances. Why don't they do that earlier if that's the way they think they can create chances?

'The rule changes about playing out from the back – defenders going into the penalty box to receive the ball from a goal kick and start moves – means we're seeing lots of mistakes and goals conceded by teams trying to play out from the back who can't do it very well and are putting themselves under pressure. At times we're seeing too much possession football without enough penetration. I would say that has changed over the last ten years.

'For example, a team switches play, and get it to their full-back who's in open space and then rather than him breaking forward, he'll stop the ball and play it back again. You've achieved your first objective by switching the play to create space and then you don't take advantage. A lot of teams do that now. Even Manchester City, who are the best team in terms of tactics, still don't make the most of certain situations when they've created space.

'I'm not saying just throw it into the box. Look how Riyad Mahrez gets inside on his left foot and puts the ball into an area where it looks threatening. Why don't they do more of that earlier in the game? There's a snobbery about in the media as well – if a cross goes into the box and it gets headed out it's all, "That was a waste of time."

'We're seeing more safety in players' passing than them trying to penetrate. I imagine it's the coaches wanting the players to be safe with their passing, keep possession, don't give it away cheaply. The players moan at each other if they give it away cheaply and what you're not seeing much of now are forward runs and penetration. Liverpool are the best at it; they make more forward runs and play more forward passes than any other team.'

Does Stewart think there is a danger of becoming dogmatic about tiki-taka-inspired possession football as we used to be about the ubiquitous 4-4-2?

'Yes, absolutely. I still see a coach on the side of the pitch saying "pass it, pass it" but you're having problems passing it because the opposition are pressing you high up the field. If they're pressing you high up the field, it's difficult to play around, so you've got to think of a strategy to bypass it. We have seen Man City bypass it quite well with Ederson. When he knows the press is too high, he goes long. Goalkeepers have got to make better decisions. They have to be good players, not just with their short game but with their longer game. They're the first ones who have to make the decision whether to play out of the back or go longer. Are we playing out from the back or sucking the opposition in so there's more space to create a three vs three or a two vs two up the pitch, then we can go longer?

'Antonio Conte did that brilliantly at Inter, with Lautaro Martínez and Romelu Lukaku over the two years he was there. That was why Lukaku scored so many goals whereas when he played for Chelsea the build-up was slow, then he had two or three players around him whenever the ball came to him.'

Crazy Gang

You might think it sacrilegious to offer Wimbledon's Crazy Gang as an example of innovative English coaching but a tactical plan, backed up by targeted recruitment, transformed a club far beyond its resources. Terry Gibson and his team-mates played a highly disciplined 4-4-2, pressed from the front and were supremely fit, by the unscientific standards of the day.

He told me it wasn't complicated, but it was difficult, 'It was tough mentally but in terms of intelligence it was quite easy. You just kept doing the same things time and time again.

'It was all repetition, grinding teams down and making them play the sort of game they didn't want to play. It was aggressive. It was basic. The 4-4-2 is probably the easiest formation to coach.

I would go as far to say we were the kings of 4-4-2 – we out-punched our weight completely. I was the highest-paid player when I joined the club on £25,000 a year which was a lot less than I'd been earning at Man United. We had players that beat Liverpool in the FA Cup Final who were on £90 a week. Some of them came from lower-league clubs on the same as they'd been at Plymouth, Swansea, or Bristol Rovers. It was an opportunity to play in the top division. We had a lovely dump of a stadium, which was another advantage. Old team-mates of mine hated playing against Wimbledon, particularly at Wimbledon. We used everything to our advantage.

'We had midfielders who weren't allowed to pass sideways or take more than two touches at any time. You're not talking first-time passes, just helping things on in one or two touches, putting it in behind.

'There was a whole language; "reaches" were long balls from the full-back behind their full-back, into the final third as quickly as possible. We had to have a certain number of reaches per game to be successful. We had to have so many crosses per game, midfielders had to win the knock-down and put it in behind again. It was very, very basic, very easy to coach, very boring to play and train every day but it led to success we had no right to.'

Wimbledon's FA Cup win in 1988 is regarded as one of the great underdog stories and it was, if you consider it was a Southern League club until 1977 – but the side that won at Wembley had finished sixth then seventh in the top flight.

Gibson said, 'There were a few clubs playing that way, but we were the best at it. We played it unashamedly whereas other clubs didn't want to be labelled long-ball merchants. Wimbledon embraced it. The supporters bought into it; if a full-back didn't smash it down the channel the crowd would get on his back. It was hard work physically. My career ended at 31 through injury and I wouldn't have bought me. I would never have bought a forward with six or seven years on the clock at Wimbledon because it was relentless.

'We were the fittest team in the league – the training was so hard. Everything was built around that physical style with those basic requirements from every position. As a forward you had to cut off the goalkeeper, who could pick up back-passes then. If you chased into the channel and your two forwards did their job, you might be able to force their defender to put the ball out for a throw-in or hook it forward and we would be favourite to win that and smash it back in again. From kick-off I unashamedly passed it all the way back to Dave Beasant. He was the first keeper to come out of his box 20 yards up field – that was playing out from the back, except he would smash it into the other penalty box. I would get chances although they might not be easy.

'I played 70 minutes in the FA Cup Final and didn't receive a single pass from a team-mate. I've watched it back: I chased, closed people down, forced Alan Hansen to go out for a throw, I pinned up against the centre-backs to make sure they didn't get a headed clearance so our midfield could smash it back in again. It was really basic football at its best.

'There's an embarrassment about playing that way now – there was then. We did it, Watford did it, Sheffield Wednesday did it. I wouldn't have paid money to watch Watford versus Wimbledon, both teams were playing exactly the same way. The offside law was different so anybody offside would be penalised. You spent the whole game sprinting back to the halfway line because you knew if the ball came straight back, you'd be offside. Defenders used to knock the ball back to the goalkeeper and then sprint to the halfway line.'

Gibson played for Tottenham, Coventry and Manchester United before Wimbledon and later joined Glenn Hoddle's Swindon:

'My toughest adaption was when I went on loan to Swindon. They had the most passes in English football, and I came from the side that had the least. I was running around never touching the ball. There was a back three with Glenn as a sweeper. They had Micky Hazard and John Moncur in midfield – really good players and I was like a spectator watching 50 passes, thinking am I ever going to get a touch?'

He coached alongside his Crazy Gang team-mate Lawrie Sanchez at Wycombe, Northern Ireland, and Fulham before moving to Spain to scout for Manchester City and Bolton, later becoming an expert commentator on Spanish football and now works for La Liga TV.

We were both part of the Sky Sports team that witnessed Paco Jémez's Rayo Vallecano side employ '*juego de posicion*', or 'positional play' if you want to sound less sophisticated. You might not recognise the expression, but you've seen it in action. We were opened-mouthed when we first saw Rayo's keeper pass the ball to his centre-back who was under pressure. They conceded lots of goals – but they won the argument.

'We used to laugh at Paco Jémez,' Terry reminds me. 'Now everybody's doing it, and no one says anything. They're obsessed with playing the ball out from the back with short goal kicks even when it's not on. If you keep doing that, you're inviting pressure. The pressing team becomes enthusiastic about it. You're thinking, "Go on play it. We'll get it back." I'm not saying play direct all the time. Do play out from the back but only when it's on.'

Jémez's Rayo side is only remembered outside of Spain by a few hardcore fans. The real shift in perception came from Guardiola's Barcelona. To Gibson, it made perfect sense for that team to use those tactics:

'Barça had Gérard Piqué and Carles Puyol dropping to the edge of the box and receiving the ball from Víctor Valdés because, remember, the ball had to leave the penalty area from a goal kick. You've got to remember everyone was dropping off against Barça, so it was the right thing to do. Why would you hoof the ball from Valdés to Lionel Messi, Thierry Henry, David Villa? It was the right thing for that side. That's the point. Now I'm looking at teams and I'm thinking, "Why? You're not going to get anywhere."

'Occasionally we have seen someone like Ederson finding a long ball. There was a realisation that if they pushed too many players on, there was a gap behind but that's not happening as much again now. It's an obsession. People think they're not allowed to play it long. You see centre-halves who don't want the ball. You see teams come under pressure and chip into the midfield and basically just give up possession because centre-forwards don't challenge. They're not set up that way.

'By all means, if a keeper catches a cross, bowl it out to the full-back or a centre-back and play into a midfielder who isn't under pressure and build your attack from there. But if everyone is set up to press then it's not on, so don't do it. It's unusual to see a team play out like that and create a chance at the other end. It looks great when it comes off, but the risks outweigh the rewards. Also, everyone is static, waiting in position. Believe me, because I used to do it, if you're one of two forwards you can split the four defenders and you have all the belief in the world, and your team-mates will back you up and you know the other team will give the ball back to you, maybe by chipping it down the pitch.

'We see goals every weekend in the Premier League and La Liga from teams playing out from the back when it's not on. If you play out at the right time you can cut through the departments of the team and create chances but if the other team aren't set up for the long ball, then do that. Don't be one track.

'People will say I'm a dinosaur, but I don't want to go back to the '80s and '90s with both teams in a 4-4-2 and goalkeepers crashing the ball up the pitch and never playing from the back. I'm just saying if you're static and you're giving the ball to players whose best attribute is defending and asking them to dribble out or receive a ball in an awkward position and you're reluctant to clear the ball then it's becoming an obsession. We're losing the art of defensive players who do everything they can to defend their goal.'

I asked Garry Birtles how he thought Brian Clough would have fared in the modern game and he brought us back to what was becoming a theme, 'I think he would have adapted. He would have been annoyed if we had tried to play out from the back all the time and got caught out because I think that's a big problem in today's game. The goalkeepers and everyone feel they have to do it every single time, even if it's tight and a mistake can be made. That baffles me because you can't do it every time.'

Birtles works as an expert co-commentator on Premier League games and watched a lot of Daniel Farke's Norwich. The Canaries were promoted twice and relegated once under the German before he was sacked midway through the 2021/22 season, before they went down under his replacement Dean Smith. Birtles was exasperated at Farke's intransigence:

'They got relegated because he never changed it. The number of games I commentated on them, and they made mistakes trying to play out from the back and got caught out. They'd be playing with Teemu Pukki and be losing the game and you'd be thinking, right, get someone on up front and try to get something because they were down at the bottom, and he wouldn't. He would substitute off one striker for another and play exactly the same way, which baffles me.

'If you're losing change tactics a bit and try to unsettle the opposition. It's very predictable now. Substitutions are usually on the hour mark, like it's in a coaching manual. The best managers are the ones who change it when it's going wrong whether it's in the first half or whenever. Others wait and wait, and the other team scores another goal and the game's gone. It's more robotic now, it's more coaching manual stuff and I'm not sure that's the right way.'

That is a word you hear a lot – robotic. Another is clones. In the era of EPPP and England DNA, with a style of play promoted by the football authorities, and coaches who spend more time with young players than ever before, there is a notion that diversity has diminished, as Matt Jackson acknowledges:

'In the Premier League, there's a big divide in quality but not in styles. So, whereas a Wimbledon, or Sheffield United for a time, would come in and upset the applecart by being direct that doesn't exist much anymore. You don't have that diverse range of players. The old adage was, "Can you go to Stoke on a

Tuesday night?" Well now you're going to get the same sort of game wherever you go.

'A large part of that is having so many foreign players but this is also the first wave of young professionals coming through that people harshly call clones. The coaching programme does encourage individuality throughout, but you get a lot of players who can do the same things because the coaching is good and comprehensive.

'Another big difference is on the athletic side. When I was playing, Daley Thompson or Linford Christie were at the peak of athletic excellence. Paula Radcliffe was in the year below me at school and was of such athletic quality that you're on the cusp of any illness tipping you over the edge into not functioning.

'As footballers we were a step away from that – we were going to the pub on a Wednesday and Thursday. You didn't get the injuries, because the intensity and pace of play weren't what modern players face. Now they're such good specimens, but have they moved to that cusp, right on the edge of being fit or really not fit? That's why we've seen more cruciate knee ligament injuries; with the pace of the game, you see injuries that we rarely saw. We're talking about a 20-year window and human evolution hasn't moved the human body on to cope with the demands at the top level of football.

'There are a lot of millionaire footballers now who are athletes first then footballers rather than the other way round. The athletic ability sets them apart rather than their football ability.'

When I watch academy games I see a contrast between the tactical pace, which can be slow, and the breathtaking speed that the players reach when they do hit their straps.

'That's the standout factor,' Jackson agrees. 'Ability, technical skill still come into it because clubs say if a kid has ability they'll wait as long as it takes. But unfortunately, you'll find there are a multitude of outstandingly talented footballers playing at the lower levels or at non-league level simply because physically they couldn't get through 90 minutes a week and a 46-game season against the supreme athletes at the top level.

'Every team would have players like that in the past. Would Jan Mølby, for all his brilliance, have been able to play at the level he reached in the modern game? I'm not sure. You would have to build a team around him. Look at the fitness levels of goalkeepers now – they're transformed, and they don't really run much further than their old counterparts did, but their athletic ability is outstanding.'

Mavericks lost

That brings us to a familiar complaint about modern football, the loss of the maverick, the character, the unpredictable star. Does the modern tactical, technical game have room for a rebel, or even an individual creative talent?

Rodney Marsh was as mercurial as they come. A winger with Fulham, QPR and Manchester City, he was picked nine times for England by Alf Ramsey, but his international career was ended by a quip. In his pre-match team talk, Ramsey ordered his players to work hard and singled out Marsh. 'If you don't work hard, I'm going to pull you off at half time,' he said. Marsh replied, 'Christ, at Man City all we get is a cup of tea and an orange.' He was never picked again.

I was on Rodney's Sirius XM show *Grumpy Pundits* and asked him about the lost breed. He said, 'I would say the cusp was Paul Gascoigne, Eric Cantona, Matt Le Tissier; I can't think of any players like that since. It's sterilised football. I remember when I heard Pep Guardiola – who, by the way is the best coach in the world – but when he talked about his forwards winning the ball back within six seconds of losing it, I thought I could never have played for him.

'It's a massive shame because football needs characters. The game should be full of characters, but mavericks are a dying breed. Jack Grealish has it in him, but a maverick has to produce. You can't just run around with great big calves getting pissed every weekend!'

We were talking after Manchester City's 2021/22 title celebrations and as we all know, Grealish having a celebratory session doesn't put him near the bracket of players from Rodney's day.

I did an unscientific Twitter poll and 90 per cent of respondents wanted more unpredictable, skilful players. That matches my real-life observation. At the England versus Germany match at the 2021 European Championship the crowd urged Southgate to bring on Grealish, who was cheered to the rafters when his face appeared on the screen. The energy from the fans was for England to attack with flair.

Southgate was vindicated. When Grealish came on, he was elegant, and England scored twice. But the match-winners were Raheem Sterling – a very modern attacker – and Harry Kane, a fascinating player, not a clone but not an obvious throwback. I guess there were England fans who wanted the manager to stick with his disciplined structure, but that is hard to express collectively.

Garry Birtles, who's younger than Marsh, also laments the loss of players like his old Forest team-mate, John Robertson. Brian Clough wrote of the Scottish winger, 'Rarely could there have been a more unlikely looking professional athlete ... scruffy, unfit, uninterested waste of time,' adding that Robertson 'became one of the finest deliverers of a football I have ever seen – in Britain or anywhere else in the world – as fine as the Brazilians or the supremely gifted Italians'.

'What a player he was,' recalled Birtles. 'But they were everywhere then: Stan Bowles, Frank Worthington, Tony Currie, George Best obviously. There were terrific players. It's sad that we're not seeing that ilk anymore – it's a bit depressing really.

'Who is a world-class player in the Premier League at the moment? Have England got a world-class player? Not sure we have. That's where it's all changed, for me, and not for the better. Players are being restrained from expressing themselves as they probably can, which I find a little bit sad. It might be down to the academy system because you get kids in there from eight or nine and they're not allowed to play with their friends at school and on a Saturday.

'It gets a little bit robotic for me, a bit predictable, you're looking for players who make something happen. Wilfried Zaha is maybe the nearest.'

Guillem Balagué has seen players who remind him of the mercurial talents of yesteryear but not at the top level, 'You get those players in non-league. They've been thrown out of academies, and they can make a career in non-league and some of them get money through it. Generally, those mavericks have been thrown out of academies because they don't have the consistency in their minds to be elite players, I think.

'Luis Suárez would probably be the exception. A maverick is like that for a reason, a maverick doesn't want rules, he wants to be his own man. Right now, the football we produce is a machine, you've got a role and you depend on the others; you have to be generous. Football is a mirror of society so whatever happens out there happens in football, and right now there's not much respect for the one who is a bit different or breaks the rules.'

How times have changed. Football frowns on mavericks but people voted in their millions for politicians such as Boris Johnson and Donald Trump, revelling in their disregard for rules and conventions.

'There's a little bit of conservatism in the idea of having "The Villain", "The Maverick", as if only one person at a time can be that,' Guillem continued. 'Yes, people should be respectful of communities and of people, but we should be respectful of those who are different and not dump them out. Don't point out who is the devil, or the maverick, just have a community where they're allowed to be like that.

'In football they all play a role and if you're a bit different then you might be the winger, you get brought on, or if you are a maverick and you want to be yourself then football is not for you now.'

Jon McKenzie agrees that the demands of modern top-level football leave little space for individual flair:

'To a certain extent we are losing the capacity to have those maverick players again, maybe just even mercurial players. The big question of the last decade was how the hell do PSG win the Champions League with a front line of Mbappé, Neymar and Messi? Is it a reality now that forwards have to be involved in off-ball defensive work for a team to hit the highest heights? No one's tuning in to watch Messi and Neymar press but that comes at a cost.

'I don't know if your question was motivated by Jack Grealish, who was a mercurial talent for Aston Villa and at the heart of everything, and he goes to Manchester City and people say, "What's he doing there?" I don't think he's been a flop, he's a creative talent and a brilliant footballer but when you're in that sort of team and system you have to do system things. People say, "Where are the Matt Le Tissiers?" But I think the Matt Le Tissiers of old become the Matt Le Tissiers of today, so be careful what you wish for.'

But haven't people always complained that life is more systematised than before? Remember Herbert Chapman's words from 90 years ago, 'Football today lacks the personalities of 20 or 30 years ago ... The life which we live is so different: the pace, the excitement, and the sensationalism which we crave are new factors which have had a disturbing influence.'

Chapman started his career before World War One and continued afterwards. The world had changed and so had football. Footage from 1901 shows what seems to be an utterly shambolic game with players doing their own thing. The march of progress in football is towards organisation and systems, away from the individual. The information revolution of recent decades has changed the world, as war did in Chapman's life. Football has changed quickly enough to leave a sense of loss. We miss the fun that comes – sometimes – with unpredictability but do we really want to go back?

The haphazard game of yesteryear had room for Marsh, Best, and Le Tissier; we welcomed the entertainment but in England they were outsiders. Pelé and later Ronaldinho were central to their Brazil teams, same with Cruyff and the Netherlands. These great players weren't sideshows. Lionel Messi is the modern exception, so breathtakingly talented that a systems manager like Guardiola built around him.

English flair players were mavericks often stubborn and feisty, or downright troubled. I suspect only characters like that could retain their individuality in a system that demands sacrifice to the team ethic. The fact that we elide the concepts of 'maverick' and 'entertainer' speaks volumes about English conservatism. People think they want mavericks, but do they? Parents complain more about a kid who loses the ball when dribbling than one who misplaces a pass. The first kid is a peacock who needs to be taken down, the second an honest trier who needs support. Perhaps it suits English football that the modern game demands system players because that has always been a strong part of our collective consciousness.

Running up that hill

One of the considerable upsides of the professionalisation of English football is the improved fitness of the players which has been significant in the success of Premier League clubs in the Champions League.

Andrea Orlandi looks on from Spain with an envious eye at the ability of English teams to run their way to success if tactics and talent aren't enough, 'At times we in Spain might have been a bit arrogant, thinking that we have the talent, and that was enough and I think now the talent isn't there, not in the levels we were used to a few seasons ago we have to change our way of training.

'We have a very strict way of training where every team from the under-nines trains the same way which is basically football-based with small-sided games, but I think there's been an evolution, and you have to adapt.

'I was at Atlético Madrid's training ground and the intensity was high, as high as it is in the UK, so they do train like modern football requires but there are different problems. The level of coaching is really high in Spain, tactically they work as hard as ever which is why you see really tight games because they nullify each other. There needs to be a change of approach in training because that's not us. When I was at Barça I never ran once, I ran with the ball, but I never put my trainers on and went to the gym and ran on a treadmill or up a hill – no chance!'

Different era, but Ray Lewington recalled his playing days in the 1970s and '80s when English players were capable of running hard, despite their bad eating and drinking habits, and an archaic approach to the science of fitness:

'We worked really hard. We did things they would never do today. When I was at Chelsea, we used to do a seven-mile cross country and they'd throw in a "fitness day" – we used to call it the Olympics. You would do say two 800s, six 400s, ten 200s and 15 100s. That would be your day's work. Hill running; going up Richmond Park. Players nowadays, I think, would refuse to do it if you said, "Right, lads, we're going up Richmond Park for a seven-mile run."

'When I tell the sports science people now what we did they say to a man, "That didn't do anything for you as a footballer, you need to do football-related running." So doing those seven-mile slogs around Richmond Park didn't do anything for us – which doesn't make me feel that clever.'

Terry Gibson can't contain his disdain for the Crazy Gang's training routine:

'We'd play the weekend and win, lose or draw we'd be training Monday and be waiting to hear whether it was a six-miler or 12-miler. Imagine that every Monday! Our training ground was on the A3 and an "A3" was six miles around the forest and up the A3. An "A3 windmill" was the same but we'd then run up to Wimbledon Common and back which was about 12 miles. It was a result if they just said we were going to do an "A3"! I'm going to be honest, I cheated like mad!

'They were pointless. I was useless at them. I used to get criticised but I'm 5ft 4in with little legs and I couldn't run 12 miles as quickly as someone else.'

Ray and Terry's careers straddled the heyday of English dominance of European football and its abrupt end after the Heysel disaster in 1985. The muscular fitness of the English was a part of our success. The later period of Italian ascendency was accompanied by doping scandals. Here is how Paolo Di Canio, who played in England from 1997 to 2004 with Sheffield Wednesday, West Ham and Charlton, put it:

'Doping in English football is restricted to lager and baked beans with sausages after which they take to the field belching and farting. English football culture is one of pure, intense competition and that is why I have always preferred it to Italy.'

The sports science might be lightyears ahead of where it was, but in time we will discover some of the current practices are flawed.

'There's been that evolution in the sports science of football,' says Jon McKenzie. 'The players are fitter, stronger and they know exactly what they have to do to be at that elite level, at the peak of fitness. Any branch of science or body of literature develops over time because there's more exposure to scenarios and we're gradually approaching that plateau at which point you'd think things would level out.

'Maybe I'm too analysis-pilled on this one but I definitely think the best teams from now would beat the best teams from 20, 30 years ago and those teams would have beaten the teams from 20 years before that. I know that's a fairly controversial opinion among average fans, but football is a cultural phenomenon which is growing and improving, and the march of progress is ever upward.'

In Jon's theoretical football match, the Old Generation XI would have a chance if two-footed tackles were allowed, there was a draconian offside law, and it was played on a winter mudbath. Could these modern players do it on a wet Wednesday in 1980?

This is another important point for grassroots coaches – adapt to the conditions. Premier League clubs have spent fortunes to get the cutting edge of turf science and technology. When Guardiola first came to England, he asked for Manchester

City's grass to be cut to 19mm but had to muddle through with 23mm because of the English climate. At academies they have near-perfect grass and artificial surfaces. If you can trust the roll of the ball, you can inculcate a culture of passing football. If you are playing in the local park and the council can't afford to pay groundskeepers, you need alternatives. That is what the contributors mean when they say don't just robotically follow the prevailing wisdom.

Match analyst Daniel Hutchings sees evidence that English football is readapting already:

'In League Two in the last four or five years we've seen a lot more teams trying to play possession-based football – Swindon for example. But since Liverpool have done well in the last couple of years, League Two football has changed again. It's going back to the old-fashioned pump it long, if you like, more direct. I never thought I would be asked to look for a 6ft 5in centre-forward but I was. It's always changing.

Daniel was already watching more League Two football than almost anyone else, so I asked whether they were already out of the other side of tiki-taka-inspired football.

'It's always re-examined. This is what's so great about football, there's no way of playing that guarantees winning games. The clubs are ultra-professional. On the analysis side there were a few clubs in League Two who didn't have analysts and they were falling behind, so they've invested.

'The older ways are coming back, not necessarily in terms of 4-4-2 and smashing balls up the pitch but taking philosophies and speed of play and bleeding into what was tiki-taka.'

Will the next development be a return to old-style direct football? Not as we knew it. It could still be effective against teams who haven't been brought up that way, but kids coming through academies aren't equipped to play Crazy Gang football. The best that old-schoolers can hope for is that Matt Whitehouse's view of adaptable, versatile footballers is realised, with space created for idiosyncratic, individual talent – and centre-forwards, and centre-backs. Developing intelligent players, giving them responsibility, and encouraging them to grow as leaders, is also how we will retain a distinct essence of Englishness and head off the danger of copy-and-paste coaches recreating a decade-old version of Spanish football.

7

Don't show them you're hurt!

'Every player had a bit of my blood on his shirt
or his shorts or somewhere ... the ball was
covered in blood.'

WHAT DOES it say about English football that one of our iconic images is 6ft 4in centre-back Terry Butcher soaked in blood, eyes wild, looking like something from a horror movie?

It was 1989, a World Cup qualifier in Sweden and a draw would do nicely. Butcher, who had joined Rangers after English clubs were banned from Europe, clashed heads with Johnny Ekström. England's physios tried to patch him up on the pitch and at half-time the doctor started stitching his injury but ran out of time. England's defensive cover was Paul Parker, an accomplished player but only 5ft 7in tall. Butcher stayed on, heading and clearing the ball with incredible bravery as his white shirt turned claret. He was clearly concussed and losing a significant amount of blood. He finished the game and helped secure the 0-0 draw that edged England closer to the World Cup.

He was a hero. One tabloid headline was 'Give Butch the VC'. He was the football reincarnation of the English Tommy from the trenches, racing towards enemy guns without a care for his own neck.

Footballers are three times more likely to die with dementia than the general public. Outfield players are four times more likely to be diagnosed with neurodegenerative disease than non-footballers. It is an age-old problem. Walter Winterbottom's *Soccer Coaching* has a 16-page section dedicated to heading practice. No surprise, Charles Hughes placed physical bravery high on his list of qualities:

'In matches, courage is required to use the head to make contact with the ball in situations where it is not unreasonable to expect defenders to use a boot. This type of courage is more to do with character than technique. Good attacking players must look to get into danger areas. Their desire to score must outweigh any considerations they have for their personal safety.'

In the 2007 League Cup Final, John Terry was knocked out when he dived to head the ball and Arsenal's Abou Diaby kicked him in the face. Chelsea won without their captain, who was later released from hospital and turned up for the celebratory night out. Even now you can still see footballers taking blows to the head and effectively getting up and getting on with it. Butcher himself told the BBC that we should phase out heading:

'Eventually I want to see football with no heading. We've seen pictures of a lot of the footballers of past generations where they've got dementia and Alzheimer's and it breaks your heart. The family are the ones that will really suffer and friends as well because it's not a nice thing to happen and it's not a nice thing to witness.'

You can't tackle these days

If you don't yet believe that football has gone soft on tackling, then good for you. I imagine you're also fresh-faced with luscious hair. Just wait. The ferocity of tackling has reduced fairly consistently for three decades. At times I thought we had arrived in the right place but now I find myself saying it, 'You can't tackle these days!'

I hear retired players younger than me bemoan the decline of aggressive physicality and remember that older pros said exactly that of their era. It is part of the human condition to regard younger generations as feckless and soft: the Father of Comedy, Aristophanes, was writing nearly 2,500 years ago and his plays are basically about the younger generation lacking moral fibre; the kids of ancient Athens were all snowflakes.

In a 1992 video, *Soccer Hard Men*, Vinnie Jones, who had just returned to Wimbledon, said, 'I get very frustrated with the referees because they don't give you an inch.' Jones was fined £20,000 for his part in the weirdly fascinating documentary. He had been a building site labourer before his first spell at Wimbledon in which he was part of the FA Cup-winning side of 1988. He claimed his early foul – a 'reducer' – on Steve McMahon, Liverpool's hardman midfielder, was pivotal in the Dons' victory.

Jones admitted, 'I let him [McMahon] just have a touch and whacked him. I hammered him, and it knocked the stuffing out of him, and he went about the field on tiptoes. They were all so shocked their man had been sorted out and it spurred on my players.'

McMahon took revenge in a league match at Anfield with a studs-first lunge which left Jones needing eight stitches just below the knee. The referee was perfectly positioned to see what was, effectively, an assault and waved play on. Jones thrived in that climate, 'The good thing about English football, they don't roll the length of the pitch if they're not hurt. I hope the continental fouls and their antics don't creep into our game because people like myself will be finished.'

I think that sort of physicality reached the peak in the first half of Jones's long career, which ran from 1986 to 1999. Ron 'Chopper' Harris, who played for Chelsea between 1960 and 1980, was a celebrated hardman but he wasn't as physically imposing as Jones. His reputation was built on ruthlessness, essentially a willingness to push the tolerance of referees by frequently fouling. By the 1980s, play was much faster, and players exploited an inconsistency in refereeing that wasn't seriously addressed until the 1990s and then took time to filter into game play, particularly in England.

The manly code meant that complaining about brutal tackling was bad form. When England played away to Scotland in 1985, the commentator for Scottish TV, Archie McPherson, revealed that Don Revie told him the home side should single out Glenn Hoddle. 'He's got to be hit hard and often, as quickly as possible,' McPherson relayed.

When Maurice Malpas cut down Trevor Francis on the halfway line in the opening minutes, McPherson was grimly triumphant, 'That was Trevor Francis, that was. No booking. A gentle reminder of what a tackle ought to be.' Over the replay he started victim-blaming, 'You can watch him going in there, just hear it. Bang! There might have just been a little flourish by Francis.'

McPherson was mis-remembering the past. If you watch matches from the 1960s and then the '80s, you see more ferocious tackles later. Les Ferdinand scored over 200 goals as a classic number nine and was the PFA Player of the Year for 1995/96 when he hit 29 goals as Newcastle came so close to winning the Premier League. He smiled ruefully when I asked him about the importance of physical bravery in his playing career:

'It was a major part of the English game, a major, major part. I think back to when I would play against Tony Adams, or Martin Keown at Arsenal and you knew you were going to get kicked from behind. I always tell people how defenders could come through the back of you.'

Ferdinand made his First Division debut in 1987 and his career spanned the first FIFA-inspired attempts to rein in tackles from behind. In England progress met resistance because we liked a good hard tackle.

Ferdinand said, 'When they changed the rules, centre-halves had one opportunity to come in from behind then the referee would give them a warning. I remember playing for QPR at Loftus Road and the ball came into me, and as a centre-forward you knew that was the one when you were going to get lifted up in the air. I remember this ball coming into me and I knew I was going to get a free kick, so you had to go for it. Adams comes through the back of me, he lifts me up in the air the referee comes running over and says, "Right, Tony, that's your one! No more!"

Tony gets up, turns to Steve Bould and says, "I've had my one, yours is the next," while I lay on the floor.'

Terry Gibson was a team-mate of Vinnie Jones at Wimbledon in the late 1980s – arguably the most notorious team in English football. As well as being relentlessly drilled, they were expected to be tough, but some went beyond that. A lunge by Jones on Gary Stevens left the Tottenham player with career-limiting injuries. Stevens was in a vulnerable position as he battled with John Fashanu when Jones recklessly crashed into his knee. Fashanu was involved in another grizzly incident when his flailing arm caught Spurs' Gary Mabbutt who was left with a fractured skull. Gibson says the Crazy Gang legend is often overblown now, but admits it was too violent at times:

'A line was crossed on a number of occasions, and players got injured. But we had players injured as well, the same injuries that we inflicted we suffered. It was a tougher era. There were two or three players noted for their brutality, their physical side – the rest were big, strong, physical but not overaggressive. It was a big strong team, everyone was over six foot except me, Dennis Wise, and Terry Phelan.

'To be honest, I played with tougher, harder players elsewhere. Every team had tough players. Graeme Souness, Jimmy Case, players of that ilk who could put their foot in; Bryan Robson, as good as he was, could put his foot in.

'Wimbledon wasn't just about 11 hard nuts kicking people, but we were a story because we had a former hod carrier in midfield who was going around kicking people. That was a better story than Bryan Robson or Graeme Souness putting their foot in.'

The old pros tend to look back on the physicality of yesteryear with a wry nostalgia, but these are the ones who made it. They stood up to the hatchet men. None of the people I spoke to were dirty players, but they all relished the physical challenge.

'We've gone too far the other way,' thinks Garry Birtles. 'The worst thing in football is the continual diving, the simulation, it's just embarrassing. When we got kicked, we got kicked hard and it bloody hurt. We were told to get straight up. I was told, "Even if it's hurt you, smile at the boy who's kicked you and run ten yards past him."

'I remember Willie Young whacked me on the halfway line against Arsenal and it hurt but I got up, smiled, and sprinted past him and he's in a dither because he's got to get back and mark me. You expected it. I played against Paul Hart, and you knew in the first ten minutes you were going to get dumped on your backside in the centre circle with him smiling down at you. It was their job to unsettle strikers.

'Ian Bowyer: if anybody went high, he'd go higher. He was a terrific player. Every team had the enforcer in the back four or the centre of midfield but because of the change of rules now that wouldn't happen because you'd get sent off. You have to reel it in and be a little bit cute. Referees have got a hard job because players throw themselves to the floor in a ridiculous manner and it's so difficult at that pace to see if there's been contact. It's a totally different game.

'They now consider players' momentum and, for me, that's ridiculous. You can win the ball fairly and because it looks worse, and the man is taken off balance it can be a yellow or red card. You've won the ball cleanly and just because the momentum takes you further, you both go tumbling over that tackle can be punished. That doesn't make sense.

'I'm definitely not saying everything was better in our day. There have been big improvements in player welfare; we had one physio and that was it more or less. There are so many people in the background now – nutritionists and people like that – that's the massive change.'

Tony Gale believes the change in the laws have driven the change in playing style, but he still sees a difference between football in England and elsewhere in Europe:

'The rules of engagement are different; there's no tackling from behind, there are yellow and red cards at the drop of a hat, so the intensity is now in the running. What you've got is an honesty in our game, on the running side and a physical side.

You get more challenges in the air and shoulder-to-shoulder than in European football. We've also had the influence of European football culture and it's perfect. You've got a bit of both and it's showing certainly in terms of our clubs in European football.

'I was seen as a ball-playing defender. I wasn't as physical as I should have been for that period, so I appreciate the ball-playing side now as much as anybody. To play like I did then was so much more difficult because I had the physical side stopping that style. The rules were such that a not-so-good defender could get away with it by their physicality, not by thinking about defending and intercepting the ball. So, there's a bit of both, I love the physical side and I wish there was a bit more of it in the Premier League, a bit more contact, but I love the fact that the rule changes have helped the skilful players.'

There is a definite sense of loss among some fans at the passing of tougher times.

'You think of direct approach, a big number nine up front,' Paul Embery remembers. 'I followed football as a kid in the 1980s and you had people like Stuart Pearce who were going in for full-blooded, bone-crunching tackles as part and parcel of the game and I think that was a good thing. I do think we're in danger of becoming a non-contact sport almost. Contact is gradually being erased. I'm a bit old-fashioned but I do like the "up-and-at-'em" approach, and I think probably a lot of fans do as well.

'I used to go and see Dagenham & Redbridge when John Still was manager, and it was long ball. The keeper never rolled it out, it was always booted out, but it was exciting, high tempo, there were lots of crosses coming in, lots of action in the final third. The fans loved it. I think that was an archetypal English game.'

But Terry Gibson believes a lot of the old attitudes are best consigned to history:

'There were players I played with who only had football careers because they were aggressive, strong and, let's be honest, dirty. That was their role. Game after game, they took as many knocks as they gave, played with injections in knees and ankles then went out and did the same again in the next game. You looked up to those players who played like warriors. Their job was to compete against like-minded players in the other team. I am really glad you haven't got those kinds of players any more who are only footballers because they're aggressive and cross the line.

'You had to learn how to tackle because I was naive when I first started. I tackled like I'd been taught as a school kid, but you find yourself up against people who are going in over the top, going through you and leaving their studs on your shin. I opened up my knee joint on a couple of occasions because I went in with the side of my foot, so the older players at Spurs told me I couldn't tackle like that. You then end up showing your studs in every tackle because you didn't trust your opponent not to. You didn't go over the top of the ball to hurt someone, but if you didn't show your studs, you were probably going to get hurt.

'I showed my son some old goals I scored on YouTube, and he laughed and said, "There were three red cards in the build-up." He's right, there were two-footed tackles flying in all over the place.

'I paid for it. I had my career cut short through injury. I liked to think I gave as good as I got but I probably didn't, and you end up at the age of 31 with terrible ankles and knees and the like. Every aerial challenge you had your elbow up for self-protection. I learned the hard way. I probably had 20 stitches before I started putting my hands up and covering my face from a centre-back. That didn't stop me getting another 20 stitches in the years after. Aerial challenges were a real threat. It was horrible at times – it was good fun – but I'm glad it's not like that anymore.'

Culture acts as a filter. I was a working-class kid born in 1971, and I loved watching and playing the game with my friends, but I was a gentle soul and the 11-a-side football scene in Teesside was too rough for me. There was no traumatic incident, no obvious psychological scar, it was just dominated by more aggressive people, as was English football in general.

Of course, that was no great loss, but a more serious question is whether Iniesta or Xavi could have come through the English system. Maybe they would; I am roughly the same age as Gareth Southgate and Steve McManaman and neither of those was an aggressive bruiser.

Keith Hackett played a role in the transition away from the era of the hardman. He was a Football League and Premier League referee from 1976 to 1994 and later head of the Professional Game Match Officials Board. He was an international referee from 1981 to 1991 and remembers stark cultural differences between English and continental officials, 'It was absolutely more physical. I remember coming off a game and the Italian assessor saying, "You English referees are so liberal with the laws of the game." But they all loved our game, by the way, it was blood and thunder and all that goes with it.

'In our era referees judged challenges in relation to intent, and then the laws changed. We have to recognise in the modern era that a player has a duty of care towards to an opponent. It doesn't matter if you're from the front, side or back in terms of a foul challenge, you can no longer use the ball as a decoy – and to some degree you no longer have to make contact with a player to endanger his safety.

'To some extent I think the law has been influenced by the value of the players and the impact on their career.'

It is natural that progress meets resistance, but a test of whether change was needed is to look at the recent past and ask yourself whether you would go back. In the football context think of tackles from behind, two-footed lunges and defenders having a free hit at strikers early in a match.

In the cat-and-mouse game of gaining competitive advantage, footballers use new interpretations of laws to buy fouls in novel ways. Watch out for players choosing not to play the ball but placing themselves between it and their opponent, anticipating contact that might bring a free kick or penalty: it is a particular favourite in VAR-governed matches where contact looks worse on slo-mo replays.

Another tactic is to wait for an opponent to get close then initiate contact and go down, leaving the officials to unpick what happened. I'd be fascinated to know whether they practice. With few players ever sanctioned for simulation, it is high-reward, low-risk. I occasionally referee kids' games and I am conscious that I let challenges go that younger (properly qualified) referees would give as fouls. I think I'm right – but Vinnie Jones thought he was right to 'give players a clump'.

Cheats

One trend with no proud father is players exaggerating the force of challenges. The matches played during the Covid lockdowns with TV coverage, but no fans, highlighted the bloodcurdling cries players let loose when they feel contact, only to jump up and play on seconds later.

Les Ferdinand used to consider it a matter of pride to play down any pain he suffered, 'Now when you see player get tackled you think, "Bloody hell, he can't carry on," because they scream as they go down. I always remember the one thing I thought was, "Don't show them you're hurt." I suppose that's changed dramatically. Any little tackle that comes in, you hear them screaming before they've even hit the ground. There was a time when you tried to pretend you were tough and pretend you couldn't feel the challenge because you didn't want to show you were hurt.'

Ray Lewington used almost identical words to describe the reaction to being fouled in his playing days from 1975 to 1990, 'You never showed you were hurt: if you went into a tackle and came out limping you got on with it – never show you're hurt, you know, they'll think you're weak. That was the talk.'

He fears it will be hard to cut out play-acting because clubs are desperate to get every advantage:

'There are a lot of people within the game who say as soon as someone is touched, they go down and it's ruining the game. A lot of people are saying it but not publicly, mainly because maybe some of their players are doing exactly the same.

'You don't have total control over players – if they fall over during a game, it's not something most of us want but maybe our own players are doing it because that's how they've been brought up. I think it would be sad when we get to the day when people in football say, "It's contact so it's a foul." Contact isn't a foul; we've gone away from that. No one is coming out and saying it yet but there's a lot of feeling that the game is being ruined because people are falling over all the time.'

Paul Embery identifies cheating as a significant factor in driving people away from the game, and he has a point – gamesmanship and uneven finances are the least popular aspects of football:

'I hate, really loathe the diving and cheating which is becoming so blatant. The game has been awful at stamping that out. If you had a serious sanction in place, if you knew you were going to get a five-game ban every time you dived, you would stamp it out at a stroke.

'Managers are totally hypocritical. They'll defend their players but if they're on the receiving end of the dive they're the first to complain. It's turned me off the top end of the game, I tend to watch more now at the lower levels.'

Keith Hackett agrees, 'We've almost got a "death" in every game. We see players rolling in agony and for me that's a real worry because those that scream bring attention to themselves but the next time the referee might ignore them.

'In fairness to them, there's greater pressure to win. Clubs have 45 players and only 25 are in the Premier League squad, so the competition is fierce, and the dark arts come into play. Players go to ground much more easily than ever, either to deceive the referee and win a penalty or to bring the referee's attention to his opponent. It's about the desire to win and to enhance reputation.'

Sports fans who don't like football often cite play-acting as the main reason. It is not new, but it is more sophisticated than ever.

Matt Crocker still believes English football is played with a large degree of integrity although he admits coaches do weigh fair play against results. I asked him whether the English still have the right to regard ourselves as a uniquely fair footballing nation. He took his time and took a deep breath:

'Good question. In terms of the academy system and how we bring up players, there's a real fairness. I think it's another English trait – we want the game to be played a certain way.'

But there were buts:

'I remember having a meeting of national coaches that got extended into a meeting of senior football club managers and one of the coaches brought up: when do we teach the dark arts? You know, how to slow the game with five minutes to go: take a throw that doesn't come on to the pitch and it's your throw in again, things like that. There was a really successful English manager with lots of experience who was horrified. He said, "No, we're renowned for being fair."

'It really divides people. I think there's still a really strong sense that we want to be a nation where we play the right way and do the right thing. When we played under-15s, 16s, 17s what other nations will do to win is unbelievable. I remember here taking under-12s to Spain for a tournament and they were giving out these friendship bands before the game and saying, "You need to wear them." It was a boiling hot day, and we didn't realise there was wintergreen on them, and the kids were sweating and wiping their eyes and getting the wintergreen in their eyes – the extremes some coaches will go to get a win!

'I was torn. Do I think there are certain things we need to do to increase or slow momentum in games? Yes. Should we cheat and dive? No. Absolutely not.

'I remember when we'd already qualified for a European finals and there was a player who had a yellow card that would carry into the tournament and there was a debate among coaches about whether we say to him, get another one now and you'll get rid of the suspension before the tournament – but we didn't do it. The integrity was important, but I don't think every coach would have that view.'

Years of watching games as a neutral has shaped my perceptions and I find myself sitting in a stadium surrounded by fans who are utterly convinced the referee has cheated their team and saying, 'No, that was a good decision.' Almost always when I see Twitter users moaning about a biased commentator or referee, it is nonsense. There is tendency in the media to portray English clubs in Europe as honest and beyond reproach, in defiance of the new reality.

A classic example came in the 2021/22 Champions League when Manchester City got the 0-0 draw they needed at the Metropolitano to knock out Atlético Madrid. Late in the game with the home side on top, Phil Foden broke down the left wing when he was tackled by Atlético's Brazilian defender Felipe – who then deliberately caught the City man in his follow-through. He had already been booked so the referee correctly decided to send him off. But first, Foden's momentum took him clearly off the pitch, only for him to roll back on, pretending it was a natural action as he writhed in agony. Atlético's ex-City defender Stefan Savić dragged Foden back over the touchline, and a pushing and shoving melee started. It was ridiculous from Atlético and suited City perfectly – Felipe was dismissed and the whole incident derailed them.

This was a clear and successful use of dark arts, but the significant parts of the English media pretend it doesn't apply to our teams. The honest reaction is to say, 'Yes, we did it because we were desperate to win.' I will offer two pieces of evidence for my case that Manchester City used dark arts in that game: they were fined by UEFA for their players' conduct and, more tellingly, Pep Guardiola told us in the press conference before the game they would match Atlético and grab every advantage, fair or foul.

Time-wasting seems to be increasingly annoying football supporters. A few people contacted me on Twitter to advocate for an independent time-keeper. That wouldn't be my choice. Time-wasting is as much about breaking your opponents' momentum as reducing the length of the match. After the incident above with Foden, Atlético weren't the attacking force they had been in the minutes before. The delay worked. The danger of an independent time-keeper is that referees might opt for an easy life and give up harrying players along. My preference would be for the officials to enforce the rules we have now or, if you want to be inventive, fine clubs who waste time. It is hard to define how much time-wasting goes on but given the level of analysis we have now, we could find a way.

You could argue that players at English clubs are more streetwise than before. Traditionally we accepted aggressive lunges and two-footed tackles as part of the game and sneered at foreigners for finding sneaky ways to cheat. At the 1986 World Cup, Diego Maradona cheated to give Argentina the lead in the quarter-final but, let's be honest, England's players took every opportunity to clog him to stop him using his mesmeric skills. The culture of English football held that fouling was fair game – it was the referee's business to draw the line – but deception wasn't. We were outliers then, and we no longer draw that idiosyncratic distinction as clearly. The growth of momentum-sapping, time-wasting is an area where the desperation to win football matches makes them less appealing to watch and we need to cut it out.

VAR-cical

Before video referees were introduced, I thought one upside would be a crackdown on cheating. If anything, the opposite has happened, as players know challenges often look worse on replays. Garry Birtles wants to call on old pros, 'You feel for referees because you see things being taken out of their hands. It's too inconsistent, it's frustrating for fans, commentators, everybody. I think it's wrong not having an ex-player in the VAR. The thing that does me is the theatricals. It's embarrassing. If my kids had been watching me play and me do that, they would have slaughtered me.'

Keith Hackett thinks the leadership of English football has been too weak:

'I understand the ref not cautioning if he's not clear but there are instances when it's clear that a player has dived or simulated, and it's not happened. One of the things I expected from VAR is that referees would be helped with simulation but that hasn't been the case.

'Referees have been weak for a long time. Weak refereeing and weak VAR – it's a declining standard of referees. I'm seeing players going down rather than attempt a shot on goal. PGMOL need to review the action and say, "Are you interrogating that?"'

He thinks VAR has added to the complacency of English referees and their bosses, 'Physically: lazy. VAR: lazy. No accountability: lazy. Management: holiday camp. That's why I'm on social media making those comments. There have been some really poor changes that have affected the game. There seems to be an energy to change the laws for change's sake. We aren't half making life difficult for refs at grassroots level.'

Jon McKenzie thinks VAR misses the point of what referees are for, 'VAR is an example of applying a sort of scientism to the game and saying, particularly with offside, this is either offside or it's not. We can constantly improve our technology so those finer margins become even finer, and we can zoom in and in and in, to accuracy of a millimetre, but who cares? When has anyone ever cared about those decisions being completely right or completely wrong?

'Football, until recently, was judged by human arbiters whose whole function was to allow the game to take place and make decisions to the best of their ability. Sometimes decisions are going to be bad. People say if there was some sort of failsafe VAR where we only apply it when there's some egregious miscarriage of justice it'd be OK, but it's gone the other way and it's more about accuracy than functionality.

'Commentators bemoan that fact that no one is able to celebrate a goal because there's a thing in the back of your mind that it can be disallowed. That changes people's relationship with the sport. It makes people feel disenfranchised, as though it's not as authentic as it once was. The same thing has happened to me because of the data revolution.'

VAR is football's collective punishment for moaning too much about match officials. Who cares if an offside decision was marginally wrong? Well, it depends on who was flagged. If our team loses out, we scream and shout and post angrily on social media – if not, then it is easy to be philosophical. We in the media are as bad, we need to avoid the easy option of stirring up aggravation and the lazy practice of focusing on refereeing rather than football. We need to collectively grow up about officials making mistakes.

Toxic masculinity

It is good to be proud of being a man but has English football's brand of masculinity been helpful or a hindrance? When Glenn Hoddle played his last game for his country after moving to Monaco, he lamented that the tough-guy image of English footballers got in the way of winning tournaments:

'At home youngsters are ashamed if they haven't got what everyone calls "fighting spirit" yet overseas their pride is hurt when they can't control the ball with their first touch – that's the difference.'

The so-called 'golden generation' of English football who are now active in the media admit their club rivalries restricted the camaraderie of the national team. In a fascinating exchange with Tony Bellew, the ex-world champion boxer turned podcaster, Jamie Carragher admitted he would struggle to change if given his time again. Bellew's response is illuminating.

Carragher said, 'You see players high-fiving each other or hugging each other before games. Hugging Gary Neville? Never in a million years! I still wouldn't do it now if I was playing. I just think the lads are a lot softer now and I'm not saying that as a criticism, I think it's helped England as a team but it's not me. When I see people in tunnels, coming off pitches I think, you know, as [his former manager Gérard] Houllier used to say, and I think he was right, "You're going to war on the pitch." You'll see them in the players' lounge, you don't need to mix with them before the game or coming off swapping shirts. That was always my mentality so I wouldn't change it, even if someone said it would help England, I'd say I want to make sure I help Liverpool.'

Bellew, an Everton fan, was delighted:

'Us fans, that's all we really want. We want to see players go on the pitch and not care about anything else apart from doing your job and getting rid of them and do whatever you've got to do to win. They're not your mate for 90 minutes; the minute you walk across that line, he's your enemy, simple as that.

'Go out, lads, and get stuck right in, let them know we're here, and if you give us that every week, we'll love you and adore you. It's great to hear a player with those values. It doesn't exist anymore. They're shaking hands and hugging and picking each other off the floor.'

Carragher responded, 'The world is softer. People talk about woke and things, listen, I think a lot of the things that have come in as life evolved and moved on are for the best but when it was football, everything went out of the window for me, even if I was playing against my former team-mates. I know my competitiveness or anger was too much for other players to handle every single day. At times when I was a footballer it was draining, and I didn't enjoy it enough.'

Bellew's appreciation of Carragher's overt will to win is not unusual. English football fans roar their approval of thumping tackles and chasing lost causes. Is there anything wrong with that chest-beating motivational style given that elite footballers have to be ultra-competitive? Yes, if it stops you being clear-headed. Chasing a lost cause might be useful in a team with no game plan, but an organised outfit can pass around that charging player with ease, then exploit their numerical advantage. Intelligence is as important as determination. Increasingly the head is as important as the heart, and not in the Terry Butcher sense.

Saul Isaksson-Hurst put it this way, 'The problem was that it was our fallback, and that's what we celebrated. We celebrated John Terry trying to do a diving header and block the ball on the floor with his head when we should have been celebrating our quality individual technicians unlocking defences.

'You still want players to have desire, that willingness to go to war but you've got to have the rationality and composure to have quality on the ball. Of course, you want players willing to fight and win the ball back. You see that with Pep Guardiola's teams off the ball the way they press like they're going to war. You want that, but it can't be the only thing you've got. For a long time, football was just, "We're going to fight, we're going to smash them." I remember even Chris Waddle in an interview saying we used to just out-run teams and beat them up physically because that's what we had. We've got to come out from that because we're better than that.'

Matt Crocker describes a different sort of strength from the traditional notion, even a different sort of physicality:

'I think there are two types of resilience – physical: can you do a James Ward-Prowse and play 90, 100 consecutive games? If you're going to win a tournament at World Cup level, you're going to have to play every few days and top players, Champions League winners, have that physical resilience.

'There's also mental resilience – can you do it, or do you look for excuses? Can you switch on at a moment's notice? Do you stay focused during games, after games and when preparing for games? If you're going to win World Cups, as much work happens off the pitch as on it. What can you do in the other 22 hours to aid your performance?

'We have some amazing physical and mentally resilient players coming through; Phil Foden typifies it. Was he a late developer? Yes. Did he have huge belief in himself when he was probably being out-muscled by so-called bigger boys when he was younger? He has trained and his club has supported him to be the player he is today. It's something you have to work on with players.'

There is no one better to speak about the relationship between football, masculinity, and mental wellbeing than Paul Mortimer: player, coach, therapist. What a career switch. I suggested to him we are in the healthier state than when he was playing in the 1980s and '90s.

'Without a doubt but that old "don't show weakness" thing is still prevalent,' he said. 'I spoke to players the other day and that's what came out of their mouths, "Don't be seen as weak." There have been positive changes to pastoral care, player liaison, sports psychologists and some clubs have therapists. Spurs were looking to have their own health and wellbeing person. They're beginning to understand the importance of emotional wellbeing.

'Where it hits the buffers is that all that work was accessible by players but not staff. I talk to staff about retain and release. They'll talk about the welfare of the players, and I'll say, "I'm asking about you." A player hears the news once, they have that conversation 15 times. If they're letting ten players go, they have to hold them emotionally ten times. If every one of them was a 10kg weight the staff are carrying 100kg, so much weight of emotion. Tomorrow, they come in and are a bit emotionally challenged and somewhat abrasive with some young lad and might leave an impression that can be so damaging but it's not their fault, it's because they're carrying all this.

'Everyone talks about how few openly gay professional footballers there are, but they don't just become gay as pros. In the academy system you'll have so many players struggling with their sexuality and they're more likely to talk to a coach at that age. I said to a coach if someone wants to drop this on you but says not to tell anyone, how are you going to deal with it?

'I'm a clinical supervisor as a therapist and I've delivered to managers and asked, "Who holds you emotionally?" I thought he was going to cry. By the way, this is a big-name manager.'

Understandably, Paul didn't tell me who it was. 'It's like a buzzword, emotional mental health, and wellbeing. It's started and it's really good, but we've got a lot of work to do. It feels like we're at the experimental stage, working out who should be getting what and where. The great thing is that lots of players are beginning to talk about it but is the support going at the same pace? I don't think so and therein lies the problem.'

As Paul says, there are schemes to help players tackle mental health problems, such as the FA's Heads Up. It is a long way from 1999 when Aston Villa manager John Gregory publicly slated his player, Stan Collymore. He was quoted by *The Guardian*:

'As a manager you can only do so much for a player; you can't wet-nurse him. I know he was suffering from clinical depression but the day after the season finished he checked out of the clinic where he was receiving treatment and went on holiday. I understand he's fully recovered but, if he hasn't, then he should pack the game in. I've tried everything to get the best out of him. Sometimes it was a cuddle and I even publicly criticised him hoping he would ram the words down my throat. I have done lots of things to try to make it work but nothing did.'

It would be unthinkable for a manager to speak like that in public now but a more sympathetic attitude to mental health problems doesn't make the root causes disappear. Money insulates you from many things but not the pressure of being a footballer. Paul Mortimer sees players young and old who aren't equipped to cope:

'I asked some players, "What would it be like if one of you cried in front of another?" Three or four of them laughed. Then we drilled down, and they don't know. They're uncomfortable, because the only emotion they're conditioned to express is aggression, that anger and frustration. That's all seen as positive. Sensitivity and showing you care, those sorts of emotions are seen as weakness.

'Football is literally about exploiting the weakness of the opposition, so we have team talks about the weaknesses. You're drip-fed that being weak is unacceptable so by 18 years old, showing emotion, sensitivity is never going to happen. It's embedded that you can't do that. So, their ability to develop a sense of who they are doesn't develop apart from "I'm a footballer".

'The playing bit is easy – if it's for them. The emotional bit is where they struggle. We players, athletes, have addictive tendencies. We're told not to give up. We're sent to bend the rules, express ourselves, challenge authority, be curious, don't

198

back down. We're sent to do that, conditioned to do those things. That's why players will drink to excess because they need to fill that gap of acceptance because we don't teach players to understand their emotions.

'I counselled a player who was penalising himself to the point where he wasn't eating so that he could maintain weight and he couldn't see anything wrong with it. This is what happens, you punish yourself because you think you're not worthy.'

Bottoms up!

British football has had a long, unhealthy relationship with alcohol, which is no surprise because British people have long had an unhealthily close relationship with alcohol. In World War One, David Lloyd George proclaimed that Britain was 'fighting Germans, Austrians, and drink, and as far as I can see the greatest of these foes is drink'.

Some of our greatest players and managers have been blighted by serious alcohol problems: Jimmy Greaves, Bobby Moore, George Best, Paul Gascoigne, Kenny Sansom, Ray Wilkins, Jim Baxter, Alan Hudson, Brian Clough, and Howard Kendall are a few names on a long, long list. In 1957, Hughie Gallacher, formerly of Newcastle and Scotland, suffered depression after his wife died, drank heavily, and committed suicide by jumping under an express train. Our collective attitude to alcohol is weird: we can't decide whether to laugh or cry, to celebrate or censure.

Brian Clough encouraged his Nottingham Forest players to drink alcohol in the build-up to their triumphant European Cup finals. Garry Birtles accepts it seems incredible to look back at how much they drank and how much they won:

'I don't know how to explain it. We were fit as fiddles. I kept ticking over so my body didn't get bogged down with crap food, drink, and everything. It's impossible to say why we were so successful; we might have won three European Cups if we hadn't drank so much!

'There was a big drinking culture. It wasn't just having a quick drink. I used to go out on a Sunday and have six pints and then go back later and have six more. That was how it was done, and I was as fit as a fiddle. In two seasons I played nearly 140 games. I had to get the club doctor out after the second season because I had blood blisters all over from exhaustion, but I enjoyed every minute. There were no mobile phones, no social media so what else did you do? You went out with your mates; you weren't chastised for going out. You weren't supposed to go out after a Thursday, you weren't supposed to play golf after a Wednesday, but sometimes I played on the Thursday.

'The Friday before one game we thought it was going to get called off. It was minus-ten at about half past five. All the cars were frozen, and the City Ground pitch was frozen solid. I went out with my mates, thinking there was no way the game was going to be on. I had about ten pints, went playing three-card-brag at my mate's house until three in the morning. Then the phone call came – Cloughie had convinced the referee to play. We won 3-1 and I got man of the match.

'It's all about metabolism. Not everyone has got the same metabolism, some people can do some things others can't. Today they think everyone's body is exactly the same and it isn't. Some bodies tolerate stuff and others don't. Nobody can prove otherwise.

'It's a mental thing sometimes. Cloughie was a great man-manager, he took the pressure off. Before the European Cup Final, he took us to Cala Millor for a week and we were playing tennis, sunbathing, drinking, no curfews, and we won the European Cup.'

Ray Lewington has similar memories – apparently all the players from their era do:

'There was a culture in English football where you worked hard, played hard. I can remember going up the motorway coming back from say Manchester and it was impossible to drink everything we had on the coach because there was so much. It was that time – we were almost encouraged to do it. Obviously, a few did it to excess but it was that sort of laddish culture that you got on with it.'

Terry Gibson was at Manchester United at the time of the infamous drinking culture that Alex Ferguson tackled in his early years at the club. Alcohol consumption was linked to notions of team building and camaraderie, and Terry says the expectation was that drinkers had to 'run it off':

'That group of players I was with at United were the kings of drinking. It was like that at every club I played with except Wimbledon where there was no social scene, no drinking culture. At Spurs there were senior players who didn't mind a drink. The routine was to play on a Saturday, and we didn't have to be in until Monday so as long as you turned up on Monday...

'It was rare that a player turned up for training drunk. They might have had a heavy night out, but they'd turn up and train, probably harder. I got lapped by Bryan Robson at Manchester United on a 12-minute run – and he'd been on an all-nighter. I could hear him coming up to lap me because he had a plastic bag on – and I hadn't been out. They put the work in. Obviously medically and scientifically it's not the right thing but the culture was, if you'd had a heavy night out, come in next day and train hard. People generally stopped drinking on a Wednesday. The rules were generally no drinking 48 hours before a game. It was in the little handbook they gave you and most of the time most the players stuck to that.'

Tony Gale thinks it's unfair to portray their generation as drunks and loafers:

'In a certain way, we looked after ourselves or we wouldn't have been as fit as we were to play the professional game, which was also played at a fast, intense rate and it was physical. We were fit. As time's gone on, science has improved, and you understand the body a lot more.

'Normal people eat more healthily nowadays. You think in the old days, what your mum and dad used to eat was a lot of shit, wasn't it? But now people understand fruit and vegetables, you've got to eat this and that, not too much carbohydrate and everything, so physicality has improved in the game, but it has in life generally, hasn't it?'

Albert Ferrer told me that Spanish players didn't do any specific physical work when he was playing. Maybe that was the key: England's culture of drinking heavily and 'running it off' versus the continental footballer's disdain for physicality. Then the scientists ruined the party.

Lee Hendrie witnessed that cultural shift, 'It had to change. You can't approach week after week with the mentality of my era and the era before because you'll get caught out. The modern English game is based around being an athlete and working on lots of finer details.

'When you'd won a game, the lads would be thinking about having a night out. I don't think the lads are like that now. It's stopped, that era's gone. I was still on the tail end but there's no way you can do that nowadays, not if you want to be at the top of your game although I'm not saying the lads don't go out sometimes.'

Excessive alcohol consumption was a key part of the hooligan years. The threat of a modern revival comes laced with cheap cocaine. Even when behaviour is good, lots of us associated watching football with trips to the pub. Other sports are the same: English cricket, rugby, racing are all excellent excuses for a booze-up. Football's popularity means it is followed by a greater array of people, and some of them aren't very nice when they're drunk. English football is intrinsically woven into English culture.

Abusing your heroes

A section of Middlesbrough's old ground, Ayresome Park, was known as the Chicken Run. I didn't understand the concept as a kid, but it was known as the place to stand if you wanted to abuse the players. I don't understand it any better now.

Our relationships now happen in both the face-to-face world and online, something my generation has had to adapt to as adults. It is changing our lives for better and for worse in ways we don't understand. Matt Jackson says mobile phones and social media have intensified the scrutiny on footballers to unprecedented levels:

'They've been more immersed in football. Social media makes a big difference – we were shielded coming through. We were still going to the pub. There wasn't the profile around players like there is now. If Everton players were seen out in Liverpool it was no problem at all. When I was at Wigan, I would shop in Asda in Wigan no problem at all, and people might just say hello and stuff, but you don't get footballers in their own community anymore.'

George Best was the probably first footballer to make the transition to superstar celebrity. When he bought a house people came to sit in his garden and look through the front window. The explosion of interest in football has extended celebrity status to lesser players than Best. Today's stars can afford huge estates with high walls, but Paul Mortimer spots an unhealthy obsession:

'I can never work out this role model thing. You only know me for 90 minutes on a Saturday, so you don't know who I am. You can't live your life like me because you don't know me. Players are put on a pedestal they don't deserve, they're not ready for and they shouldn't have to deal with. Players are now set a higher standard of behaviour than fans. Fans can abuse players, but the player can't have a go back because, "We pay your wages!"

'Football has changed. Fans used to have a moan at players if they weren't playing well but generally supported them. Now it's not moaning, it's abuse. We live in a society where the average man in the street's wage is going down and the average wage in the Premier League is about a million a year – an average squad player. Phone-in programmes, rolling news, players are now in your front room and fans think they own them.'

According to Capology, Cristiano Ronaldo was the highest-paid Premier League player in 2021/22 on a gross £515,385 a week, or £26.8m a year. Manchester United players occupied four of the top five positions, but the team fell well short of Champions League qualification. Jadon Sancho didn't suffer financially by taking a circuitous route to the Premier League – he was reportedly paid £350,000 a week gross. Kevin De

Bruyne's decision to hire Analytics FC paid off to the tune of £400,000 a week.

The numbers are hard to justify in a country where people are struggling to pay rent, mortgages, and energy bills while food bank usage booms. But are footballers to blame? If you believe in free markets, then what is the problem? They're easier to tax than people of similar wealth. They haven't bribed or cheated their way to the top. You don't get to play for Liverpool because your dad knows someone, or you went to the right school. I would argue it is a structural problem in football that certain clubs are able to suck in so much of the money but scan through the *Sunday Times* rich list and ask yourself how everybody got that rich. Was it a good idea for Chelsea to give Timo Werner a contract worth £271,000 a week? No, but he didn't put a gun to their head. Criticise his technique and his finishing, say he's not worth the money, but there is no excuse for the abuse of players we now see, particularly online.

In 2018 Mortimer was commentating when West Brom's Jake Livermore confronted a West Ham fan who had taunted him over the death of his baby son:

'He [Livermore] lost it and was climbing into the stand because the fan was abusing him about losing a child. People think that's acceptable. Fans have a right to criticise performances – not a problem at all, but the colour of my skin, my sexual orientation, whether I've got a disability have got nothing to do with it. We've moved into an environment where nothing is off limits.'

Football takes racism more seriously than in the playing days of the ex-pros I interviewed but that was an incredibly low bar from which to judge.

'I can remember the whole Shed End at Chelsea shouting at me, "You black bastard!" I was 19. I was terrified,' Mortimer recalls. 'It was overt and it mirrored society at the time because I was getting abused in the street as well.

'Society has changed so therefore football has changed but this overt aspect is creeping back into stadiums, slowly, week after week there are black and ethnic minority players complaining about being abused from the stands.

'I don't think in football we know how to deal with discriminatory behaviour. We keep saying it's a mindless minority. OK, but I think we have to go through the majority to get to the minority. If part of a stadium is shouting racist abuse, that whole stand is shut down and when they come back, they'll police themselves. Points should be deducted, and clubs should be thrown out of competitions if they don't behave, simple as that.'

Talking about racism brought us to the subject of black managers in England, or rather the distinct shortage of black managers. Almost 30 years after the formation of the Premier League, Patrick Vieira became the tenth black manager in the competition. Mortimer believes the problem is obvious:

'Football doesn't want black managers because otherwise there would be black managers. Historically, black and ethnic minority players have been seen as physically gifted, not intelligent. Most owners aren't going to trust a black guy with their money because where in their life have they seen black people on a par with them? Look at the areas they socialise in. Are people of colour managers, titans of industry, leaders? No, so why would an owner trust a black guy?'

Of the nine black managers who preceded Vieira in the Premier League, five of them had less than half a season at that level, having been appointed in precarious circumstances.

'Look at black managers and how many of them lose a job, get another, lose a job, get another. The Sam Allardyce factor. It doesn't happen,' said Mortimer.

'Name a black coach who would have got the Newcastle job the way Eddie Howe got it. I look at Frank Lampard, Steven Gerrard. Gareth Southgate got special dispensation to manage in the Premier League – he didn't have the qualifications. That doesn't happen to black managers. Roy Keane starts at Sunderland. Paul Ince at Macclesfield, Sol Campbell at Macclesfield.'

Since 2018, the FA has aimed to appoint black or ethnic minority coaches for all its 28 national teams. For Mortimer it is a small but necessary step:

'We're having to manufacture opportunities, quite rightly too. We've been talking about this for 20 years. Ledley King was assistant manager to Mourinho at Spurs and when Mourinho went, Ryan Mason got the job. Chris Powell was there who was an established manager. They didn't give it to the established manager, they gave it to someone with no managerial experience. What links Ledley King and Chris Powell? If they'd been white, it wouldn't have happened, let's not kid ourselves.

'Terry Connor got the Wolves job when no one else would do it because it was a crap job. Chris Ramsey got the same thing at QPR when it was a crap job, and they were going down. When Alan Pardew left West Brom they gave the job to Darren Moore, temporarily, knowing full well he was never going to get it. He did such a good job that, in my opinion, West Brom went, "Crap, we'll have to give it to him." The next season they were fourth in the table, and they sacked him. Doesn't happened to white guys.

'What had Lampard done to get the Everton job? He was terrible at Chelsea. He's got the job because he's Frank Lampard. I'm not blaming him. I see him as a lovely guy and one of the Premier Leagues best-ever players, but should he have got the jobs he's got? In my era Ashley Cole was our only world-class player, in my opinion, but where's he coaching? Why wasn't he given the same opportunity?

'It's not just a football problem. It's a societal problem. I know I walk into a room, and I can change the temperature just because I'm a black guy. One of the problems we have in this aspect of implicit bias is expectation. Someone's expectation of me is what will get a me a job or not. I'm not expected to be intelligent and smart. I'm expected to do as I'm told and be physically gifted.

'I got the [UEFA] A licence, and I was thinking about the pro licence which cost £8,000. The PFA could pay half so that's not a problem but why would I do it when I know there's no job at the end? I met the criteria before the pro licence came along and never got a sniff. Me and a good friend went for the same job and later he said, "I'm gutted I got a rejection letter." I never got a letter. Six months later I still hadn't got a letter. His existence was acknowledged, mine wasn't. The issue is the lack of opportunity.'

It is not only about fairness. Genuine diversity opens pathways for talented people. Over 100 black players have appeared for the England senior men's team since Viv Anderson became the first in 1978, and there were 11 black players in the most recent squad. Mortimer says there's a straightforward matter of practicality:

'There was a spell when in England's under-15 to under-21 probably 60 per cent of the players were black, yet they had no one reflective of them on the staff. No one understood them because all the coaches were white and came from a position of authority. How to do understand a 16-year-old black boy if you've never come across a 16-year-old black boy before?

'They've got a scheme now at the FA with black and ethnic minority coaches being attached to each level, which is great because if that's what had to happen then so be it. We have to use the rules because there's a block on offering black and ethnic minority coaches the same opportunities.'

Asian network

When we talk about race in English football, we need to break it down. There is a blocked pathway for black players becoming managers but for British-born South Asians the problem is becoming professional players at all.

Zesh Rehman made his Premier League debut for Fulham in 2004 and for years he remained the only player with two Pakistani parents to feature in the top flight of English football. Players of mixed heritage such as Hamza Choudhury, Neil Taylor and Michael Chopra have played – and there are now some promising South Asian players including Arjan Raikhy and Zidane Iqbal close to breaking through.

Zesh Rehman's brother Riz was a professional at Brentford but broke his leg and moved into non-league. He now works for the Professional Footballers' Association as a player inclusion executive and has been trying to unblock pathways through the Asian Inclusion Apprentice Scheme.

He said, 'Any South Asian players from under-nines upwards who sign with an academy will get access to mentors from similar backgrounds – typically people a few years older who've been through it. It's for families too. I've found they have tons of questions so it's always good to have a network of people from similar backgrounds.'

When we spoke, there were 116 South Asians out of 12,000 kids in the academy system, spread around 48 different clubs. It was more than Riz had expected and he describes it as a step in the right direction. He is steadfastly optimistic that we will soon start seeing British-born South Asian kids following his brother's footsteps:

'Since Zesh there have been a few others of mixed heritage but now you've got parents who were born and bred in England, who grew up watching football. A lot of the parents in the system are 45 or 50 and their kids are 16, 17, whatever. Those parents grew up loving football, so it was natural for them to support their kids' dreams. When their parents first came to England it was about working, making money, education, which is right, education should still be the focus. Now I'm seeing the ones who were born and bred in England, the way they were brought up, how they talk is British through and through, they see themselves as English first rather than any other ethnicity. I think in the next four, five years we'll see more coming through.'

Riz sees a flourishing grassroots community of South Asian footballers that doesn't yet connect with the academy system:

'The data shows that the Asian kids are playing just as much if not more than their black and white counterparts, but I've found that Asian parents and Asian clubs don't have networks.

'Lots of grassroots clubs know scouts and know where to push a promising player whereas a lot of the Asian clubs are new and don't know the elite pathways. Without that you're going to be stuck in grassroots clubs and Asian clubs which don't progress.

'Last week I had a talent ID day with Arsenal and took 100 young players. Arsenal selected six to come back to the development centre. They said that without this day they don't see these kids and there was some real talent. They said these were better than some of the kids in the academy.

'We want clubs to really sweep the country for the talent, I'm helping them to put a strategy in place to diversify their recruitment and ask how are they going to look into the untapped community to find hidden gems.'

Zesh retired from playing in 2022 and joined Portsmouth's academy as head coach of the under-18s – the first British Asian to get such a senior role at under-18 level. The Rehman brothers were brought up watching Aston Villa from the Holte End before they moved to London when Zesh was scouted by Fulham. Riz's positive experience in football underpins his optimism.

'I've been going to football since I was aged eight at Villa Park. My dad always said when he went in the Holte End in the '80s with his Villa scarf on he was welcome. We never experienced any racism as fans from a young age. We were the only Asians sat there. I can't speak for everyone because I know there have been isolated incidents but I'm happy to take my nieces – they support Crystal Palace, they wear the head scarf, no issues.

'I've got to look on the positive side. I don't really talk about barriers facing young people. I focus on the pathways and the journeys, using their networks because if the focus around Asian kids was always on the negative then parents aren't going to push their kids towards football.

'If football was racist, I wouldn't be getting into clubs, but football has welcomed me with open arms, they want to listen. If you're good at what you do, the clubs will let you in. There are pockets of fans, but football reflects society. It is impossible to monitor everyone or educate everyone. It's embedded in society but it's not going to deter me or Zesh, we want to go right to the top.'

Not such a man's game[12]

The professionalisation of football is nowhere more evident than in the women's game. Long after the lifting of the infamous ban in the early 1970s the authorities remained steadfastly indifferent and women's football languished as an amateur sport, sustained by dedicated pioneers.

In 2003, Fulham chairman Mohammed Al-Fayed abandoned his one club mission to bring the women's game in England into the modern era, frustrated at a lack of institutional support and the indifference of rivals. Jump to 2020, and Chelsea were paying £250,000 to buy Pernille Harder. In 2021, they signed Lauren James from Manchester United for what could end up being £200,000.

People are watching more than ever. The Women's Sport Trust reported a near four-fold increase in viewing hours of the FA Women's Super League – up from 8,830,000 in the 2020/21 season to 34,048,000 in 2021/22 – thanks to a new deal involving Sky Sports and the BBC. Forty-five per cent of the viewers for the 2021/22 season were female, in comparison to 33 per cent in 2020/21.

The FA Women's National League Strategy 2022–2025 puts a series of demands on clubs in terms of player support and infrastructure. The grassroots girls' game has thrived in response to FA financial backing and ever more open-minded attitudes.

Sue Smith won 93 caps for England between 1997 and 2012 and is now a co-commentator for Sky and the BBC. She remembers a gulf in standards between club and international football:

'As an England player we did tactics every day when we were away, either on the field or in meetings. We'd analyse the team we were playing – what they were good at and what they weren't good at, hours and hours of set pieces on and off the pitch, so many individual clips looking at yourself on the ball and off the ball. Now that's something the girls do now at club level.

---

12 This was written before the Women's Euro 2022 victory

'Clubs have got video analysis which was coming in when I was playing for England but at club level, we didn't always have that. We obviously had coaches but not people videoing matches and training sessions. I used to love watching myself back because you'd pick up certain things and maybe think I wasn't as bad as I'd thought and vice-versa.

'Even the teams lower down are doing it. Players will be watching games and analysing tactics. When I was playing, it was very much, "They play 4-4-2. We're going to play 4-4-2. This is how we're going to play. They've got a good left-winger, a midfielder who's really skilful or a centre-forward who's good in the air." It was very basic whereas now it's in depth. As a left-winger you'll know everything about the right-back and if she doesn't play, you'll know about the right-back who could potentially play, whether they're quick or slow, good on their right foot or their left foot. It's huge now.'

This book would have to be twice as long to analyse women's football in sufficient depth but some of the trends are the same as the men's game. Sue has seen the English women's game go abroad for talent on and off the field and change in style as a result:

'For me, sideways and backwards means a safe, easy option. Good decisions aren't necessarily playing short every time. The best teams can play longer or threaten behind or play through or around. They adapt. As a forward I wanted my players to be a bit braver but that's the attacker in me saying that. I want the ball forward, but I get that as a midfielder or defender you might want to play safe and make sure you don't lose it. That's probably an influence from Spain and Italy and from foreign coaches coming over.

'Arsenal had Joe Montemurro, an Aussie coach who was very possession-orientated. I know it's the Arsenal way – pass, pass, pass, keep the ball. Sometimes they overdid it when they could have created more chances and scored more goals; they try to pass it into the net – that was a criticism of Arsenal women.

'He went and they got a new manager, Jonas Eidevall, and it changed to being more direct. If a long ball is on, they'll play it and they're not afraid to go forward quickly and play with energy and intensity. They've been really successful doing that, and the players enjoy it. Is that his way or has he looked at the players and thought that would work? It's probably a balance. Foreign coaches and players coming over has definitely influenced the women's game being able to play in different ways.'

There is more money and greater professionalisation of women's football in England and who could complain in those circumstances? Perhaps unsurprisingly, I can. One of the biggest traditional names in English women's football is Doncaster Belles, the South Yorkshire club that had a strong team when the women's game was briefly shown on Channel 4 in the 1990s. In 2013, the FA announced that Manchester City would replace the club by then known as Doncaster Rovers Belles in the top tier.

How modern. A club funded by a Middle Eastern autocracy with a dreadful record on women's rights would take the place of a traditional English team that had helped build the game in the face of official indifference. Money outweighed history. Doncaster now play in the fourth tier.

I was afraid I was being churlish given that the women's game is getting long-deserved recognition and funding, but Sue agreed that it would be a shame if the iniquities of men's football were transposed wholesale on to women's football:

'That is the worry. You look at last season and Chelsea and Arsenal were pretty much runaway leaders. Man City had a nightmare in terms of injury so you would have had the top three, then a middle bit and then clubs that haven't had that much investment. Birmingham were always going to get relegated because of their training facilities and lack of funding and investment in the squad. They were never going to compete with Arsenal and Chelsea. Look at Chelsea's bench – it's full of top-quality internationals who'd get into any team. Birmingham's bench is full of kids with no experience in the WSL. My worry is that it's going to be the same in the women's game, that you're going to have a couple of runaway leaders.

'The FA are looking at how to help the teams that don't have the investment – but the richest teams are the best teams and that's always going to be the case. The FA massively wanted Liverpool to come up because that's huge for the WSL because of the name because of the men's team but could they have helped Birmingham?'

Data analysis from Dave Carbery at the University of Bath shows that women's leagues are considerably less competitive than men's – not only in England. He observes that the pattern mirrors the earliest days of men's leagues in England and Scotland. However, the men's game did have a long period where it grew far and wide before the concentration of wealth gradually made it less competitive. It is normal that a sport would have uncompetitive periods as it becomes established and grows but we have got to be mindful of locking that in.

'It's been like that for a while,' says Sue. 'When I was playing, Arsenal won everything. If you could finish second to Arsenal that was a big achievement. When I was at Leeds, and we finished second – and got to the FA Cup Final and got beaten by Arsenal – that was an achievement.

'They were the team to beat because they had the most money. They were able to give players jobs, pay them. Then it went to Man City because they put a load of money in and got a load of good players. It's like the men's game – you don't want it to be a two-team race every season.'

Is that inequality inevitable? No. There isn't the same concentration of success in American sports where they actively level the playing field. Salary caps are problematic in a global sport because we want great players in our country – and relegation is essential. But there are plenty of potential devices.

Why, for example, is any of the TV dividend distributed as prize money when we know beyond doubt that richer clubs finish higher in the league? It is subsidising the wealthy. For women's football to continue to grow to its potential, fans need to believe the trophies won't be divided up between the same few clubs.

That might show the men's game that genuine competition is worth striving for.

Modern football, modern Britain

In so many ways football is a nicer place because society is a nicer place. You might not think it from your Twitter timeline or watching *Question Time*, but most people are less racist, less homophobic, less discriminatory than ever. I know that is easy for me to say when I am never on the receiving end, but I do believe the culture war industry exaggerates the scale of divisions and amplifies the voice of people most hostile to change.

Some change is bullshit. On the football field, for example, there is no justification for diving, time-wasting, and cheating – it is not some great cultural advance learned from our neighbours. No excuse – 'the other lot do it' or 'it's referees' fault for being inconsistent'. It is good to question modernism because some of it is dogmatic nonsense. That doesn't mean tolerating bigotry, and we need to be as vigilant for any creeping growth of loutish and abusive behaviour – in real life and online. There have been some high-profile accusations of appalling criminal behaviour levelled at footballers, but I don't see evidence of a trend that is worse than before.

In 2022, Blackpool's Jake Daniels came out and became the only openly gay current English professional footballer. As far as I can tell the reaction was incredibly welcoming. Daniel Hutchings, the match analyst who helped me with this book, came out in January 2022 and told me his experience has been positive and affirming. My fear for Jake is that we place too big a burden on him. He's a kid who had played ten minutes of senior football. He can't single-handedly solve football's homophobia problem.

The men's game does have a homophobia problem. We know that because there wasn't an out gay male footballer in England between Justin Fashanu and Jake Daniels. Thomas Hitzlsperger and Robbie Rogers both played here but weren't out at the time. That is a chasm – and it is cultural. Too many all-male settings in Britain are homophobic. The nature might have changed, and the tone softened but the persistent use of casual homophobic insults is enough to create a barrier, and for gay boys to choose not to play football. As we have seen with Jake Daniels, the top end of the game is more enlightened than ever so let's be hopeful that as the culture in younger groups changes, we will see more gay men playing the best game of all.

8

The best league in the world?

THE LAST day of the 2021/22 Premier League season had something of everything. Not a single position had been sorted before kick-off and the title race went to the wire. Manchester City clinched it by coming back from 2-0 down to beat Aston Villa. Liverpool were never in provisional top position because they were drawing with Wolves. Like City, they won in the end, but it was thrilling. Tottenham hammered Norwich to claim the final Champions League position and Leeds won at Brentford to stay up. There were 39 goals in ten games. It was a marketing department's dream.

People clearly enjoy what the Premier League serves up. Average attendances were higher than ever before at 39,989. Broadcasters from around the world are eager for a slice.

We have the richest league in the world. Fourteen of the top 30 clubs in terms of revenue are English. Leeds had just been promoted when they appeared at number 23 in Deloitte's Money List. Manchester City surpassed Real Madrid to claim the biggest revenue of any football club: £571m to Madrid's £567m, although the source of City's wealth was less susceptible to pandemic-related setbacks than traditional giants with huge fanbases. Premier League spending power saw players of the calibre of Christian Eriksen playing for 13th-placed Brentford, while 14th-placed Aston Villa were able to buy Diego Carlos, a key player for Sevilla, who finished fourth in La Liga.

But for Thibaut Courtois's amazing performance in the final, an English team would have won the Champions League for the second season in a row. Six of the last ten finalists have been English. Real Madrid's dramatic, miraculous run prevented a second straight all-Premier League final. The most accurate measure of the strength of a league at the elite end is the UEFA coefficient where clubs are rated on their performance in European competition over a five-year rolling period. The Premier League has been in first place for the periods ending 2021 and 2022, after eight years led by La Liga.

I think that is a comprehensive case. The counter involves asking whether this glittering juggernaut was worth the cost. Let's start with Matt Crocker, Southampton's director of football operations, who believes the Premier League retains its unique intensity:

'Absolutely, that's what makes it special and different. There aren't many leagues where you can be 3-0 down, or 3-0 up and lose 4-3. It's not all the time but you're still watching games with a spirit of not giving up, that resilience. I think that's a real positive, I guess that's the bulldog spirit that helped the Football League and the Premier League. That's what the Premier League has grown off the back of, I guess, what makes it exciting and sellable in hundreds of countries around the world.'

He told me the running stats had stood up through the games played in empty stadiums during the pandemic:

'The players were still covering the high-speed sprinting distances – the stats are all there. Fans want to see themselves on the pitch. If your job is working in a factory and you know the blood, sweat and tears you've shed that week, you pay your money to see that from your team.

'I've always liked players buying into that sense of representing your fans and your community and that plays in with the bulldog spirit of what English football and Englishness is renowned for, roll your sleeves up, some of the stuff around the coastal nation, protecting the borders, the history stuff. We're a country of amazing resilience over years and years. Maybe that got lost in our identity of English football, but it has always been part of Englishness.'

Competitiveness

You've heard it said that there are no easy games in the Premier League. Repeatedly, I'm sure. I'm sorry, but the old adage doesn't stand up to scrutiny. Manchester City collected 458 points in the last five seasons, losing only 21 games. They've scored 485 goals and conceded 143. They averaged 91.6 points a campaign with an average goal difference of 68.4.

The bottom-placed teams have collected just 16, 21, 23 and 22 points in the last four seasons. This is similar to Serie A (17, 20, 20, 27) but La Liga's worst club has claimed 32, 25, 30 and 31 points. Public perception lags behind the reality here.

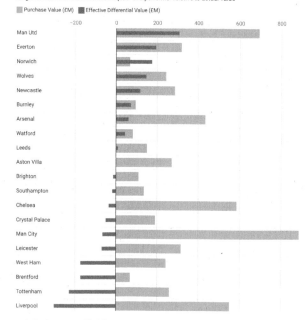

SQUAD VALUE DIFFERENTIAL
PL 2021-22: Squad *effective* value vs *actual* value

Comparison of Transfermarkt stated total squad value and linear regression predicted squad value based on actual goals scored in 2021-22 season. Values in £M
Larger effective differential means squad "overperforms" relative to actual value

results data: https://www.worldfootball.net
market data: https://www.transfermarkt.co.uk
Chart. @carbery_dave · Created with Datawrapper

Euro Leagues 2021-22 Season Ranked Competitiveness

Premier-League ■ Serie-A □ La-Liga ■ Ligue-1 □ Bundesliga ▨ Scottish-Premiership
▨ Eredivisie □ Primeira-Liga' ▨ Austrian-Bundesliga

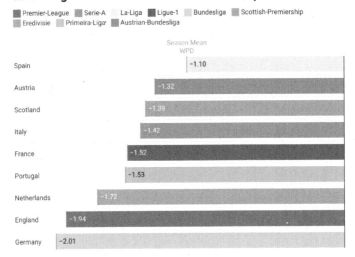

individual match WPD value calculated as:
winner's & loser's normalised league table position difference * by goal difference * by goals for
seasonal mean is average of all match WPD

Chart: @carbery_dave · Source: @fbref · Created with Datawrapper

Premier League Historic Competitivity

Examination of Historic Seasonal Win Positional Differential
in Premier League 1992-93 to 2021-22

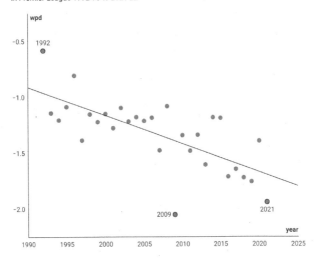

Individual match WPD value calculated as:
winner's & loser's normalised league table position difference * by goal difference * by goals for
Seasonal mean is average of all match WPD values for that season

Chart: @carbery_dave · Source: worldfootball.net · Created with Datawrapper

ADDED VALUE
PL 2021-22: Goal Difference v Squad Total Purchase Value

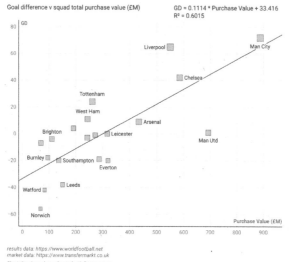

Goal difference v squad total purchase value (£M)

GD = 0.1114 * Purchase Value + 33.416
R² = 0.6015

results data: https://www.worldfootball.net
market data: https://www.transfermarkt.co.uk
Chart: @carbery_dave · Created with Datawrapper

Dave Carbery, an academic with the University of Bath, analyses football data. He created a model to examine whether the Premier League is as competitive as we like to believe. The Win Position Differential measures results along with the position of the teams in the table when the match kicked off.

Dave was motivated by a conversation after a game of five-a-side in which his friend repeated the dogma that the Premier League is uniquely competitive, 'Anyone can beat anyone.'

'Obviously, it's literally true,' he conceded. 'A lot of people see what happens at the top of a league structure as a reflection of competitiveness. Clearly there are draws and cases where teams further down beat teams further up, but I looked at it with a view to all the results that make up our headline final day, all 380 games.'

You can read Dave's methodology in his blog, but I needed it spelling out in non-scientist terms, so I asked him if you draw a line plotting competitiveness in the Premier League over the years is it wiggling downwards?

'Absolutely right. In 2009/10 there was a significant downwards movement, that was the most uncompetitive year but if you take that out the trend is very clear, it really is. It's telling us that it's getting less competitive. The ten years from 1992 backwards there is almost as clear an upwards trend of it getting more competitive. Could that be correlated to English clubs being banned from Europe?'

Remember this is measuring results across each Premier League season. The 2009/10 title race went to the last day with Chelsea clinching it with an 8-0 win over Wigan. It is perfectly possible to have exciting battles, even as football becomes less competitive.

When Manchester United won the first Premier League title they claimed exactly two points per game. In 2017/18 Manchester City claimed 2.63 points per game and 2.45 in 2021/22. I suggested to Dave that competition throughout the league has declined as the game has become richer:

'I think the numbers strongly support that statement. I suppose it would be a reasonable sense of causality but certainly there is a correlation with those years leading to changes. Over the last five or ten years that money has come from different sources. Teams being supported by nation states is a different level altogether than just being funded by TV money.

'I can imagine the inflationary pressures getting ridiculous. I don't know how high up the fire will get; I suspect that while you're in the Premier League it's fine but the pressure to try and stay there is going to get crazy. And while three teams continue to be relegated, some of those teams that go down are going to be in deep doodoo.'

We will get to the distorting effects of parachute payments shortly.

Comparing selected top divisions in 2021/22, Spain's was the most competitive followed by Austria, Scotland, Italy, France, Portugal, Netherlands, England, and Germany. That isn't the whole story, of course. Real Madrid won La Liga by 13 points, and we want stories, rivalries, and knife-edge finishes. Liverpool pushed Manchester City to the last day, having won the title in 2019/20 and collected over 90 points in three of the last four seasons. Jürgen Klopp and Liverpool's highly acclaimed backroom operation have been as important for the notion of Premier League competitiveness as Leicester City's title win in 2015/16.

Southampton's 9-0 defeats against Leicester and Manchester United in 2019 and 2021 respectively have been the biggest losing margins in any of the big leagues in recent years. No side has hit eight in a La Liga match since 2018. Serie A was given a shot in the arm when Juventus's stultifying run of nine straight league titles finally ended in 2020. Inter and AC Milan have both won the championship since – with a thrilling race in 2021/22. Competitiveness is the obvious failing of the Bundesliga. Bayern have won ten consecutive titles and their eight-point margin in 2022 was the narrowest since 2019. We shouldn't judge the success of a league solely by comparison with others – the blight of anti-competitiveness afflicts other leagues as Champions League money distorts domestic competitions. Globalisation has helped create a concentration of wealth and power in society and football is no different.

Of course, as I write about competitiveness in the summer of 2022, I leave myself a hostage to fortune. Maybe Manchester City will slump, maybe Nottingham Forest will be top by the time you pick up this book. I'm going to guess not. More likely is a Manchester United revival; a club that size should always be relatively close to getting things right.

The Premier League does seem to have a waiting list of oligarchs and billionaires who want a slice – we will get to the ethics of club ownership later but the arrival of Saudi money into Newcastle did create a potential new power at the top. When I was growing up it never occurred to me that Chelsea or Manchester City would challenge for the league title but in 2021, their Russian and Emirati owners watched them go head to head in the Champions League Final.

Competitiveness throughout the Premier League may be gradually declining, but it was never particularly even in terms of who won it. In its early years, Manchester United were too good for the rest in too many seasons. It was important that

Blackburn Rovers and later Arsenal rivalled Alex Ferguson's team, at least for a while. Supporters' money funnelled to clubs via TV channels and ticket sales attracted rich foreign owners which had the triple effect of adding new challengers at the top, inflating transfer fees and wages, and widening the gap with the chasing, or let's say trailing, pack. After Roman Abramovich's 2003 arrival at Stamford Bridge, Chelsea, Manchester United, Arsenal and Liverpool all qualified for the Champions League every season until 2010.

In the late 2000s the Premier League threatened to become dominant in European competition, claiming six of the eight Champions League semi-final places in 2007/08 and 2008/09, but Barcelona's victory in 2009 was the start of a decade of Spanish success.

The revival of Premier League clubs in Europe is a result of the vast stash of cash being spent more wisely than before. Politicians who argue that throwing money at problems is no guarantee of solving them might have pointed to the Premier League for much of its existence, but deep pockets won through. Once again, top managers have been lured to England. I believe them when they talk about the atmosphere at English stadiums but huge budgets matter too. Manchester City's money won them titles under Roberto Mancini and Manuel Pellegrini, but their points tallies bounced up and down. The owners wanted Guardiola, a tactical innovator, renowned for football that was both stylish and successful, and put in place the sporting leadership to attract him. Then they spent vast sums on players, professionalised their backroom set up and, in 2017/18, became the first Premier League club to reach 100 points. Liverpool thrived under Klopp, thanks to the German's leadership and some smart transfers. Chelsea won the 2021 Champions League after following Liverpool's example of recruiting German ingenuity in the form of Thomas Tuchel, and, of course, an expensive squad.

Guillem Balagué again sees the dividend of English football reaching out for help – and paying top dollar:

'Is the Premier League the best? For what? The quality of the players? Well, they pay more than anybody so, of course, you're going to have lots of very good players but why don't the top, top, top players want to come? Why wasn't Ronaldo here at his peak? Why hasn't Messi arrived?

'Is the Premier League best for clubs that have got more solutions? For coaching? Absolutely. In Spain, Xavi, [Carlo] Ancelotti and [Diego] Simeone are in charge of the top teams. A guy who's just starting to learn, a guy at the end of his career and a guy who has only one way of playing. It's quite poor compared to what you're getting in England. It's finally spending its money really, really well, because it gets the best coaches, the best in every department (except Man United). Everyone has or is aiming to get the best, professionalise and do the back-office stuff really well. We are lagging behind in Spain.

'Man City and Liverpool aren't there only because of money. Man United had the same money and kept failing through the same mistakes. We'll see how Erik ten Hag gets on but the people taking decisions won't understand fully what he's trying to do. Aligning the people who make decisions and the people who come in to lead teams is crucial. Many clubs have done that, a lot of them have experience from abroad or have listened to people from abroad.'

But money does buy points. Or least it should. I guess it is easier to become a negative outlier by making bad decisions, than a positive one.

Dave Carbery has analysed this, 'If you measure league positions against cost and get a straight line to plot whether a team is up-performing or down-performing, you see Liverpool have impressively been getting more from their transfers. Man United have been exactly the other way round.

'Liverpool spend lots but spend cleverly with a strategy. They do a lot of due diligence on players, how they'll fit in, personality, playing style, age range, whereas instinctively a lot of us feel that Man United are blunderbussing money on to people for t-shirts.'

If you compare the overall cost of squads to performance in the 2021/22 season, Liverpool did best, followed by Tottenham, Brentford, West Ham, Leicester, and Manchester City. Manchester United were bottom, followed by Everton and Norwich. You might remember the criticism of Norwich's playing style from our ex-pros. The Canaries spent lightly by Premier League standards and they either spent it badly, were let down by tactics – or, more likely, a combination of both.

You might not believe competitiveness is king. Or you might not think it is worth paying the price for the changes required to create it. The NFL in America is hugely competitive in terms of who wins it, but clubs accept the rules aimed at levelling the playing field, in the knowledge that there is no relegation.

Fans of top clubs are less likely to embrace any rebalancing. Trophies, prize money and ultimately new supporters gravitate to the rich clubs. English fans with their family and community links are less likely to change allegiance than people in emerging worldwide markets. Surely that is one reason that foreign owners of big clubs don't care about the depth of English football.

Goals

Guillem Balagué asked a fair question: to claim the Premier League is the best in the world you have to know what you want. Goals? We are mid-table. In 2021/22 there were 1,071 at 2.82 per game, which was a single goal less than 2018/19 – but more than the Covid-hit seasons with reduced capacities or empty stadiums. That was better than La Liga (a miserly 951 goals at 2.5 per game in 2021/22). Spanish football is very tactical, lower sides aren't being hammered and referees allow teams to disrupt their opponents' momentum.

If you want goals, watch the Bundesliga where there were 3.12 per game in 2021/22. It had more goals than La Liga, despite having only 306 matches compared to 380 in Spain, England, France, and Italy. If your perceptions are already challenged by La Liga being competitive, then look at the goals per game in Serie A. The Italian top flight has outscored the Premier League by 277 over three years; its goals per game was higher than the Bundesliga in 2020/21. So, in the land of *catenaccio*, the scoring rate went considerably higher in the seasons when attendances were lower. Is the Italian version of this book complaining about there being too many goals?

Bums on seats

It seems that competitiveness isn't the main driver for attendances, at least based on the Bundesliga's popularity in its own country. There were still Covid restrictions in other leagues in 2021/22, so let's take 2018/19, the last full season before the pandemic. The Bundesliga was a clear winner with a hugely impressive 43,445 average gate. The Premier League was second with 38,182 and that figure rose once stadiums were open again to an average of 39,989.

La Liga was a distant third in 2018/19 (26,935). Italy's Serie A's average was 24,931. Ligue 1 was fifth with 22,833. The Championship's average of 20,075 deserves an honourable mention – hugely impressive for a second tier.

Healthy ticket sales are clearly positive but not proof that a league is objectively better. The efficiency of the ticketing process, price and clubs' attitude towards fans are important. People scoff when I suggest that English clubs treat their supporters well but compared to La Liga it is true. We have a £30 price cap on tickets for away supporters; at the end of 2021/22 already-relegated Alavés charged Cadiz supporters €150 for what was a crucial game for them. Rayo Vallecano don't sell tickets online. My Spanish journalist colleagues shrug and say it's 'cultural' but La Liga would get more money for its TV rights if viewers weren't looking at half-empty stadiums. Fans going to games in Spain may feel less commodified than their English counterparts where clubs are far more adroit at parting us from our cash, but here at least the football industry gives the impression it cares whether fans turn up.

The price of watching football in England varies tremendously. Tottenham have the most expensive season tickets, with the priciest costing £2,025. Their least expensive option is £807. Going to see Manchester City is a bargain by comparison. Even after an overall increase in the season ticket prices, City's least expensive season ticket is £350, while the most expensive is at £980. Manchester United have frozen season ticket prices for an 11th consecutive year. They range from £532 to £950. Liverpool's cheapest season ticket costs £685, while the most expensive is £869. It is not just a north-south divide. West Ham reduced their prices for their cheapest season tickets to £299; their most expensive is £1,025, rising from £945 in 2021/22. Wolverhampton is the most expensive place to watch football in the West Midlands. Their cheapest season passes cost £590.

What is the secret to the huge attendances in Germany? A wave of stadium development ahead of the 2006 World Cup put the Bundesliga way ahead of Spain and Italy – and compared to elsewhere, being a German football fan is very cheap.

The *Frankfurter Allgemeine Zeitung* calculated that an average Bundesliga fan could attend 17 home matches, buy a new home shirt, two beers and a bratwurst per game for less than €500 or £428 a season. Bayern Munich supporters can buy a standing season ticket for the Allianz Arena for €145 or £124, which works out at just over £7.29 a match.

The right amount of football on TV

I am biased here, having made a living from reporting and commentating on televised football, but I think football on TV is a wonderful thing. I remember when there were no live televised league games and life was bleaker. I love watching football – Premier League, Championship, Champions League, La Liga, Bundesliga, whatever. If I can get to the stadium all the better but televised football has opened up a world of possibility for watching the greatest sport. It was a tremendous boost that football was on TV when we were told to stay at home for the lockdowns.

I appreciate that progress has come with loss – as the interests of match-going fans are often secondary to needs of TV. It is an obvious failure by a club to get their pricing structure right whenever games are played in front of empty seats – but I think we are in a much better place than before the Premier League existed.

The importance of TV in English football is highlighted by how much of the clubs' revenue came from their broadcast deals in the period covered by the latest Deloitte report: Wolves 87 per cent, West Ham 83 per cent, Leicester 82 per cent, Everton 76 per cent contrasted with Bayern Munich's 42 per cent, PSG's 36 per cent, and Zenit Saint Petersburg 20 per cent. I should note that this period was hit by the pandemic, and West Ham's average attendance in 2021/22 was an impressive 58,370. The gap between the top of Deloitte's Money List and 20th narrowed in the Covid years – having tripled over the previous 15.[13]

The Premier League is superbly run and marketed. The TV coverage is brilliant and highly professional. The widespread use of the English language around the world helps, as do the cosmopolitan playing squads. The Premier League should be protective of its relationship with domestic broadcasters: both the paid platforms, and the BBC. The siren song of streaming services is fraught with danger of exacerbating the lack of competitiveness and leaving a smaller audience. The BBC and ITV can't provide the depth of coverage of Sky Sports and BT; mix-and-match remains the best solution.

Inflation

According to football finance blogger Swiss Ramble, Chelsea's wages were £333m in 2022, which is over six times the £56m bill when Abramovich bought the club. Major rivals have responded: Manchester City's wage bill was £355m, Manchester United's was £323m and Liverpool's £314m. Since 2012 Liverpool's rate of wage growth has been sharper than Chelsea's.

Kieran Maguire of the Price of Football blog writes, 'In its first season, 1992/1993, the Premier League total wage bill for

---

13   Deloitte's and Swiss Ramble's analysis on Twitter

all 22 clubs was just over £97m, with players receiving an average annual salary of £106,000. By 1999 the average Premier League annual salary had increased to £474,000. In 2010, on the back of increasingly lucrative TV deals, the total amount spent on wages had increased to £1.39bn with the average player salary increasing to £1.57m.

'By 2020, the amount spent on Premier League wages has doubled, rising to a staggering £2.8bn spent with the average annual salary in the Premier League, now a mouth-watering £3.79m.'

English clubs could have chosen to use the surge in TV money to literally give away match tickets and merchandise but, of course, they didn't. There is always a rival somewhere to be outspent. Alan Sugar called it 'prune juice economics'.

Magic of the cup

No day in the calendar stirs the nostalgic juices of English football fans like FA Cup third round Saturday. Every interview, TV package, commentary introduction and newspaper article is heavily seasoned with misty-eyed reminiscence. Ronnie Radford, Mickey Thomas, Tim Buzaglo, Roger Osborne, Ian Porterfield, mud, Bovril, sheepskin coats and orange balls. Jumpers for goalposts.

I commentated on Wigan versus Blackburn in 2021/22 and Rovers manager Tony Mowbray was at it, 'When I was a kid the FA Cup used to be the biggest matches of the season culminating in that FA Cup Final with your dad and all his mates with the curtains drawn and the beers flowing and the bacon sarnies. What a day! All the women were out of the room, and it was full of, like, 20 men cheering on a football team. That's how it was when I was a young kid. It felt like a privilege to be in that room with my dad and his mates watching the FA Cup final, but times have changed.'

They have indeed. Just a few decades ago, winning the FA Cup was as big a deal as winning the league. Two main things changed – Premier League riches and TV accessibility. Mowbray was born in 1963 and as a kid would have been able to watch highlights on *Match of the Day*, if he stayed up late, *Sportsnight* seemingly randomly in midweek and, living in the north-east he will have watched *Shoot* on Tyne Tees. We saw hardly any live club football on TV, so FA Cup Final day was thrilling, even the coach rides and the special edition of *Mastermind*. The FA Cup is still important, but its elevated status has gone. My kids will join me to watch the final two minutes before kick-off.

Mowbray's eyes weren't glistening in that press conference. He knows hard-headed modern football has no time for sentiment:

'Are Blackburn Rovers going to win the FA Cup this year with Manchester City, Liverpool, Arsenal, Man United, Tottenham Hotspur, Chelsea – probably not. We'd like to have a good run because that can keep the confidence and the excitement of the fanbase going and you can draw one of those big sides and it's a great day out for the fans.'

But tellingly, he added, 'The most important thing is that there's no replay, so we don't end up with a backlog of fixtures.'

They were chasing promotion to the Premier League which would have meant Mowbray keeping his job and Blackburn keeping their best players. As it was, they lost a thriller at Wigan and faded from the promotion race anyway.

The FA have done a great job of keeping ticket prices relatively low and games are on terrestrial TV. We haven't given up on the FA Cup; it has settled into mid-table status, not unlike cup competitions elsewhere.

The days when big clubs didn't feel they could commit to the League Cup, and we saw victories for Blackburn, Middlesbrough, Birmingham, and Swansea, seem to be gone. The competition has been dominated by the elite and for the last nine seasons it has been won by Chelsea, Manchester City, Manchester United or Liverpool, with City claiming six of those.

Death Star finances

We can have our reservations about finances, playing styles, cynical play and yearn for greater competition, but if people are turning up and tuning in then presumably, they're happy. So why change anything?

Kevin Miles, the chief executive of the Football Supporters' Association, says English football must be mindful of its future wellbeing:

'There are a lot of things you can rejoice about in English football. We're seeing the top players in the world in stadiums that are generally of world-class quality; they're safe, they're comfortable. English football generates so much money that can be invested in the sport, which is great, but it has to be sustainable.

'Football hasn't just been going since 1992 – the FA Cup is 150 years old. There's a long tradition of football through the whole pyramid. Football is not like any other business. The relationship between clubs, which are companies, and the fans, who are customers is not like the relationship between any other commercial enterprise and their customer base.'

Football agent Craig Honeyman might be a less obvious source of caution, but he also believes the success of the Premier League must be shared for the benefit of the game as a whole.

'We need a more sensible approach to how money is distributed from the Premier League,' he told me. 'While I was really disappointed that City got knocked out of the Champions League, people I speak to in Europe were delighted. They didn't want an all-English Champions League Final. They were delighted that Leicester got knocked out of the Conference League and delighted that West Ham got knocked out of the Europa League. They don't want this English dominance because the Premier League has become this Death Star for the rest of Europe and the Football League.'

The scorching heat of top-level competition has been used to justify rule changes in favour of the clubs who have already stacked up every advantage. They always want more. They demand competition changes, such as the restriction of FA Cup replays to help them with fixture congestion. If they want fewer games, they could get knocked out, but this is deemed an affront. Winning the double of Football League and FA Cup was regarded as a magnificent achievement a relatively short time ago. In 2021/22 Liverpool were two games from completing the quadruple and Klopp was still passionately demanding favours with fixture scheduling and extra substitutes. The latter was allowed. The rich clubs have better squads so it should work in their favour; although perhaps hard-running defensive teams might be able to stay fresher and we might see a dip in goal scoring. It will be hard to unpick.

Basket case

Prize money is a problem that can be solved with a little political will. At lower levels it is still a welcome reward for clubs that perform brilliantly but generally, it widens the divide as the same teams dominate in the league, the cups and Europe. They sign better commercial deals, demand bigger shares of broadcast contracts and subsequently hog the prize money, locking in a cycle of reduced competition. In 2020/21 champions Manchester City received £43,287,000 in 'merit' payments from the Premier League; bottom side Sheffield United got £2,164,340. Here 'merit' means using considerably bigger resources to sign better players and finish higher in the league – then get rewarded with a share worth over £41m more than their poorer rival.

Honeyman, who examined the effect of budgets on the success of clubs in the second tier for his master's degree dissertation, highlights the dangerous effect of the lure of Premier League riches:

'The Championship is a complete and utter basket case. If people called in their debts tomorrow, the league wouldn't exist. The majority of debts are to owners. The revised parachute payments of 2017 changed the face of competition in the Championship because if you've survived one season in the Premier League you get three lots of parachute payments that total £100m – at the same time a Championship club is getting £7.9m a year in solidarity payments and TV. How can they compete with clubs that have got vast sums of money and have assets in their squad that they paid for while in the Premier League?'

The figures above for Sheffield United's merit payments don't tell the whole story. One of the strengths of the Premier League has been that a chunk of its broadcast revenue is shared evenly – in 2020/21 that was £84,841,628. Losing that on relegation could be catastrophic for clubs committed to eye-watering player wages. Parachute payments were introduced when the Premier League was formed to help bridge the gap on relegation.

But in 2017, Premier League clubs voted themselves bigger parachute payments and the Championship has suffered since. Sheffield United were paid £46.62m in 2021/22. They will get another £38.17m in 2022/23 – and if they don't go up, they will get another £16.98m the following season – which is 55 per cent, 45 per cent and 20 per cent of their Premier League money.

In 2020, EFL chairman Rick Parry told a parliamentary committee, 'We have six clubs in the Championship receiving parachute payments which means on average they get £40m per club; the other 18 get £4.5m each.'

Craig's study of ten years of Championship spending (2011–2020) and points accumulation showed a massive imbalance:

'Any club that is managed appropriately after relegation should finish in the top six. If they're mismanaged, then it can go wrong. Sunderland and Wolves both got relegated with parachute payments which is a frightening prospect.'

He divided each season's Championship into three tiers of high, middle and low spenders and discovered that only one club – Huddersfield in 2016/17 – were promoted from the bottom eight spenders. A club in the top eight spenders has a 70 per cent chance of promotion over a ten-year period. On six occasions over the ten years, the top spenders were promoted. In 2019/20, Stoke finished 15th having spent £141m for 56 points, an incredible £2.5m per point.

I'm not a Nottingham Forest fan but I was happy when the once-great club returned to the Premier League for the first time this century, even if they had gambled on big wages. That is another problem: clubs such as Bournemouth and Brentford took a chance and went up so they can tuck into the Premier League feast. Others fail and are left teetering on the edge of collapse – such as Derby County who were mismanaged by former owner Mel Morris.

Craig Honeyman advocates a change in financial fair play rules that link spending by EFL clubs to revenue. FFP is designed to stop owners gambling their club's future by putting in money for transfers and wages in the form of loans, which can later be called in. Expenditure therefore has to be linked to income.

'My personal feeling is that if a wealthy owner is willing to put money in that's fine, but that money should be put in in advance,' he argues. 'You could say, "This is your turnover, and you can't spend more than that unless your owner puts up the money." For example, if it's going to be £60m above turnover and you commit to that for three years then the owner puts a £180m bond into the club. That would be sitting on account and couldn't be taken away. At Stoke, the Coates family would be more than willing to put that money into a bond and invest heavily to try to get out of the division and compete with the clubs with parachute payments. What you've got is chairmen overstretching the resources of their clubs to compete with rivals who've got parachute payments and it's going to a leave a huge mess.'

That makes sense. FFP aims to protect clubs from reckless owners, but it restricts the essential oxygen of competition – unless accompanied by significant redistribution of income. Another danger is that FFP doesn't necessarily stop bad practice but punishes it afterwards. Derby were relegated with a 21-point deduction after Morris walked away – 12 for going into administration and a further nine for FFP breaches.

Honeyman thinks football might be pushing its luck too far. He cites companies such as BHS, Staples, Toys "R" Us and Blockbuster that have gone bust while football clubs survive, 'We lost Bury but we've only ever lost a few professional football clubs. They're taken over by a consortium or by fans' groups like Portsmouth, who had that dizzy dream and had to be rescued. They don't disappear; they're invariably rescued but I honestly think there'll be a big club that goes bust, probably in the Championship.'

Jon McKenzie also sees hazards in football's gamblers' paradise:

'If you want elite football played in the best way by probably the best talents the world has ever seen, football is in a good way because we have thrown so much money into the development and understanding the game. It's at that pinnacle.

'But football is essentially a Ponzi scheme at the moment. We need to keep getting bigger and bigger investors to operate the way that we have. Once you hit the Saudi PIF and the UAE, and Qatar there's nowhere else to go. No bigger investors exist. At some point the bubble will bottom out or burst and then I don't know what'll happen.

'In the past, clubs would go bankrupt and supporters would pick up the pieces and take on the debt because it was manageable. If a big club goes bust now who can offset that debt? The fans certainly can't. I wouldn't be surprised if in the next few years, a really big club just hits the pan and that's it. Hopefully that isn't the case, but I do think there'll be a reckoning at some point.

'People in my industry would like to think that smart people will be the ones who survive. There's a lot of uncertainty and everyone likes to pretend things are fine and maybe it will be, but I think a lot is dependent on things not going bad and it won't just be the Burys of the world who suffer.'

Has English football been hijacked?

'I'd rather everyone look and get
excited about football.'

Amanda Staveley, 2022

Has the top flight of English football been hijacked by dirty money? Are the people who own and run clubs alien from the fans, concerned with their own glory and wealth? Or worse, using the beautiful game as a front for ugly regimes?

Some people don't even like the debate and would rather we keep politics out of football. The argument runs that in the modern globalised economy an entity bursting with commercial potential like a Premier League football club can no longer be owned by the archetypal local lad made good. They need people with serious wealth, or access to it. They will hire the sharpest brains across the various departments in which top clubs excel. Without big hitters, England will go back to the late 1980s and early '90s, looking through a grubby window at the best football can offer, revelling in a misguided sense of purity, watching enviously as continental teams win European trophies.

It is not as though other leagues are made up of ethically inspired workers' collectives. Remember when the best club team in the world was AC Milan? That was built by Silvio Berlusconi: billionaire, politician, crook. The so-called fan-owned clubs of Real Madrid and Barcelona are hardly that; power rests with presidents drawn from the ranks of the rich and powerful. Under the stewardship of Josep Bartomeu, Barcelona ran up massive debts despite selling its soul to Qatar. People look enviously at the German model where 50 per cent plus one share must be owned by fans. That has helped keep tickets cheap, but the trade-off has been domination by Bayern Munich and a reduced impact on European competition from the rest.

The golden goose

When Len Shackleton, a winger with Newcastle, Sunderland, and England, wrote his autobiography in 1956 he called a chapter 'The Average Director's Knowledge of Football' – it was a single blank page. That was in the days of the maximum wage when footballers like the great Tom Finney worked as a plumber, and Jimmy Hill swept chimneys, despite playing in front of huge crowds. There was no glory era of perfectly run football clubs.

We moved from top-division clubs being owned by butchers, road hauliers and paternalistic aristocrats, through shiny-suited stockbrokers, to foreign billionaires and nation states. In lower divisions there are still local owners but fans of Bury, Chesterfield, Blackpool and a host of others would tell you that having a chairman with a British birth certificate doesn't guarantee everything is rosy.

The Premier League's mantra when the issue of regulation is raised is, 'Don't kill the goose that laid the golden egg.' A new era dawned when Roman Abramovich bought Chelsea in 2003. The only other foreign owner at the time was Mohammed Al-Fayed who had moved to England decades before he bought Fulham.

Chelsea had a reputation for style over substance. In recent years they had won the FA Cup in 1997 and 2000 and the European Cup Winners' Cup in 1998 but only one league title, in 1955. There were rumours the club might go bust and outside its fanbase there would have been little sympathy, given its past association with hooliganism and its boorish, confrontational chairman Ken Bates. A stream of stars soon arrived, and José Mourinho came from Porto, where he had earned a reputation as the best young coach around. Premier League championships followed in 2005 and 2006. I remember a caller to a radio phone-in arguing the rules would have to be changed or Chelsea would win the title forevermore.

Instead, Manchester United and Sir Alex Ferguson rallied and won four of the next five Premier Leagues, generating substantial revenue that allowed the great manager to regenerate his squad. United had been owned by the Edwards family until it was floated on the stock exchange in 1991, raising what now seems a paltry £6.7m. An attempt by Rupert Murdoch to buy the club met passionate and well-organised fan resistance and was eventually quashed by the government. But the defences had been breached and two Irishmen, best known for their horse-racing operations, John Magnier and J.P. McManus became major shareholders. In a bizarre twist, they became embroiled in a row with Ferguson over the ownership of the racehorse Rock of Gibraltar. The Irish pair began selling shares and in 2005 the club was acquired by American tycoon Malcolm Glazer.

Manchester United had a massive worldwide fanbase, was financially sound and successful on the pitch. Glazer bought it with capital that came mostly from loans, the majority of which were secured against the club's assets. He effectively bought arguably the biggest football club in the world with its own future revenue. Interest payments would cost the club £60m a year. Glazer also used payment-in-kind loans which were eventually paid off in 2010. According to Swiss Ramble, the club still has significant debts resulting from the takeover.

The trophies still arrived while Ferguson was there but after his retirement United underperformed to an extraordinary degree, at least in terms of winning trophies. Off the pitch, United continued to milk its stature and popularity and commercial revenue grew. There was cash for transfers but no effective sporting plan. Manchester United should be fighting Bayern Munich, Real Madrid, Manchester City and Liverpool for the Champions League, not scrapping to even qualify. Thankfully the leveraged buy-out wasn't the future of football – at least until American company ALK took over Burnley in 2020 and loaded debt on to the club.

Abramovich was very different. When UK government sanctions forced him to sell in 2022 after Russia's invasion of Ukraine, he was 'owed' £1.5bn. He had been the most generous owner in the Premier League era – pumping his money into the club's transfer pot. Chelsea also spent fortunes paying off managers sacked by the trigger-happy Russian, but they did win the Champions League in 2012 and 2021, the Premier League five times, the Europa League twice and the FA Cup five times. Some people cite that as evidence that hire-and-fire worked; I believe they would have won the league more often had Abramovich been more patient with his better managers.

Sportswriter Matthew Syed said in 2013 that Abramovich, like other Russian 'oligarchs', made his money in a rigged privatisation in cahoots with the then Russian President Boris

Yeltsin and when Vladimir Putin came to office figured that an international profile would help protect him from reprisals.

'He was never in Chelsea to make a profit ... he bought Chelsea for protection. He knew there was a risk that Putin would come after him – as he had with other oligarchs – for his role in this very dubious business practice under Yeltsin and he knew the best way of protecting himself from being got at by the Russian authorities was to associate himself with a highly visible British asset and he chose Chelsea FC,' Syed told Sky.

Over time, Abramovich's relationship with Putin thawed although he denied there was a close connection. That didn't stop the UK government sanctioning him as part of its crackdown on Russian financial influence after the invasion of Ukraine.

Sportswashing

Another model of elite football club ownership propelled Manchester City from Alex Ferguson's 'noisy neighbours' to perhaps the most feared side in the world. City was listed on a private equity market from 1995 before being bought out in 2007 by the former Thai prime minister Thaksin Shinawatra for £81.6m. City bought new players but finished mid-table in 2008, whereupon Thaksin sold the club to the Abu Dhabi United Group Investment and Development Limited, essentially an arm of the state of Abu Dhabi, for £200m. They immediately broke the British transfer record to sign Real Madrid's Robinho for £32m.

It took a while – and a lot of the regime's fossil fuel receipts – but City have become the dominant club in English football, winning four of the last five Premier League titles up to and including 2022. Players of the quality of Kevin De Bruyne and David Silva came to the Premier League – and in 2012 Sergio Agüero's title-clinching goal provided one of English football's most exciting moments.

City's owners would also point to the development of the area around the Etihad Stadium as evidence of the wider benefit of their presence, although the restaurants, bars and housing have come with rising house prices and rents. An economic system that throws up winners and losers can hardly be blamed on a football club but the flow of Abu Dhabi money through Manchester City hasn't solved any fundamental problems.

City were accused of cheating to get around FFP regulations by disguising owner-investment as sponsorship revenue and in February 2020 given a two-year ban from European competition by UEFA. The European governing body launched its investigation after German newspaper *Der Spiegel* published leaked documents in November 2018. City's lawyers convinced the Court of Arbitration for Sport that UEFA's case was unfair because it used illegally obtained documents that distorted the picture. The ban was overturned and the fine reduced. It was massively important for the club, which would have faced financial turmoil without Champions League revenue to balance against its investment in the team.

Instead, the damage done was to the credibility of FFP. One of the main contenders to win the Champions League had been found guilty but the case hadn't stuck. The conclusion widely drawn was that big clubs with rich owners would employ the best accountants and lawyers to plot a route through any regulations the governing bodies thought up. Football reflecting society. In 2021, City announced the highest revenue in world football, €644.9m. It was an impressive performance for a club that has only the sixth-highest average attendances in the Premier League behind Manchester United, Arsenal, West Ham, Tottenham, and Liverpool.

UEFA has now removed the words 'fair play' and has new 'financial sustainability regulations' that limit the ratio of player wages, transfers, and agent fees to 70 per cent of revenue and profit on player sales. Rich owners will be able to put more money into clubs. Spending on youth football, infrastructure, community, and women's football is no longer exempt from the regulations.[14]

---

14 Swiss Ramble

FFP wasn't without problems. The strongest reservation was that it locked in success for existing big clubs. As UEFA director Andrea Traverso said, 'Competitive imbalance cannot be addressed simply by financial regulations. It must be addressed in combination with other measures.' I fear we will be waiting a long time for significant other measures.

Motives

Did Khaldoon Khalifa Al Mubarak of Dubai grow to love football watching Shaun Goater skating across a muddy pitch at Maine Road? Was Yasir bin Othman Al-Rumayyan inspired by Mirandinha signing for Newcastle in 1987? Or was there some other reason for autocratic Middle East states to buy popular underachieving English football clubs and try to win the Champions League?

The concept of sportswashing is not new: see the 1934 World Cup staged by Benito Mussolini's fascist Italy and the 1936 Olympic Games held in Nazi Germany. The idea is that a damaged reputation – country, company, individual – can be repaired and polished by association with something much-loved and fun. At nation state level, owning a football club can help buy acceptance in democratic, liberal countries for regimes with poor human rights and a history of corruption.

Sacha Deshmukh, Amnesty International UK's CEO, said after the Saudi takeover of Newcastle United, 'We wish Newcastle fans and their team well, but we remain deeply concerned about how our football clubs are being used for sportswashing. Football clubs being purchased for the purpose of trying to distract from serious human rights violations isn't confined to Newcastle, and sportswashing isn't confined to football – but the Saudi takeover has obviously brought the issue of human rights and football governance into sharp relief.

'Despite assurances about a supposed separation from the Saudi state, ownership of St James' Park is now very much about image management for Crown Prince Mohammed bin Salman and his government.'

To be fair to Amanda Staveley, the quote at the beginning of this section is out of context. She said, 'I'd rather everyone look and get excited about football … than be involved in war.'

It's not exactly Mahatma Gandhi but, yes, football is better than war. It does, though, encapsulate the point of sportswashing: don't look here, look there.

Staveley, the private equity investor who fronted the Saudi Arabian takeover of Newcastle and stayed on as part-owner and public face of the club, was speaking at the FT Business of Football Summit in the early days of the 2022 Russian invasion of Ukraine when it had emerged that Abramovich was likely to lose control of Chelsea. It was a sumptuous sermon of amorality, an ode to sportswashing, 'We're always going to have geopolitical issues. The world is never going to not have problems.'

Note the rapid dismissal of moral issues, the shift to the personal and the positive. Her voice showed real emotion when she addressed Abramovich's looming loss, 'I'm really sad today that someone is going to have a football club taken away because of a relationship they may have with someone. I don't think that's particularly fair, actually, to be honest. But I also think that we have to hold all of our relationships to account, and we've also got to remember with Saudi that it's an incredibly big, important country that I love, I love the people there. It is a young vibrant population and I've seen Saudi change so much. And I'm not talking now as Newcastle, I'm talking as me, these are my thoughts because I've really got to know a lot of people and I'm excited but I'd rather everyone look and get excited about football than be involved in war.'

The other 19 Premier League clubs objected to the takeover – ironically including Manchester City – but the government approved the sale. Why wouldn't they, given that British companies had sold over a billion pounds of military hardware to Saudi Arabia during its conflict with neighbouring Yemen?

In with the purchase price sportswashers acquire a private army of defenders who jump to condemn anyone highlighting their practices as bitter or biased. Labour MP Chris Bryant was the most public pursuer of Abramovich after Putin's invasion and received a torrent of abuse.

He tweeted, 'I have never known so much hatred as I have received in recent days from Chelsea fans over the sanctioning of Putin's long-term mate Roman Abramovich. Sorry, but Abramovich washed his dirty money clean through sport.'

On that note, to save me from hassle I should point out that the autocratic Qatari state owns Paris Saint-Germain and has put money into Bayern Munich, Barcelona, Real Madrid, AS Roma and Boca Juniors and, of course, the 2022 World Cup. FIFA also gave the 2018 World Cup to Putin's Russia. Sportswashing is everywhere, not just England and not just football.

I'm not sure the regimes get full value for money. Saudi Arabia's PIF has stakes in a long list of companies including Boeing, Disney, and Facebook. I have no idea when they bought these because it brought nothing like the heat of investing in a football club. They buy British property, shares of British newspapers, they deal directly with democratic governments and individual politicians. Why doesn't that provoke the sort of response the Newcastle takeover did? For example, this paragraph from Amnesty's press release after the completion of the deal brought to wider attention something I had never heard of:

'We hope fans, players and Newcastle United backroom staff will look seriously at the human rights situation in Saudi Arabia and be prepared to speak out about the jailing of people like Abdulrahman al-Sadhan, whose 20-year sentence for tweeting was upheld just hours before the Newcastle deal went through.'

I can understand the cynical reaction of Manchester City and Newcastle fans: it might be wrong to take the money, but another club would have done so. Abu Dhabi is an ally of the UK. British soldiers are embedded in the Saudi army. Arsenal were criticised for signing a sponsorship deal with Rwanda, then the British government signed a much bigger one to send refugees there. Why should football clubs be held to higher moral standards than the government?

The neo-liberos

From the off, the Premier League was about money and control. The UK economy is about as deregulated as you will find. The rich prosper, and we are relaxed about where they or their money came from. The deal is that they drag everyone else up. Failing that, they had better distract us or influence the political system.

Paul Embery, Brexiteer and trade unionist, believes English football's ownership model is simply a reflection of the country, 'It's a symptom of a much wider economic and social phenomenon. Football has been caught in the wash of significant changes in global markets and the fact that now we have a much more liberalised economy and capital is able to flow around the world more and more. It's a symptom of that, which has upsides but considerable downsides as well.

'It's not only football that's been sold off. We've seen our utilities sold off; we've seen large parts of our manufacturing base sold off. It speaks to a wider debate about whether we want any sort of national economy, whether as a society we're quick enough to recognise the downsides of that neo-liberal approach with the liberalisation of capital and the effect it has on global wealth inequality for example, environmental standards, democracy. I don't think it's something that football can fight on its own.

'I think it's as much of a shame that we don't own vast chunks of our own railway network, for example which is owned by foreign investors.'

The last English-owned club to win the Premier League was Arsenal in 2004 in the days of Peter Hill-Wood, who inherited his shares from his father, who got them from his father before him. His friend and fellow director Sir Roger Gibbs had been a class-mate at Eton. Another director was Sir John Chippendale Lindley Keswick, another old Etonian and merchant banker known as 'Chips'. These weren't the lads from the North Bank, but Embery retains a fondness for the days of the old-school-tie brigade:

'My brother is an Ipswich fan, and they used to be owned by old-school owners the Cobbold family who owned the Greene

King Brewery. They were doing it for the love of the club and the connection with the area. They weren't in it for the money, to make a fast buck and they took this small provincial backwater club to UEFA Cup winners.

'It always brings a bit more if you can have owners who are doing it for the right reasons, and they invest in local talent. When it's so commercialised, as it has become now, and people decided to own a football club almost as a plaything, it takes the sheen off.'

The not-so Super League

When you are in the business of persuading people that you should get to keep your incredible wealth and privilege, it is never wise to overplay your hand. Yet in April 2021 the 'big six' English clubs acted with uncharacteristic oafishness when they announced they intended to form a European Super League with Real Madrid, Barcelona, Atlético Madrid, Juventus, Inter and AC Milan. They hadn't spent time buttering us up, they had no broadcast deal in place, no loquacious advocates in the media and the launch itself was ham-fisted with no public face other than a rambling TV appearance from Real Madrid president Florentino Pérez. He argued that the Premier League's wealth distorted European competition and forced their rivals to take dangerous risks or drop out of contention for trophies. The proposal was received with less hostility in Spain where there is a greater concentration of support for the two giant clubs.

In England it was met with fury and derision. There were Covid restrictions in place, but fans turned up in great numbers to protest outside grounds. A Chelsea fan's placard caught the mood, 'We want our cold nights in Stoke.' Supporters and commentators made it clear they valued the English league most. Champions League nights are fun, but our fandom is rooted in domestic rivalry.

The lack of relegation in the ESL proposal touched a raw nerve: American sport has many qualities but the lack of fear of going down – or hope of going up – robs sport of half of its narrative. At the time, Manchester United, Arsenal and Spurs were looking far from super – and Juventus were in a run of being knocked out of the Champions League by Ajax, Lyon, Porto, and Villarreal, none of whom were deemed worthy of the ESL. At other times, Nottingham Forest, Aston Villa, Hamburg, and Steaua Bucharest might have been considered part of the elite, too important to fail.

The English clubs felt the burn and quickly distanced themselves from a project they hadn't even bothered advocating for. It made little sense for them anyway. The first part of Perez's argument was sound – the English do have a huge advantage. Why would they walk away from the source of their power – a domestic competition able to command massive broadcast fees, foreign investment, and packed stadiums? It showed that the people who run the richest, most powerful English clubs didn't care about Englishness. Their presence here is transactional and if there was more money to be made uprooting to Asia or America then off they would go.

The Spanish and Italian clubs haven't given up on the concept and I wouldn't be surprised for it to come back as a Southern European proposal designed to take on the might of the Premier League. The incompetent launch was even more baffling when you consider UEFA was already in the process of kowtowing to the richest clubs with an expanded Champions League. If the ignominious failure of the ESL gave UEFA a strong hand against the greediest clubs, it hasn't chosen to play it.

Happy fans

Fascinating research by Sporting Intelligence for the *Mail on Sunday*, published in March 2022, revealed that most fans of Premier League clubs were opposed to clubs being run by nation states, wealth funds and oligarchs but club bias shone through brightly. Winning football matches matters.

Eighty-five per cent of the nearly 11,000 who responded supported the appointment of a regulator but, no surprise, fans of Manchester City and Newcastle were most opposed. This is a real block on cleaning up the ownership and running of the sport. Imagine if the chief candidate for the regulator's job says he or she doesn't think owner-funding of clubs is a problem and they should be allowed to put in as much money as they want – now how would Manchester City and Newcastle fans respond? Is there such a thing as a truly independent regulator – or would they come with their own set of biases?

The fans were also generally happier with the owners of their clubs than would surely be the case lower down the leagues. Brentford's Matthew Benham was the most liked by his club's fanbase, no surprise given that he is a fan and under his leadership they climbed from League One to the Premier League. The next most popular English owner was Brighton's Tony Bloom – an old colleague of Benham's until they fell out. Norwich's Delia Smith was tenth, despite the Canaries being bottom of the league at the time. Being English doesn't guarantee popularity – West Ham's joint owners David Sullivan and David Gold were 17th; the unpopular move away from Upton Park was at play here. Premier League fans don't object to foreign ownership as a matter of principle – although I would suggest local owners are given more leeway. No prizes for guessing that the least popular owners among their own fanbase were the Glazers.

The Premier League fans surveyed were largely unmoved about fans involvement on boards; given a chance to make suggestions, only five per cent raised that as an issue. Meaningful, properly enforced FFP was the top concern and in third place was the related topic of owner-funding hidden as sponsorship. Supporters wanted robust and effective fit and proper persons' tests. Others called for a regulator to impose limits on cash withdrawals by owners from clubs; caps on ticket prices; gambling and crypto product bans; protections to stop stadiums being sold; a ban on the stockpiling of players outside first-team squads and caps on agents' fees. It is worth stressing the survey was of Premier League fans – which I think accounts for the issue of fair distribution of broadcast revenue figuring only tenth on the list of concerns.

Les Ferdinand wasn't the only person who made the point about fans' expectations of clubs spending money:

'Let's get it right, it's not just the managers, if you're a fan of Man City, Arsenal, Tottenham, any of these big teams in the Premier League, you're not happy with us saying, "We'll bring a youngster through the system."

'The supporters' mindset is that if we're not spending 50, 60, 70 million on some players then we're not competing. Every now and again we can bring a young player through, and they say, "yeah", but I know if he's not good enough they'll want us to go and spend 60, 70 million. We need to change that mindset.'

Agents

Erling Haaland's move from Borussia Dortmund to Manchester City in the summer of 2022 came with a £51m transfer fee and a £34m agent's fee. If you think those proportions are wrong, then the man who designed the deal would have agreed with you. Only the late Mino Raiola argued that it was the transfer fee between clubs that was the strange part.

Sadly, the Dutch-Italian superagent died before the carefully planned deal for the explosive Norwegian striker was finalised and it was left to his partners to collect the cash. Haaland and his dad Alfie were quids in too. Dortmund had little cause for bitterness having got 89 games and 86 goals from a player who would probably have gone to a richer club two and a half years earlier had the inventive deal not been struck. Manchester City got one of the outstanding young players in the world for £85m in transfer and agent fees – madness in the normal world but cheaper than Paul Pogba, Romelu Lukaku and Jack Grealish.

FIFA's new proposals for regulating agents would outlaw such a deal. They want a ten per cent cap on what the agents representing buying clubs and player can receive from any transfer, limits on what those acting on behalf of selling clubs could also make from deals and on rewards to family members, unless they are an agent.

They also want to set up a clearing house through which all transfer payments would go. The governing body would like their new rules to be in place by 2023/24 – some very wealthy agents plan to make them dance through the courts first.

Few people would argue against reform. Some years ago, FIFA effectively gave up and the system has been a mess since. Raiola was reportedly paid £41m when Pogba moved from Juventus to Manchester United for £89m in 2016. United allowed the Frenchman to leave for free in 2012 and again in 2022. It is hard for football to plead poverty when it comes to supporting grassroots and lower-league clubs.

According to FA figures published late in March 2022, in the period including the summer of 2021 and January 2022, so not including the Haaland deal, Manchester City spent £35m on agents. Manchester United paid out £29,036,141, Chelsea £28.2m, Liverpool £22,136,224, Arsenal £18,652,818 and Tottenham £13,938,231. Watford paid agents £12,593,435 on their way to relegation – no doubt grateful for parachute payments to come. The average for spending between the 20 Premier League clubs was £13.6m. Brentford were the lowest spenders at just under £3.5m.

In the Championship, Fulham were by far the biggest spenders on agent fees at £10.2m with West Brom next at £4.1m. Sheffield United, Bournemouth and Stoke spent over £3m and Nottingham Forest were sixth – with fees of £2,388,090.

Most of Craig Honeyman's clients are at EFL level and he prides himself on positive long-term relationships with players and clubs, but he agrees there is bad practice around:

'In some cases, the criticism is fair. It's like any industry, builders, plumbers, or anything. There are good and bad. There isn't a TrustPilot for agents, so we all get tarred with the same brush.

'There are some great people in my industry. There are some smart, considerate people but there are also some truly awful people and sometimes they give all of us a bad name. The media play a part. The greedy agent line comes out time and again.

'My worry about the potential independent regulator is that agents are an easy target and sadly we're not protected by being in the EU anymore, so our government can do whatever the hell they want.'

Honeyman insists there is nothing fundamentally wrong with agents working in football:

'Recruitment agents and estate agents get paid a percentage that's much higher than a football agent. Some recruitment agents get paid 17 per cent of someone's annual salary for placing them in a job. Recruitment agencies work in football and they're putting in chief executives, sporting directors and chief medical officers and no one talks about them.'

Before he was an agent Honeyman worked in human resources and remembers coming off worse in negotiations with experienced trade union shop stewards, but he doesn't think the players' union, the PFA, can properly represent their clients in the high-rolling world of modern football:

'When clubs, players and agents are aligned things run incredibly smoothly but if one of those parties is out of line, it can all tumble down quickly. Players need agents through good times and bad.

'If things are going smoothly, they need agents to negotiate deals to make sure they're getting their market worth. If they're moving to another club, they need guidance and, let's be honest, clubs use agents to move players they don't want. Agents are engaged to move a player and clubs pay handsomely for moving assets that have become liabilities.'

The Premier League has been the richest in world football for a long time but until recently that wasn't reflected in trophies won. I wondered whether that was partly down to haphazard recruitment.

'I think that's fair, to a certain extent,' said Honeyman. 'One of the issues we have is the "Premier League tax". I dealt with a La Liga club who wanted to sell a player but the price for a Premier League club was £10m higher than if he went to Serie A or the Bundesliga. How is that right in the world? They say they'd be short-changing themselves if they sold him to the Premier League at the same price as elsewhere.'

Remember Lucas Pérez? His hometown club Deportivo La Coruña paid around €1m to sign him from Greek side PAOK in 2015. He had one full season at Depor and scored 17 goals in La Liga and there was speculation he was about to sign for Valencia for €8m. The next thing I knew, Arsenal paid £17m. He had one season with the Gunners before being loaned back to Depor and was eventually sold to West Ham for £4m. How on earth did those negotiations go?

Honeyman says the better-run English clubs are less of a soft touch now, although there is no way round paying heftier fees than continental rivals:

'The way Liverpool manage their ins and their outs has been very smart. City and Chelsea have historically spent vast sums of money and then you've got the middling clubs that still spend. Look at Brighton; if that was, say, Ajax bidding, they wouldn't pay the same fees for the same players.

'It's a lot less wild west now, there's a lot more information, more transparency but English clubs in the top two divisions still spend considerably more than anybody else because the Premier League have such vast sums.'

Fan-led review

The government seized on the spirited opposition to the European Super League shambles and announced a fan-led review of English football, albeit one that was driven by a Conservative MP. Tracey Crouch and her panel did speak to supporters' groups and none of the football governing bodies or leagues had a veto. Crouch, an FA level one qualified coach, wrote the report. This is how it starts:

'I believe there is a stark choice facing football in this country. Build on its many strengths, modernise its governance, make it fairer and stronger still at every level, or do nothing and suffer the inevitable consequences of inaction in towns and cities across the country – more owners gambling the future of football clubs unchecked, more fan groups forced to mobilise and fight to preserve the very existence of the club they love and inevitably more clubs failing with all the pain on communities that brings. As was remarked to the review, clubs are only one bad owner away from disaster.

'For those who say that English football is world leading at club level and there is no need to change I would argue that it is possible simultaneously to celebrate the current global success of the Premier League at the same time as having deep concerns about the fragility of the wider foundations of the game. It is both true that our game is genuinely world leading and that there is a real risk of widespread failures and a potential collapse of the pyramid as we know it. We ignore the warning signs at our peril, and I hope this review protects the good and the special but sets a clear course for a stronger national game with the interests of fans at its heart.'

If the report is implemented there would be three main ways to guarantee fan involvement in the running of clubs:

Golden share
This would essentially be a veto on heritage issues. Remember Hull City's proposed name change, Cardiff's red shirts and, more egregious, Wimbledon being moved to Milton Keynes? The existence of the golden share would hopefully result in it never being used.

Shadow boards
These would be representative of the fanbase and would have regular contact with the people who run the club.

Independent director
Without power, shadow boards might become blown-up fans' forums, so clubs have to appoint at least one director to consider supporters' interests.

The interconnected nature of the recommendations makes sense when you consider the EFL's argument that 25 per cent of broadcast revenue should go to its 72 clubs. Well-run Premier League clubs could reasonably baulk at being asked to send money to the likes of Derby when they were under Mel Morris's stewardship. Fairer distribution of TV revenue has to come with better governance and ownership tests. It is reasonable to ask exactly who the money is being shared with.

This would all be overseen by an independent regulator chosen by a government-appointed panel. In practice, OFCOM, OFSTED etc aren't immune from political pressure but it is important to try. There was opposition from the Premier League, as you would expect. Angus Kinnear of Leeds United was widely mocked after he described the proposals as 'Maoism'.

I was sceptical when I first saw the report because there had been reviews of football governance before and nothing significant changed. After all, if you want nothing to happen, commission an inquiry. But after speaking to the FSA's Kevin Miles, I am more optimistic.

'There are two or three key differences this time,' he said. 'Firstly, this was fan-led. There was a panel of experts from around the game, but the evidence was driven by supporters' groups. I think we heard 130 hours of evidence and getting on for 100 hours of that came from supporters' groups from up and down the country and throughout the pyramid, pulled together by the FSA.

'In the past these processes were trying to find solutions everybody could agree to. In practice that meant that you either end up with split reports or a lowest common denominator consensus.

'There have been plenty of examples that show the regulatory regime we've currently got isn't adequate so this time action will the taken. The regulator will be there and if football gets its act together then fine, but if it doesn't the powers will already exist to do something about it. Football will be independently regulated by statute and that is a departure.'

Labour criticised the review panel composition with the reasonable point that only Miles was a fan representative, so he set himself a four-stage task:

'I had four very broad-brush tests against which I measured the outcome: 1. Would it prevent another European Super

League breakaway? 2. Would it prevent another Bury, part of the professional pyramid, going bust? 3. Would it provide for a fairer distribution of money with investment into grassroots games? 4. Would it provide an audible voice for supporters at all levels of the game?'

He thinks the proposals met his target and insists the crucial task now is for the whole package to be implemented, not broken up or watered down.

'It's not an a la carte menu; the parts are interdependent. If we see the whole thing implemented, that would build on and not jeopardise the successes the professional game has seen in past decades.

'It should mean that communities aren't at risk of losing their football club because it has been run in an unsustainable way. It should take out the mad casino gambling of the Championship where clubs are spending 200 per cent and more of their turnover on wages in an unsustainable gamble to try to get into the Premier League. Clubs are one change of ownership away from disaster, or an owner running out of money or interest from collapse.

'It should allow for a greater distribution of money, a greater investment in grassroots, the women's game and elsewhere, but it should also celebrate the successes we've had in English football. There's a lot to be proud of.'

Miles is hopeful that Crouch will be able to persuade her fellow Conservative MPs that their jobs could depend on keeping football fans onside:

'People talk about "our" club, and it's not because you own it, it's because it's part of your identity. They have a huge role to play in cultural identity and community fabric. It's not like any other industry, so it has got to be sustainable. Chelsea owed £1.5bn to Roman Abramovich personally, so on average he loaded £80m of debt per annum on to the club. That is completely unsustainable without him. You can't have a situation where a club as important to the country as Chelsea is at risk at the whim of one owner.

'At a time when there's more money in the game than ever there's more danger of financial crises than ever. Look at Derby, going absolutely to the brink over their unrealistic spending. That's built into the system of how the money is distributed, how performance is rewarded, the structures of the leagues. We want a successful game, but we want a sustainable game.'

But agent Craig Honeyman doesn't like the idea of an independent regulator:

'I read the review. There were 16,600 participants and the questions were incredibly leading – asking if the current regulator is fit for purpose, without explaining what the FA actually does. No one ever says the FA have invested this much into children's football or doing great work in women's football. All I read is more and more negativity, and that's what the punters are picking up on.

'Tracey Crouch might be brilliant, but she's an MP representing a party, so she has to toe a party line. I'm not in favour of a lot of it. If that regulator was one of the finest legal and financial minds in the country then bring it on but if it's self-serving politicians, no thank you. If it's Gary Neville, no thank you.

'People don't understand the relationship between the FA and the Football League. The FA was for rules and regulation. The league was set up for a competition. Everything should come under one umbrella from a governance point of view which should be the FA. We don't need another body. It needs modernising like any other organisation, but if you filled the FA with fantastic legal and business minds, got an unbelievable business-minded chief executive and said, "Go and govern football; these are the aims" – you could let them get on with it.'

I disagree with Craig here. I think there has been a lack of clarity in the FA's role since the Premier League broke away from the Football League in 1992. It is a governing body but also a commercial organisation. A virtual free-for-all in English football has had its positives with a rich league attracting global talent, but it has come with built-in dangers.

Premier League clubs are missing the point when they argue against regulation. Sport is, by definition, regulated play. In the 'real' economy, a mid-sized business that over-performed like Leicester City in 2015/16, would have been bought by Manchester

City or more likely PSG or Chicago Fire. Coca-Cola owns Fanta, Sprite, Dr Pepper, Monster Energy, Relentless Energy, the list goes on. If Angus Kinnear thinks it is Maoism to have football clubs, cornerstones of our communities for longer than any of us has been alive, regulated and protected he should remember that they already are. Games are 11-a-side, no matter how big your budget is. There is a strong correlation between resources and league positions, but the laws of football mean each game at least kicks off with hope for the underdog. Football should be mindful of the deep desire among fans, and by extension broadcasters, for genuine competition. The Premier League was built on more than a century of English football.

The Premier League may yet mount a successful rearguard action against the review's proposals, but that would be a short-term win that undermines its own strength. Marcelo Bielsa didn't master the English language in nearly four years in Leeds, but he got a decent grasp on the soul of English football.

He was asked about the short-lived, ill-fated Project Big Picture, in which Liverpool and Manchester United's owners suggested giving financial aid to the EFL clubs struggling in the Covid pandemic, in return for a smaller Premier League.

'If anything describes English football it is League One and League Two,' Bielsa said. 'As a spectator of football in this country, I feel these two categories have the essence of English football. If there is anything to distinguish English football, it is the spirit you compete with. This spirit is no better represented than in these lower categories.'

Project Big Picture soon died unloved. Bielsa understood English football better than the American owners of two of its most historic and best-loved clubs:

'With any structure, we can't interpret it without looking at its history and Leagues One and Two are a description of what English football was in its essence in the beginning. It's the nucleus, the heart, the essence of football in this country. This is a view of mine and perhaps I am wrong, but it is important you do not forget the history of where you came from.'

9

Grassroots

LET'S FINISH at the bottom. There was rumble of discontent during the last Euros at England fans singing 'Three Lions'. The line 'It's coming home' is apparently now interpreted as arrogance by fans elsewhere. I doubt many people are really agitated but those who are should grow up. The line is clearly a historical reference to the indisputable fact that Englishmen invented modern football. No one claims England's national team has been a roaring success over the years. One World Cup won on home soil before most of us were born is paltry. Brazil, Germany, Italy, France, Spain, Argentina and Uruguay have won more major tournaments than we have! We're overdue.

But we have two claims to be the greatest football nation. The Premier League is the best in the world, depending on what you value, and there is more depth to English and Welsh football than any other country.

Average attendances in the National League in 2021/22 were 3,191 – that's non-league football, the fifth tier. In November 2021, 12,843 people watched Notts County versus Solihull Moors. Four teams in the National League averaged more than Empoli who finished 14th in Italy's top division. Wrexham averaged more than four clubs in Serie A, two in Ligue 1, Rayo Vallecano in La Liga and Greuther Furth in the Bundesliga.

It goes deeper still – two regional divisions at the second tier of non-league and another four steps of the football pyramid below that. If I'm free on a Saturday, I might watch Oxford

City in National League South or Didcot Town in the Southern League Division One Central. I wish I could find the man who shouted, 'Have the confidence to kick it long!' when a Didcot player passed the ball across his own defensive line in the derby against Wantage Town. For the 2022/23 season Didcot will be in the same division as two teams from Biggleswade, neither of which is Guillem Balagué's Biggleswade United who are in the Spartan South Midlands. Biggleswade has a population of 21,000.

'I can't get enough of it,' Guillem told me. 'I did my UEFA B badge and wanted to see if I could apply the stuff I was hearing. Someone said to me, "If you think you know about football, prove it."

'We went from two teams to four senior sides and an academy. Once I saw so many people with such a connection, it was a hook. I give more to it than anything else and I get much more from it than I put in. That can only happen in England. The depth of feelings at the last game of the season, the depth of emotion throughout my time at Biggleswade, you just don't get anywhere else.'

Not everything is rosy. When I interviewed Tony Gale, he was the chairman of Southern League Premier Division South Walton Casuals and he told me about his 17 years at the club. Then they folded. Essentially, Tony had run out of energy after so many years of finding sponsors and volunteers. It was debt-free, and he was only willing to pass it on to someone who would run it on the same basis.

'People talk about money trickling down from the Premier League to the Championship, but no one talks about it trickling down to the grassroots,' Tony said. 'When you think how much goes on an agent, it's unbelievable – it could keep leagues and leagues of non-league clubs going for years. The money coming into the game is good, the way it goes out of the game isn't.'

I asked Tony how he felt giving up a project to which he had devoted so much and worked on with his son who was the team manager:

'Relieved because it was a lot of work. But flat as well because it was 17 years and we'd just had our best season ever. I suppose it was a good time because it would've been hard to replicate that without significant money coming in.'

Walton Casuals played in a council-owned stadium so had no bar receipts – the lifeblood of many a British sporting club. They intend to keep their academy going, confident that it is easier to get corporate backing for youth projects than for men's non-league football.

I asked Tony whether the football community does enough for non-league:

'Absolutely not. It's a scandal. The prize money for the cup competitions keeps being cut year in year out. Non-league suffers and obviously the big boys get their money. I know I earn my money from my commentaries in the Premier League but there should be a filter down into non-league. It's important for the country, for people's wellbeing and community. It's not all about the big boys in the Premier League. I've been part of that, but lower down the scale is so important.

'The people who play football also watch Premier League games and because we've got so many non-league teams, Sunday morning football and all that, our supporters generally have a better understanding of football than anywhere else. That's why when we go to World Cups, European Championships, so many of the fans are British because we love our football. It starts from the bottom all the way up to the top, so the bottom mustn't be forgotten.'

I asked Jon McKenzie whether the scientific developments funded by Premier League wealth have a trickledown effect to the rest of the football community:

'A lot of what is happening at the top has so much money pumped into it that the clubs at the bottom can only try to mirror it. There will be some trickledown, but we know that trickledown economics is largely a myth and I suspect the same is probably true in football.

'The big clubs forget about how important grassroots football is. You see the European Super League and the desire by the big clubs to hoard everything for themselves and part of me thinks those clubs cannot live without the grassroots. The elite sides think they can; they think they're responsible for all the good things in football but they're not.

'You need players being developed at every level and maybe in this country you've lost that grassroots development compared to, for example, Germany where you play for your local club and if you play well you move to a bigger club and then a bigger area and you're slowly funnelled up.

'English clubs are looking to hoover up talent but without grassroots football, you don't have a clue who's the best. You can't run that sort of operation top-down. You're dependent on the clubs at the bottom to get the kids to a level where you can start deciding who are the best ones. Anything that threatens the health at the bottom of the pyramid will start to affect the health at the top.'

The professional game often talks about youth football in terms of the talent it could potentially supply, but that is a tiny fragment of the benefit of kids playing the game. Youth football gets a bad write-up from the media, and we usually only hear about it in the context of bad behaviour. The truth is that football has created a wonderful cross-generational community network that is hard to rival in any other walk of life.

Winning nothing with kids

Architect Darren Blake coached Tynemouth United under-nines through to under-17s. He got into it via the most common route, making sure his son had a team. The existing coach decided to streamline the squad and create an 'elite' focused on winning trophies – a 'mini Mourinho' as they're known.

Darren's son was 'streamed out' so he faced the classic dilemma – take it on or let it fail. He joined forces with his mate Phil, a data analyst no less, and coached the 'waifs and strays' for eight years.

'They loved it, but they weren't very good footballers,' Darren said. 'Half of them couldn't kick a ball straight but you could see the potential and for me that was the enjoyment. They'd been rejected, but they loved playing football and we wanted to capture that love in an environment that nurtured them.'

The FA has a curious job, looking after senior England teams who are trying to win the World Cup while nurturing clubs like Tynemouth United under-nine seconds, who, let's be honest, are probably not packing future internationals. The FA's coach education emphasises a positive environment. That is wise; the adults should be supportive, while the kids are as competitive as suits them. They would be delighted with Darren's outlook:

'We concentrated very much on enjoyment. Every kid got about the same game time and if we lost it didn't matter. And we lost a lot. In a list of priorities, that was about number ten. The main things were fun, learning about the game, developing as kids, and being sporting – trying to progress but in a gentle supportive way.

'Our league had two divisions and we finished near the bottom of the Second Division nearly every year for about five seasons. We'd lose 10-0 or 8-0 and occasionally come up with a good result, maybe a draw against a team we'd previously lost to or edge a win against one of the weaker sides and it begun to get better and better. One of the nicest things was coaches saying to me, "You can see you're doing the right things, stick with it because they'll get better." And season upon season, we edged up the league. By under-13s, under-14s we were threatening promotion and winning more than we were losing.'

Of course, it is possible to have a positive, progressive environment and play direct football. There is no automatic correlation between a supportive attitude and possession-based play although Darren's experience on Tyneside suggests football culture has changed:

'Most teams were trying to play possession-based football, playing from the back, drawing players on, breaking the lines to move progressively up the pitch. Rarely did you see a team playing direct – that old English style of game really, really wasn't there. Over the nine seasons, we played two or three teams playing that way. Some were more direct than others, but we adopted a philosophy of trying to play through the lines, keeping the ball to feet, keep the skill level high and creating chances. It took a long time but ultimately it paid dividends and they got better. Sometimes they'd score a goal that resulted from the goalkeeper passing out, had about nine or ten passes and finished with a tap-in for a striker and you'd think, "Yeah! It worked!"'

But it is not all like that. I recently spent a weekend at a grassroots tournament watching dozens of teams play frantically in eight-minute slots, firing the ball forward on hard, bobbly, sloping pitches. Long passes weren't working, and they didn't know how to mix it up. Coaching direct football is easy. If you find round pegs for round holes, you can have a competitive team comparatively quickly – the effort to reward ratio is reasonable for busy people. No one I spoke to for this book advocated that – the debate is over how much you emphasise players' ability to adapt their style of play.

In 2021/22 I saw a team superbly equipped for playing downhill, largely thanks to a goalkeeper who could shell the ball a prodigious distance. They did everything but shout 'charge' as they chased down the slope. But they needed work on their uphill tactics, judging by how they unravelled in the second half. In the Junior Premier League, which I describe as an academy league for non-league clubs, most teams play the football Darren describes. I must point out that the team at the beginning of the book wasn't his. It was a lower-division grassroots team and a JPL side, one of whom, I maintain, should have adapted their way of playing.

A report by Utilita published in the summer of 2022 found that 2,600 grassroots clubs had folded in 12 months. Another 6,000 felt they were at risk. The *Price to Play* report asked 1,000 parents of footballers aged five to 16 how the pandemic and the cost-of-living crisis had affected their kids' teams. The northeast was the worst hit area. It painted a bleaker picture than I expected; in my experience children's football is considerably healthier than the men's grassroots game. That was Darren's view as well:

'I think that's fairly evident. Kids teams are well run. Tynemouth United are based at a local comprehensive school with seven or eight pitches for matches and training, and an indoor gym for winter training. We had dedicated cabins for kit and the area was fenced off. The only gripe was people walking their dogs but that's nothing new to English football – removing dog shit is a rite of passage. Parental support was always strong, the younger the kids, the stronger the support.

'One big challenge was managing parents' expectations. Obviously, their kid is the best player, and should be playing all the time. We always tried to make sure everyone was treated reasonably. It's a juggling act. It was all about communicating your philosophy.'

Unfortunately, Darren's team didn't survive the lockdowns. A combination of 'postponements, illness and girls' meant they couldn't sustain it. Darren is an old friend of mine – we were at the same university and played a lot of football together. I didn't purposefully seek out people whose sides had folded but coincidence had it that two of the interviewees in this chapter had that experience.

The unbeautiful game

If it is tough to sustain kids' teams, with eager parents who drive them around, still harbouring the hope their child might one day be as good as Timo Werner and earn £271,000 a week, imagine running a men's grassroots team through a pandemic and cost-of-living crisis.

Jon Walton is another friend of mine, a senior assistant producer at Sky Sports and player-manager of Jeff's Chippy in the Central London Super Sunday League. Chippy were formed in 1997 by a group of Sheffield exiles who named the club after an old sponsor from their youth football days.

They played at Clapham Common, but the pitches were a mess, so they moved to the Dulwich Sports Ground. In 2021/22, Jon's first season in charge, they finished fourth, as CSKA Clapham won the league. Beaujolais Fun Boys finished bottom, which doesn't sound like fun. At least one of the 14 teams in the league has folded and when we spoke Jon was afraid one or two others might go. The season was still a success because they got to the end with almost every game played after two disrupted years.

'The standard varies massively in our team and in the league,' he admits. 'Our best 11 is very good, nowhere near semi-pro but decent Sunday league level but because we've been struggling for numbers, we've had to get loads of players off Gumtree and it's a lottery. We got a lad who didn't know how to take a throw-in. The team that won the league are very good, but their oldest player is 26. Our oldest player this season was 50, and our oldest regular is 41.

'The main challenge is getting players to commit. We've had 26 league games and play in two cups so that's 30 weekends to get 11 players, ideally 14. Last season we used 42 players.'

There was a time when men's Sunday league football was a central feature of the English landscape. In the 1950s and '60s there were 120 football pitches on London's famous Hackney Marshes. Not so now.

'We've played at Hackney Marshes four times this season and there have been a handful of games, maybe ten or 12, going on. Most of the pitches aren't being used,' said Jon.

So why, with English football booming in so many ways, is something so integral to it struggling to keep its head above water? Jon can't identify a single cause:

'The growth of five-a-side is one. Everyone we try to sign plays five-a-side in the week. It's very accessible. You could play every night if you want. Grass pitches are terrible on the whole. Would you rather play on a 4G carpet or on dodgy Clapham Common with potholes and mud?

'Running costs are crazy; £40 for a referee is fair, but in Dulwich a pitch is £120 so that's £160 a home game. We charge £10 subs to a starter and £5 for a substitute, so we lose money on home games but make it up when we're away.'

Once upon a time we were told the Premier League would send five per cent of its revenue into the grassroots of the game

– imagine! It would be wrong to say none of the wealth has been shared – you see a lovely clubhouse here and there, but overall it has been pitiful. While grassroots football relies on rundown council facilities it is doomed to struggle.

In 2021, the FA launched a grassroots strategy called 'Survive, Revive, Thrive' and one of its aims is to 'deliver 5,000 quality pitches'. The body described the plan as ambitious. I would say confusing. Too many things are crammed under the grassroots umbrella and the FA has too many problems to solve. The old-fashioned idea of men playing on a Sunday with and against people from their local area is low on the list. I hope I'm wrong.

Pitch quality massively influences playing style and if we do get a network of wonderful 4G surfaces around the country it will change English football further. I haven't played 11-a-side football for years, and I am always eager to hear from Jon about how the fashions at the top of the game filter into Sunday league.

Jon explained, 'For the first five seasons I was at Jeff's Chippy we played 4-4-2 and I always thought we were relying far too much on individual brilliance from a striker because it was so rigid. But you've got lads turning up who haven't played 11-a-side for years and they know what they're doing in a 4-4-2.

'When I took over, I spent a lot of time thinking about it, bought a tactics board off eBay and tried to make us go 3-5-2. For the first friendly I tried to explain the theory behind it. We'd play out from the back, because we had three centre-backs who could play and the wing-backs would give us width so we could play into the channels that way and keep the ball, while obviously maintaining some stability.

'It was a disaster, an absolute disaster. I'd done the research, but I didn't really know where I was playing in a back three. The wing-backs didn't have a clue whether to push on or go with their runners which they've always done. The midfielders were on the defenders' toes and the strikers were totally isolated. It was a disaster so I switched back to 4-4-2 because everyone would know what they're doing. I felt a bit stupid for trying to force a style on everyone.

'But later we went through a tricky patch – mainly due to availability. In three consecutive games we got completely played off the park. It was the first time I'd ever lost three in a row, and I was the manager now, so I had to think of something to make us more solid. So, we went 4-5-1 to make us more solid. The extra person in midfield helps massively in terms of keeping the ball and defensively it's another person to help when we're trying to win it back.

'One team in our league played 3-5-2 but they play on a college's massive 4G pitch and it obviously suited their style. On the whole people still play 4-4-2 although in recent years more teams have been playing one up front – which becomes incredibly easy as a centre-back to be honest.'

Jon is also a Carlisle United fan who has watched in despair as League Two defences interpret the Cruyff-inspired football we see at the top. Note: he stressed to me later that he regards Keith Curle as a legend:

'In previous years under Keith Curle, we tried to play out from the back, but we really forced it. We had a keeper who wasn't confident on the ball, centre-halves and full-backs who might say they want to play that way but couldn't. They didn't have the ability. It's so, so frustrating. As a fan looking on, it costs more goals than it creates. I would rather give our striker a header to try to win and pick up the pieces, than force it out of the back and lose that way. Pep Guardiola has a lot to answer for in terms of goals conceded in League Two.

'Managers think it's in-vogue and the "right" way to play but there is no "right" way – there really isn't. One of my favourite managers and teams is Tony Pulis's Stoke. They played their style absolutely to perfection. It might seem stupid but there's no way Pep Guardiola could have kept that Stoke team in the Premier League – although Tony Pulis couldn't have done what Guardiola does with Man City. It was the perfect manager with the perfect players, that he'd obviously recruited, playing the perfect style to keep them in the Premier League for so many years. It was great seeing all these teams with world stars getting paid however much, the transfers fees clubs had paid, and they couldn't deal with the long throw.'

Jon is also an active England fan who is optimistic about the team's prospects. He sees no contradiction in backing both Tony Pulis and Gareth Southgate:

'Gone are the days where we're forcing players into a system that doesn't work. People tell me Trent Alexander-Arnold is the greatest right-back in the world, but I've never seen him play well for England because he doesn't suit the system. We play short passes through midfield and Liverpool bypass their midfield. He hits these long raking crossfield passes which England just don't do, so he doesn't suit the system.

'Southgate knows his system, which is massively important, but he'll change it up. It works because to make it at that level in the Premier League you need to be able to play with the ball. Harry Maguire, John Stones, Kyle Walker. Reece James and Luke Shaw are all at top clubs who play that way. In League Two, you're just not used to playing like that so to force your style on those players doesn't work.

'The FA have finally got their ducks in a row and we're progressing players through the age groups. After that success at under-17 and under-20, we're seeing enough players from those squads come through which is exactly what the FA wanted. We should have been doing it years ago.'

Organic soil: an analogy

If you dig beneath intensively farmed land, you find little sign of life. By contrast, organically farmed soil is rich, moist, and teeming with earthworms.

The intensive farm has made more money and filled lorries full of food but how long can it go on exploiting the same strip of earth? For a while. The farmer has cash to buy strong fertilisers, better tools, and irrigation. It might get him through until he sells up.

In my analogy, the organic farmland is a century-plus of football with roots in communities throughout England and Wales. The Premier League came along, intensively exploited that fertile soil and became the richest in the world. The old owners extracted their wealth and ran. New owners came who can't remember the old organic farm and aren't from round here anyway, so why should they care? The soil is still good for years yet.

Why should a Premier League owner care about Walton Casuals, Tynemouth United or Jeff's Chippy? Because the richest league in the world grew in the most fertile soil in the world, that's why. Without that community of people buying tickets, subscribing to TV channels, playing, coaching, refereeing, driving their kids, organising tournaments, and arranging fixtures football would be just another arm of the entertainment industry, fighting with Netflix and virtual reality games. Grassroots football isn't there to supply kids to academies. It is the soul of English football.

The people in charge of the rich clubs can't keep demanding every advantage, hogging the money, and changing the rules without compromising the future health of the game. After the Premier League had been pressured by government into helping EFL clubs survive the lockdowns, Aston Villa CEO Christian Purslow asked, 'Do Tesco give corner shops a £250m loan facility?'

He missed the point. The Premier League giving the kiss of life to the leagues below is more akin to Tesco making sure British farming doesn't go to the wall, which would be a good idea, by the way. It makes no sense for the top of any industry to spoil the ground beneath itself, especially when it is hard to tell a potential rival from a customer.

The Premier League does allow some trickledown, and under threat of political intervention it will open its taps as wide as it is forced to. We will see whether we end up with an effective independent regulator but remember that where regulators exist, wealthy companies mount lobbying operations to protect themselves.

The clubs should be less afraid. They should listen to the wider football community because they need the roots of English football to be strong; selling TV contracts around the world inflates the bank accounts of players, agents, and owners but that money is spent as soon as it's earned.

For all my reservations about sustainability, football in England is brilliant. Check out every other sport by comparison. They see football as a behemoth squeezing their space. When I was a kid, Ian Botham and Daley Thompson were as famous as any sportspeople; now football dominates.

Brexit presents challenges but not in the same measure as in other industries; this is not farming, healthcare or hospitality. We can live without importing unexceptional footballers. Big clubs will still be able to buy foreign players. The EPPP revolutionised the development of young footballers in England and Wales, but the big clubs had to be placated by being allowed to snap up the best young players for small fees.

Doom-ladened predictions of TV exposure spoiling football were simply wrong. The game is better for it. People who can afford to can watch more matches than ever with some excellent coverage. Premier League highlights and live FA Cup games are on terrestrial TV. We will soon be able to see Champions League highlights on the BBC; it is a shame there are no live games, we've missed big European nights on terrestrial TV. The English game has adapted well to new technology which is critical in keeping kids interested. Football should resist the temptation to chase quick dollars by restricting access.

Match-going fans must be cherished, not rinsed for cash. The Premier League should set a target of competing with the Bundesliga to be the most fan-friendly competition, which means pushing prices towards the cheaper end currently offered and being sensitive over kick-off times.

People hate the dark arts of football and of all the issues this is probably the easiest to solve: use VAR to give retrospective punishments. We all need to be honest and call it out, especially when our team is doing it.

Greater diversity has strengthened football. Commitment to the women's game is real. Opening pathways for British Asians to participate lags behind but Riz Rehman's optimism was encouraging. Clubs putting faith in black managers would show their anti-racism stances are meaningful. The FA wants to help grassroots football thrive, but it is juggling too many balls and men's Sunday football needs help.

Another analogy: British cuisine

I like British food although I appreciate other people don't. I've seen a lot of the world and I've never found a steak and kidney pudding and roast beef restaurant. But if you don't like stodge, it's no problem. We found a solution.

If I want to eat out in Oxford I can have Slovak, Caribbean, Polish, Thai, Japanese, Italian, Indian, Turkish, Chinese, French, American, Spanish, Portuguese, Vietnamese, and I can still go to the pub for Yorkshire puddings. If what we had was a bit too basic for the modern palate, never mind, we opened up the doors and welcomed creativity from abroad. I'll stop before I find myself claiming English football is the chicken tikka masala of the world game.

English football has gone through a step-change in the last decade or so, and it is generally better for it. Greater investment in youth and coaching means clubs are producing lots of good technical players, although the lack of diverse styles in academies is probably contributing to a shortage of centre-forwards and centre-backs. Fans expect to see the ball passed on the ground and you hear it referred to as playing 'the right way'. It isn't a settled debate but there is a clear direction of travel. People who think we have already drifted into a new dogmatism point to the tendency for teams to play out from the back even when the risks are unduly high. There is a way to go in terms of tactical appreciation. We are still in a generation with lots of copy and paste football.

Pathways into the Premier League are hard to negotiate. It would be great to see reserve team football return but that would require a cultural shift in clubs. Hothousing kids is joyless and leaves emotional scars. Clubs know it is a danger and want their young players to have an enriching experience but are they prepared to make that happen? Not while very young kids are being driven around the country to play 40 minutes of football.

Have we lost our way? No. Football in England is great. It is a wonderful thing for your kids to do, a source of entertainment, friendship, and cross-generational community. Traditionalists should accept change isn't always bad, but innovators should be mindful that rapid change leaves a sense of loss. Tread respectfully and don't break things for the sake of it. Recognise that new ideas will become tired dogma if you don't question everything. A successful generation of English managers will only emerge if we encourage original thought. Don't be afraid of challenge.

Is the old style of English football gone? Yes, largely, but we are learning to adapt, we are learning to learn, to value intelligence as much as bravery. Football has always progressed and hopefully always will. I'll finish with a request to coaches and players around England and Wales: don't hoof the ball up the pitch and hope for the best or your players won't fulfil their potential – but for the sake of us old guys, remember you don't have to pass through the high press if it's not on. If you need to, get it kicked!